Talking Black

Other titles in the Women on Women series:

Daring to Dissent: Lesbian Culture from Margin to Mainstream
(ed.) Liz Gibbs

'Radical, readable and feisty, this new collection of essays from very different dykes gives us all the courage to insist on our difference and the energy to dissent.'
Patricia Duncker, University of Wales, Aberystwyth

Challenging Conceptions: Planning a Family by Self-Insemination
Lisa Saffron

'This pioneering book will be invaluable for lesbians contemplating motherhood.'
Angela Mason, Executive Director, Stonewall

Portraits to the Wall: Historic Lesbian Lives Unveiled
Rose Collis

'In this all-too-slender volume, Collis has captured the danger and exuberance of some dozen historic lesbian lives. The book is well researched and accessible, journalistic and witty.'
Fiona Cooper, novelist

Healing the Whole: The Diary of an Incest Survivor
Yvette Pennacchia

'This is a poignant and moving book. I am sure it will help incest survivors to know theirs is a shared journey, the rest of us to empathise and all who have been bruised by life to understand ourselves a little better.'
Clare Short MP

Lesbiōt: Israeli Lesbians Talk about Sexuality, Feminism, Judaism and Their Lives
(ed.) Tracy Moore

'There is no world without politics and with the intimacy of their words, these women invite us to re-examine what it really means to be a lesbian in the larger world. The stories of their lives suggest hope for change and for peace.'
Jewelle Gomez, novelist

My American History: Lesbian and Gay Life During the Reagan/Bush Years
Sarah Schulman

'Sarah Schulman's collection combines a lively sense of recent history and some wise political reflections with vigorous dispatches from the activist front line. It makes a challenging read.'
Mary McIntosh, University of Essex

Talking Black

Lesbians of African and Asian Descent Speak Out

Edited by Valerie Mason-John

CASSELL

Cassell
Wellington House, 125 Strand
London WC2R 0BB

387 Park Avenue South
New York, NY 10016–8810

First published 1995

British Library Cataloguing-in-Publication Data
A catalogue record for this book is available from the British Library.

ISBN: 0-304-32963-0 (hardback)
0-304-32965-7 (paperback)

Typeset by Fakenham Photosetting Limited, Fakenham, Norfolk
Printed and bound in Great Britain by Mackays of Chatham, plc

Contents

In memory – I dedicate this book

In memory of all the Black lesbians
who,
walked before us,
stood before us,
fought before us,

In memory of all the Black lesbians
who,
created the way,
paved the way,
led the way.

I dedicate this book
to all the Black lesbians living in the world,
to all the zamis, khushes, wiccas, matis, samtikims and dykes
Black women loving Black women.
To the ideal of a harmonious community,
to which I aspire.

I dedicate this book
to all the Black lesbians living in this world,
to the path of our destinies which we follow,
to the community,
the loving and spiritual friendships with one another,
which I enjoy.

Here may no idle word be written,
here may no idle word be read.

I dedicate this book . . .
to the existence of all Black lesbians.
I dedicate this book
to the practice of a Black lesbian community.
I dedicate this book
to the development of love and wisdom among us.
I dedicate this book
to the emancipation of all lesbians and gay men
living in this world.
I dedicate this book
with living memory
I dedicate this book.

Preface

EIGHT years ago I was living in the notorious lesbian housing co-op Blue Moon, on a road where several of their houses were situated. There were at least six out Black lesbians living on the same road, one of whom was Dorothea Smartt. She inspired me, and later I learnt she had inspired many other lesbians of African and Asian descent too. She was the fairy Goddess mother who put together the Black Lesbian Support Network resource pack, sending it out to all the Black lesbians she met on her travels. It had information about Black lesbians in Britain, and how lesbians existed in Africa, Asia and the Caribbean long before the arrival of the colonizers. The pack provided written proof of the existence of Black lesbians as far back as AD 500, and how some had created their own societies. It destroyed the myth of lesbianism as a white phenomenon and gave affirmation to many of us who lived in isolated areas.

I first met Dorothea at a National Union of Students Lesbian and Gay conference in Manchester during the early 1980s. She asked me if I would support her in requesting a Black lesbian gathering, and so together we fought for the right to a Black-only space. It was my first experience of a Black lesbians-only group and, coupled with receiving my pack, marked the beginning of a new journey. A year later I moved to London and by coincidence found myself living on the same road as Dorothea. During this time we wrote an article together about Black feminism on both sides of the Atlantic, for the now-defunct *Spare Rib* magazine. It was an exciting assignment, we read widely, and discussed and debated many issues. On completion of this feature, I said to Dorothea: 'I can imagine you in five years' time, you'll be writing and editing books.' She looked at me and smiled. Who would have known I was projecting and predicting my own future? This book, therefore, has been inspired by all the Black lesbians I have ever come into contact with. Each and every one has taught me something about myself, or stimulated thoughts in my mind. It is also inspired by those who commented on *Making Black Waves*, the first publication about Black lesbians in Britain, written by myself and Ann Khambatta. Their opinions helped to shape the content of the book.

When I was asked by Cassell to write a book about Black lesbians, my initial response was, oh no, not another one. I had just handed over the manuscript for the first one, and I thought, here we go again, I'm being typecast, they must think I can only write about Black lesbians. After a few days, however, I realized that what we really need is a whole library full of books about Black lesbians. I decided upon an anthology; I knew there were many Black lesbians scattered around Britain, all of whom had something different and important to say. So I set about putting together a synopsis and finding Black women to contribute. I was also inspired by the contributors. They were all quite chuffed at being asked to contribute to the first anthology by lesbians of African and Asian descent living in Britain. Some even said they believed it was a great honour. I too share the same sentiments; it is an honour to be editor, and for each contributor to agree to work with me on this exciting project. I am very proud to make another contribution to Black lesbian herstory.

I have been stimulated, stirred, aroused, ignited and thoroughly affirmed by our beauty and creativity. I hope Black lesbians from all over the world will also experience some of these emotions while reading this book. I also hope that white lesbians, Black and white gay men, and the heterosexual communities will also appreciate the honesty and sentiments documented and will begin to understand our culture, politics and sexuality.

This is a book for everyone. It is a long-awaited testimony of Black lesbians living in Britain.

Acknowledgements

MY thanks are many. The support of all my friends in different ways has helped me to produce an exciting book. I would like especially to thank all the contributors for keeping to their deadlines, and for writing challenging and stimulating chapters. I would like to thank my friend, Suzanne Roden, for her moral support, for kicking me into gear and reminding me to go to the gym, swim and party too, while working intensely on the book. Thank you for reading the manuscript, and giving me positive feedback. Thank you to Dorothea Smartt, who also read the manuscript and made invaluable suggestions for the final draft. I thank my spiritual friend, Carolyn Entwistle, who was there when I needed her, for holding me close, metaphorically, when I was feeling down. Thanks a billion to my Sangha family: Zenobi, Jack, Bibi, Colette, Lorraine and Edwina, who provided me with all the intimacy you expect from a relationship. Thank you for making me laugh, for my cuddles and hugs. Thank you for being there even when I tried to reject you. Thank you to Susan and Irene who kept me calm and sane while working on the book, and to Jenny White who let me know it was OK to be angry, and who gave me courage. Thank you to Jennifer Dean who supported me in the eleventh hour, and made me feel I wasn't working alone. Thank you for your enthusiasm and excitement. Thanks to Lola Flash for being so proud to have her image on the front cover, and for telling people about the book, and to Adeola and Anita who continually affirmed me while editing the book. Thanks to Max Boucher for his technical expertise, and to Bread 'n Roses for the administrative support. Also a big thanks to Deborah Hart at Microsyster, for staying so calm while working out how to print the manuscript. Thanks to Liz Gibbs who saw the need for more books about Black lesbians in

Britain. Thank you to Maya Chowdhry for the supportive telephone calls, and to Jo Odin Fraser for her supportive letters.

Finally, I would like to thank my children's home-sister, Shirley Henry, and her daughter Katrina, for providing me with a chill-out space when the pressure was on. And to my foster mother, who has always believed in me. Thank you for telling me, sixteen or more years ago, that I should write.

About the Editor

Valerie Mason-John is from the African Diaspora, and was born in Cambridge, where she lived with a single-parent white foster mother until the age of four. When her foster mother retired, she was placed in a Barnardo's home in Essex, and raised by a Polish house-father and English house-mother. Aged thirteen she met her white foster mother of today, and went to live with her in Kent at a later stage in her life. She was educated at Ilford County High School for Girls and Leeds University and later completed a post-graduate course in journalism with Business Press International. Since then she has worked as a freelance researcher for the BBC, Channel Four and the Arts Council of Great Britain, and was a feature writer for the Black national newspaper, *The Voice*, as well as a staff reporter for the national lesbian and gay newspaper, the *Pink Paper*. Her articles have appeared in the *Guardian*, *Social Work Today*, *South London Press* and various other publications. She was co-author of the first publication about Black lesbians in Britain, *Making Black Waves* (Scarlet Press, 1993). She has also travelled extensively, working as an international correspondent and a radio presenter while in Australia, where she lived traditionally among the Yolngu tribe in Arnhem Land. She has also just completed a fifteen-month course on physical theatre and mime at the Desmond Jones School, and now describes herself as an artiste of the 1990s. She says: 'I write poetry, short stories, fiction and non-fiction, and dance; I harmonize them together through acting and presenting.' She is currently a co-editor of *Feminist Arts News*, and writes regularly for *Capital Gay*. She has two more books in the pipeline, a collection of short stories and poetry and a retrospective of feminist art, both due to be published in 1996.

About the Contributors

Linda Bellos

Linda Bellos was born in London in 1950; married in 1970; and gave birth to two children in 1974 and 1976. In 1980 she came out as lesbian, and left her husband, divorcing him in 1983. Her father is Nigerian and mother white Jewish. Both were manual workers, living in Brixton, where she grew up and attended secondary school. She was the first Black woman and Black lesbian to join the *Spare Rib* collective in 1981, and has been active in numerous lesbian and feminist groups. Between 1984 and 1986 she worked at the now-defunct Greater London Council Women's Unit. She was one of the organizers of the Women against Violence conference in 1982, the Black feminist conference, 'We Are Here', in 1983–84, and the first Black lesbian conference, Zami 1, in 1985. Linda became vice-chair of the Labour Party Black Sections in 1984, a councillor in Lambeth in 1985, and the leader of Lambeth Council in 1986. Since ceasing to be leader in May 1988, she has worked in local government, and during the past two years has been working as a freelance management consultant and writer.

Maya Chowdhry

Maya Chowdhry is of Asian descent. Her father is from India, and her mother from England and Scotland. She is a writer, film-maker, live artist, and winner of the BBC Radio Young Playwrights' festival with *Monsoon*, published by Aurora Metro Publications. She is also author of the play *Heart and Heaven*, recorded for BBC radio. Her poetry appeared in the anthology *The Popular Front of Contemporary Poetry*, and she co-edited a collection of poems, *Putting the Pickle Where the Jam Should Be*. She also directed 'Running Gay' for the Channel Four series *Out*. Maya is currently a co-editor of *Feminist Arts News*, and of a book due to be published in 1996, *A Retrospective of Feminist Art*. She lives and creates new works in Sheffield.

Lola Flash

Lola Flash is an African-American photographer based in Britain. She recently curated her own exhibition, 'The Gay A–Z'. Her images often reflect the ambiguities of racial and cultural identities. She has worked for the American lesbian and gay press, and is now working for the lesbian and gay media in Britain. Her photographs appear on the covers of the Cassell Women on Women series.

Anne Hayfield

Anne Hayfield is a Black (Afro-Asian) lesbian feminist who has fought misogyny and racism for many years. She works for Lesbian And Gay Employment Rights (LAGER), where she has helped hundreds of lesbians who have struggled against extreme prejudice and abuse. She is currently using training as a method of effective change and empowerment. Anne is also a writer, and has had several reports published about the discrimination which all lesbians and gay men experience in today's world.

Savitri Hensman

Savitri Hensman was born in Sri Lanka, where both her parents originated and now reside. She came to England as a baby, and grew up in London. She was one of the founding members of the Black Lesbian and Gay Centre Project, where she worked for eight years, and was an organizer of the sixth International Lesbian and Gay People of Colour conference. Savi is committed to her Christian faith, and believes that Christianity originated from the continents of Africa and Asia. She is also a writer and poet; her poetry has been published in *Flood at the Door* (Centerprise Publications, 1979) and various other anthologies. Savi is currently working as a freelance trainer.

Tina Kendall

Tina Kendall is of Jamaican and English heritage. She was born in Bradford and grew up with white parents, and with many Black brothers and sisters. She started reclaiming her heritage at age twelve, and describes it as 'a lifelong adventure'. She is a poet, novelist and scriptwriter. *Lightning on My Tongue* (Onlywomen Press, 1994) is her first collection of poetry. She lives in many different places with her three children, who help her make the most of life and keep her optimistic.

Quibilah Montsho

Quibilah Montsho, BA, is of African descent and lives in Manchester. She has recently committed herself to the path of Zen Buddhism. She describes herself as a Black poet, writer, performer and workshop facilitator. She has been active in promoting the unity between lesbians of African and Asian descent, belonging to several groups in Manchester. In October 1993 she appeared in the Channel Four television programme *Doing It with You Is Taboo*, which discussed mixed-race relationships between Black and white lesbians and gay men.

Adowa Okorrowa

Adowa Okorrowa's parents are from Guyana. She is a writer, poet and performer. She has been involved in Pan-African and Black lesbian politics for many years. She is one of the founding members of Zamimass. She says: 'I am currently exploring my spirituality and creativity.'

Anita Naoko Pilgrim

Anita Naoko Pilgrim is of mixed racial heritage, with one Japanese parent and one English parent. She was born in Scotland in 1963, but grew up in Sierra Leone, Thailand, the Cameroons and England. She was educated at Whitestone Comprehensive School, Stroud Technical College and King's College, Cambridge. She describes herself as a bisexual woman, who is currently in a long-term relationship with another Black woman. She works as a writer, plays rugby, grows herbs and keeps tropical fish. She currently contributes to *Capital Gay*, and is the presenter of a poetry programme for Brazen Radio.

Seni Seneviratne

Seni Seneviratne was born in Yorkshire in 1951 to an English mother and Sri Lankan father. She is a writer and singer who has branched out into photography, combining all three skills in her performances. She is also co-editor of a collection of poetry entitled *Putting the Pickle Where the Jam Should Be*. Her work has been published in various anthologies. She now lives in Sheffield with her teenage daughter.

Sakthi Suriyaprakasam

Sakthi Suriyaprakasam was born in Sri Lanka, and moved to Britain in 1982. She lives in London and works for the Black Lesbian and Gay Centre and the Greenwich Lesbian and Gay Centre. She has been particularly active in issues concerning younger lesbians. Sakthi enjoys raving, having fun and debating.

Ulanah

Ulanah is of African-Caribbean descent, who was born in Jamaica but grew up in the north of England. She is working as a healing artist, educational psychologist, rebirther and psychology lecturer. Because her work is creative and intuitive, involving painting, drawing, writing, chanting, singing, breathing and creative visualization, she calls herself an artist. She performs her poetry alone, and as part of a performance duo called ASHE, a Yoruba word, meaning the power to make things happen.

Introduction

THIS book focuses on Black lesbians with one or both parents descending from Africa and Asia and its subcontinent. Therefore, it looks at the contribution made by African, African-Caribbean and Asian lesbians living in Britain. I hope that other lesbians, Black and white, can use this book as a model and framework to write about their specific experiences, because it is important that we continue to document our lives and herstories.

While working on this book, I was still promoting the first publication about Black lesbians in Britain, *Making Black Waves*. The same questions repeatedly came up at readings, and from lesbians I bumped into on the scene, so I thought it would make sense to document some answers in this book.

Why a book about Black lesbians only? My initial response was why write a book about feminism, or socialism, or capitalism? However, I replied: 'Almost every book about lesbians living in Britain is about white women. Almost every Black lesbian who came out before 1993 has been unable to find literature about Black lesbians either in Britain or the countries from which we originate. In fact we are bored with reading only about white Edwardian and Victorian ladies' tea parties, when we know that we existed too.'

But shouldn't there be a book for all of us? Warmed up by the first question, my reply would be: 'Ideally yes, but Black lesbians have been waiting years for this ideal to be realized. When white lesbians have had the resources to write books, rarely have they included our experiences. They simply forget, or state they don't know any Black lesbians. Therefore in reality, no. Until there are as many books about Black lesbians as there are about white lesbians, only then can we begin to look at this ideal.'

Why another book about Black lesbians, when there is one already out on the market? Prepared for the onslaught, I reply: 'Well, as people keep on reminding me, *Making Black Waves* is an extended pamphlet, therefore the space to write about us was limited. While it gives a concise and compact overview, there was no room to examine in depth our contributions to British lesbian culture and the issues which affect us. Indeed, the existence of only one book about Black lesbians is an indictment, when you begin to consider all the countries we originate from.'

My favourite question came in two forms: *Is the book only for Black lesbians? Can white lesbians read it?* After the initial shock of this question, I replied: 'A book about Black lesbians living in Britain is about the history of all women, all lesbians, and all Black people in Britain. It is about our survival in this country and also our contribution to British culture. If you are interested in this subject or happen to fall into one of these categories, well perhaps the book is for you.'

Why didn't you talk about sex? This last question was almost always asked by Black lesbians. 'This time the book includes sex and sexuality in at least two chapters. However, it is only a beginning. And I hope that much more is written about this subject in the future. It is another book.'

While editing this book, I have been careful to respect the opinions of each contributor, adding other beliefs where I felt it was necessary. As Black lesbians our voices have been denied, oppressed, censored and excluded by racism, sexism and homophobia. Sometimes even Black women in our own communities have taken it upon themselves to deny the right of others to speak about issues of which they don't approve. I believe in the freedom of speech, the freedom to disagree, the freedom to take risks, and that we must take responsibility for what we say. Hence, by talking and documenting debates we have a model from which to work. I hope each chapter will stimulate others to write, offer analysis and critiques of Black lesbian culture.

The first three chapters set the scene. 'Herstoric Moments' provides a herstorical chronology of events in which Black lesbians have played a part since the 1970s. It documents some of the most profound events and significant organizations which helped to pave the way for Black lesbians to come out in numbers in the 1990s. 'A

Retrospective: Black Together under One Banner' by Savitri Hensman and 'A Vision Back and Forth' by Linda Bellos offer personal analyses of the development of Black lesbian herstory in Britain. While Hensman explores coming out through the Black political movements and discusses the relevance of Black as a label, Bellos looks at her own coming out through the women's liberation movement and socialist movement.

Personal and lively voices are documented in the chapters, 'Some of Us Are Younger' by Sakthi Suriyaprakasam, and 'Some of Us Are Older' by Seni Seneviratne. Both chapters make it quite clear that being a Black lesbian in Britain involves more than taking a lover and having a good time. Through the voices of four older Black lesbians, including herself, Seneviratne makes us think about the reality of ageing in Britain, and Suriyaprakasam explains what it is like for young Black lesbians coming out today.

Similarly, the chapters 'Several Faces of Discrimination' by Anne Hayfield and 'Behind Locked Doors' by Quibilah Montsho make us realize that being a Black lesbian is tough. Hayfield offers an analysis of discrimination perpetrated through immigration laws, education and housing, and explains why Black lesbians are more vulnerable to discrimination than any other group of people. Montsho suggests that 60 per cent of Black lesbians will come into contact with the mental health system during their lifetime. Fed up with a system which is racist, homophobic and sexist, she suggests that we should look towards alternative therapies for healing. In 'Healing through My Own Eyes', Ulanah offers a personal healing guide and tools to deal with our oppressions. She shares her knowledge of African/Asian spirituality, Buddhism and meditation. *Talking Black* would not be complete without 'Holding the Banner High' by Tina Kendall, who explores the humorous side of being a Black lesbian in the 1970s and 1980s.

This anthology covers subjects ranging from herstory, sex and sexuality and discrimination to personal healing. It explores the impact lesbians of African/Asian descent have made, and looks at how we have influenced lesbian culture, literature, film-making and fashion. *Talking Black* adds one more title to the list of publications about Black lesbians in Britain. It is the beginning of a wealth of Black lesbian literature to come, for there is much more to be said.

Chapter one

Herstoric Moments

Valerie Mason-John

Setting the context

BLACK lesbians have been living in Britain since their foremothers and forefathers were transported here in the late fifteenth century. Evidence of the births of people of African and Asian descent in Britain exists from 1505 onwards, and many of our ancestors were brought to this country in their thousands, and against their will, to work as domestic slaves during the sixteenth and seventeenth centuries. The fact that same-sex relationships existed in Africa, the Caribbean, Asia and its subcontinent long before colonizers came, means that some Black women who had sexual relationships with the same gender must have been transported to Britain during the slave trade. Living in a new and hostile environment, people of African and Asian descent needed to stay together in their own communities for survival, protection and security. The existence of racism, sexism and homophobia in British society has meant that the documented herstory of Black lesbians is brief. It has taken almost twenty centuries for the herstory of white women in Britain to be documented, for a record to be made of their contribution to British culture, and this documentation is only the beginning. It could take another ten centuries to pass before the contribution of Black peoples to British culture is properly recognized, credited and recorded.

In 1984 came the publication of the first comprehensive history of Black people in Britain, *Staying Power*, by a white historian and teacher, Peter Fryer. A year later Virago published *Heart of the Race*, the work of three Black women, Beverley Bryan, Stella Dadzie and Suzanne Scafe, which documented for the first time the lives of Black women in Britain. In 1987 the first book edited by Black lesbians of African and Asian descent appeared, *Black Women Talk Poetry*, a collection of poetry by Black women of all sexualities. The editors, Da Choong, Olivette Cole-Wilson, Bernadine Evaristo and Gabriela Pearse, came together in 1983 to set up the first Black women's publishing press in Britain, Black Womantalk. Since then the collective has published one other title, *Don't Ask Me Why* (1991), a collection of short stories and poetry by Black women. Although Black Womantalk still exists, and is working on another book, the collective has completely changed, and both Black heterosexuals and lesbians are on the editorial and publishing team.

The first publication about Black lesbians, an extended pamphlet documenting the lives of lesbians descended, through one or both parents, from Africa, the Caribbean, South and South-East Asia, the Middle East and other parts of the world, was published by Scarlet Press in November 1993. *Making Black Waves* was written by myself and Ann Khambatta. This pamphlet marked a beginning of the documetation of Black lesbian lives in Britain. Prior to this, the herstory of Black lesbians could only be found by leafing through old newsletters, defunct publications such as *Spare Rib* and *Outwrite*, and in anthologies and conference reports. With very little money and support, Black lesbians managed to record significant events, bequeathing an invaluable source of information for today's writers, whose work in turn will inspire the next generation of lesbian and gay authors.

The movement

A separately organized Black lesbian movement is perhaps the response to our exclusion from the Black heterosexual world, the women's liberation movement and the white lesbian and gay community. The herstory of lesbians which has been uncovered, recorded and celebrated is predominantly about white middle-class women. In fact, it is dead white lesbians who dominate the bookshelves: Radclyffe Hall, Djuna Barnes, Vita Sackville-West, Eleanor Roosevelt and Romaine Brooks are just a few of the names which we repeatedly come across when searching for lesbian herstory. The documented rise of the women's movement during the 1970s mainly records the contribution of white women, including some white lesbians, through photography and writing. Although the 1980s have witnessed the beginning of the documentation of Black lesbian literature, it has been normally by women of African descent from the USA. Therefore, it has been important for Black lesbians living in Britain to begin documenting their own contribution to the movement before it is lost.

The herstory of the Black lesbian movement is typified by the struggle to have our gender, race and sexuality placed on the agenda. The Black political movements of the past – Garveyism, Pan-Africanism, the Black Power and civil rights movements – were all dogged by debates, splits and silence around gender and sexuality. Gender was most definitely not a priority issue, and the consideration of sexuality was completely ignored. Due to such conflict it was felt among some Black people that Black women could not afford to be separatist over certain issues and debates, because of the need to work together with Black men to overcome racism. In fact, it can be said that organizations such as Manchester Black Women's Co-op and Southall Black Sisters, who spearheaded the 'Stop the SUS' (Suspect Under Suspicion) campaign; Zanus Women's League; East London Black Women's Organization; the Organization of Women of African and Asian Descent; and other Black lesbian groups were all a response to the years of struggling to be recognized as women in the Black political movement, as lesbians in the Black feminist movement and as Black in the women's liberation movement and the lesbian and gay community.

Black lesbians were isolated, they had lost their allegiances among white women and with the Black heterosexual community. A whole feminist herstory had been written excluding the contribution of Black women. White women, whether lesbians, feminists or lesbian feminists, were not interested in American chemical companies polluting first-nation countries, or in the illegal mining in Namibia; in fact, they were only concerned with their immediate needs.

Although there has been a separate movement, Black lesbians have always been part of the wider Black, feminist and lesbian struggles. Many were always active in the Black liberation movement and others took part in Women Against Violence Against Women (WAVAW), the women's liberation movement, the Gay Liberation Front, antinuclear campaigning (Greenham Common) and Reclaim the Night marches, between the late 1960s and 1980s. Our herstory has been shaped by our oppressions. However, Black lesbians have risen above their oppressors, and achieved monumental feats, despite the odds stacked against us.

African and Asian unity

Although the Black political movement had initially brought men and women together, Black women, unhappy with their declared position in the movement, found the need to organize autonomously, and used the opportunity to forge links with other Black women they had met in the global Black struggle. As a result, the Organization of Women of Africa and African Descent (OWAAD) was founded in 1978. However, during its first year, it was argued that if OWAAD was to address issues concerning all Black women effectively, women of African and Asian descent should stop organizing separately around the issues of racist attacks, deportations, Depo-Provera and the question of forced sterilization of Black women in Britain. This shift towards forging links together was sealed in 1979 when OWAAD changed its name to the Organization of Women of African and Asian Descent. As the first documented and cohesive national network of African and Asian women, it united Black women from all over Britain, and had a profound influence on Black British women's politics. To ensure links were maintained, a newsletter (FOWAAD) was printed. However, rifts soon began to appear in the organization, and one of the major splits occurred over the issue of sexuality. Black lesbians, although they were most definitely at the forefront of the organization, found themselves to be invisible. Some remained in the closet, while others were continually silenced, and those who were publicly out caused a furore. From its outset there was a noticeable absence of debate around this issue; sexuality was perceived as being too sensitive to speak about publicly. The prevailing opinion was: 'How could members waste time discussing lesbianism, heterosexism and bisexuality when there were so many more pressing issues?' One of the first out and visible Black lesbians in public and in the media, Femi Otitoju, remembers the conference which caused the damage, 'A woman announced, there is no space for Black lesbians, so let's have a workshop over here.' She remembers some Black women being abusive and hostile, and hurling insults. She recalls: 'Some women stood up and said we're lesbians and we're offended and upset. I remember thinking, shush, you damn fools.' An ignorance of the background to the struggle and/or a hostility towards feminism from the newer members, together with the failure of the organization to take on board the differences, meant that OWAAD had a short life, and it folded in 1982. Although members of OWAAD failed to unite with each other over some issues, it was an important chapter in Black women's herstory. It campaigned against immigration authorities and virginity tests at ports of entry, it demonstrated against state harassment, battled against expulsions in education and fought many unjust laws. OWAAD for all its faults had much of the vibrancy and energy a Black movement needed.

Positive results came out of the rise and fall of OWAAD. Black lesbians belonging to the organization came together in 1982 and formed their first group, called the Black Lesbian Group, based in London. It is claimed that Black women travelled from Scotland, Wales and all over England to attend the fortnightly meetings. A fares pool was provided by members for women who needed expenses for their travel. However, the group struggled for survival. It initially asked to meet at Brixton Black Womens' Centre, but was denied access because some of the workers were concerned that a lesbian group on the premises would add to the hostility it was already experiencing as a Black women's centre. Black lesbians of mainly African descent and some of Asian descent eventually found space at the now-defunct centre, A Woman's Place, based in central London.

OWAAD's driving force

Members of Brixton Black Women's Group (BBWG) were part of the motivating force (along with other politically active Black women around Britain) which founded the national organization, OWAAD. BBWG was set up in 1973, in response to redefining what the Black and feminist movements meant to them. Its members were an amalgamation of Black women from the women's and the Black liberation movements. In its early days the group's politics was influenced by socialism. Some women preferred not to call themselves feminists because it would link them to the women's movement which had many racist attitudes. Others identified as feminists, but emphasized that feminism stretched beyond the narrow concepts of white middle-class women. During the early 1980s the group had a strong core of members who identified as Black socialist feminists. Although the question of lesbianism featured quite low on the agenda, many of the BBWG founding members were lesbians.

The group met at the Brixton Black Women's Centre, which was established by the Mary Seacole Group. This group aimed to provide a meeting space, gave support and advice on housing, social security and to mothers. Skills such as sewing, dress-making and crafts were shared. Although the crafts group collapsed over an argument about their political posture, the BBWG survived, and opened up the centre's doors to the public in 1979. This group was involved in various campaigns which affected every aspect of being a Black woman.

Black lesbians worked at the centre along with Black heterosexual women, and continued to serve all Black women until 1986, when the workers learnt they had been working in a condemned building, and suffered a cut in funding. This marked the end of an era; all that is left is a derelict building with an unfinished mural of Black women working together. 'Groups like Brixton BWG were just one of the strands which, when woven together, helped bind the political practice of the Black community as a whole. They were in many ways simply a continuation of the Black groups which had existed ever since our arrival after the war.'[1] There were thirty or more groups like the BBWG (with a strong input from Black lesbians) scattered throughout Britain during the 1970s and early 1980s.

Renaissance Black lesbians

In 1984 a group of white lesbians set up Britain's first lesbian archive, to preserve the contribution lesbians had made to British culture. During the 1970s Black lesbians had taken part in many campaigns which affected women and Black people, but this was not being recorded. Similarly, in setting up this archive, the contribution made by Black lesbians was overlooked. The archive reinforced the white-only image of lesbians through the books and information it collected, by the workers and volunteers it employed, and through its membership. Five years after it opened, a Black employee, Linda King, was taken on to try and redress this imbalance. She explored the relevance of the Lesbian Archive and Information Centre to the Black lesbian community, and how it could be improved. During her four-week contract, she collected interviews, transcripts and photographs of Black lesbians (some of which are only available to Black lesbians), and compiled a report. One of the points raised in the interviews was the fact that Black lesbians had contributed to the intellectual and cultural interests of all lesbians in Britain.

Making our mark in the 1980s

The 1980s was a decade in which Black lesbian activity flourished throughout Britain. After the first Black lesbian group was set up in 1982, Black lesbians took the initiative to organize groups, meetings and conferences on a grand scale. During 1983 a Chinese lesbian group was launched after three lesbians of Chinese descent met for the first time at a conference on lesbian sex and sexual practice. In 1984 the 'We Are Here' conference marked the first time that Black women had come out publicly as Black feminists. An organizer, Dorothea Smartt, recalled: 'It was unashamedly a Black feminist conference where Black lesbians were welcome.' The conference planning group was open to all Black women including out Black lesbians.

From discussions at the conference several initiatives were launched: an incest survivors' group; a Black women writers' network; a mixed racial heritage group; '*We Are Here*' newsletter and the Black Lesbian Support Network (BLSN). The BLSN offered advice, information and support to Black women questioning their heterosexuality. It also collated articles by and about Black lesbian lifestyles from all over the world. It was forced to close in 1986, as the exhausted volunteers moved on to do different things in the Black lesbian community. However, the collated articles are available from the Lesbian Archives in central London. The '*We Are Here*' newsletter covered many issues, including health, incest, definitions of Black feminism, Black lesbian mothers and reports about such ongoing national and global campaigns as anti-deportation fightbacks and nuclear testings in Africa. This also folded in 1986, a year which saw the closure of many women's, gay and lesbian, Black and left-wing groups in London. The abolition of the Greater London Council (GLC) in 1986 initiated a period of severe cutbacks in funding for many community-based groups.

However, despite the effects of a Thatcherite government, some groups did spring up and survive. During the mid-1980s a Black lesbian group was established at Waltham Forest Women's Centre, but folded after two years; and in the London borough of Camden, a Black lesbian group, which was set up next to the Camden lesbian project in 1985, still exists today. In this same year several black lesbians were involved in the establishment of the Lesbians and Policing Project (LESPOP); this project was forced to close in 1990 due to a complete cut in its funding. Black lesbians of Asian descent also launched a group, but this folded before the new decade. Funding was secured for a research project on Lesbians from Historically Immigrant Communities, which included testimonies from lesbians of African and Asian descent. Although the work was never published it can be found in the Lesbian Archives. Most of the groups which were set up for Black lesbians during the first half of the decade existed in London, but there were groups in other parts of Britain.

The impact and effect of these groups (with a donation of £11,000 from a white working-class lesbian weekend) culminated in Zami 1, the first national Black lesbian conference to be held in

Britain. In October 1985 over two hundred lesbians of African and Asian descent flocked to London to attend this herstorical event. It was a natural high in itself to be in one space with so many other Black lesbians, and it was a proud moment for those Black lesbians who had been part of the struggle for visibility and recognition during the preceding decade. Delegates discussed issues of coming out in the Black community, disability, prejudices between lesbians of African and Asian descent and various other topics. As with all conferences there were differences of opinion, in this case over the question of who was and was not Black. However, such debate was not surprising when so many Black lesbians from all over Britain had come together for the first time, the political thinking of OWAAD, and of London, had not necessarily filtered its way all over the country.

Zami 1 was and still is one of the greatest achievements of Black lesbians. It paved the way for further conferences, gave confidence to those Black lesbians who were frightened of coming out, and most of all it told the general public that Black lesbians do exist, and in numbers. In the same year Black lesbians were instrumental in setting up Britain's first lesbian centre in Camden, London, and during the latter part of the 1980s, Black lesbian groups were established in Birmingham, Manchester and Bradford, together with a group for Black lesbians over forty and a group for younger Black lesbians in London.

At the turn of the decade (April 1989), Black lesbians organized the second national conference, Zami II, in Birmingham. Unlike the first conference, Zami II was open to other Black lesbians with one or both parents from the Middle East, Latin America, the Pacific nations, to indigenous inhabitants of the Americas, Australasia and the islands of the Atlantic and Indian Ocean, along with those of us who are descended from Africa, Asia and its subcontinent. Over two hundred women came together and debated the issues of sex and sexuality, sexual relationships between Black and white lesbians, motherhood and many other issues. From this conference a group of women initiated a group for lesbians and gays of mixed racial heritage (MOSAIC), which still exists today, and which held its first conference in 1993 in London. In 1991 two Black lesbian groups were set up in Nottingham and

Bristol, and in 1992 a day-long event was held where Black lesbians could discuss the issue of safer sex and HIV and AIDS.

During the early 1990s the rise of Black lesbian activity reached a plateau, and is now beginning to dwindle and stagnate. Although 1992 saw another Black lesbian conference in the North, only a few groups have been founded. There have also been Zami (events of Black lesbians) days in Birmingham in 1993 and 1994.

Organizing with Black gay men

To a lesser extent Black lesbians have also organized with Black gay men. 1981 is a landmark for Black lesbians and gay men organizing together, as it was the year when the Gay Asian Group became the Black Gay Group. Although the group was initially dominated by men, women soon became a more visible presence when it renamed itself the Lesbian and Gay Black Group in 1985. This group went on to secure funding for a Black Lesbian and Gay Centre based in London. The project survived seven years of looking for sufficient funds and suitable premises, but in 1992 the centre was finally launched, and two years later it still exists as the only centre in Britain serving Black lesbians and gay men exclusively.

In 1988 Shakti, a network for South Asian lesbians, gays and bisexuals was set up in London. Since then, other Shaktis have sprung up in major cities, providing a fundamental resource for the Asian community. In 1990 Black lesbians and gay men came together to organize the sixth International Lesbian and Gay People of Colour conference in London, when over three hundred people came together from all over the world to discuss issues which concerned them. During this same year Black lesbians and gay men came together and formed Black Lesbians And Gays Against Media Homophobia (BLAGAMH), which led to one of the most successful campaigns against the Black media in Britain this century. This had centred on the ferocious attack made against lesbians and gay men by Britain's most successful Black newspaper, *The Voice*. During the last three months of 1990, it carried malicious and homophobic stories, including a report on the Black British footballer Justin Fashanu, and printed Whitney Houston's remark that she was not a 'Lesbo'. The paper's columnist, Tony Sewell, wrote:

'Homosexuals are the greatest queerbashers around. No other group are so preoccupied with making their own sexuality look dirty.' BLAGAMH, along with the support of the National Association of Local Government Officers (NALGO), initiated a successful boycott of *The Voice*, instructing local authorities not to advertise in the newspaper. After almost a year's battle, BLAGAMH won a full-page right-to-reply. *The Voice* also promised to adopt an equal opportunities policy and ensure positive coverage of lesbian and gay issues, a commitment which the newspaper has so far upheld. BLAGAMH continues to monitor the Black community, and has challenged ragga artists like Buju Banton and Shabba Ranks over their use of misogynistic and homophobic lyrics.

That same year (1990) saw the establishment of Orientations, a group for lesbians and gay men of Chinese and South Asian descent. Groups have also been formed by Black lesbians and gays in Manchester, and, in 1991, by Black lesbians, gays and bisexuals in Bristol. All three groups exist today. The short life of Black lesbian and gay groups is typical of the whole lesbian and gay community: as soon as one group disappears, another emerges.

Art and literature

Since the late 1970s there has been some visibility of Black women's writing in Britain. The majority of it has been by heterosexual women of African descent living in Africa, the Caribbean and the USA. The late Audre Lorde, American-born Caribbean poet, novelist and essayist, was perhaps our first Black lesbian icon here in Britain. Since then Asian lesbian writer Suniti Namjoshi and African-Scottish writer Jackie Kay have come to the forefront of Black writing in Britain. Their work is acclaimed both nationally and internationally. Writers such as Barbara Burford, Maud Sulter and Meiling Jin have also made inroads into established British women's publishing houses.

The feminist publisher, Sheba, currently run by Black lesbians, is one of the few women's publishing houses which has made a strong commitment to producing the work of Black lesbians in Britain. However, the lack of interest from most publishing houses has meant that Black lesbians in Britain have created their own initiatives to publish the work of all Black women, including themselves. The Black Womantalk collective is an example of this. In 1990 a Black lesbian, Maud Sulter, set up Urban Fox Press, which published *Passion: Discourses on Blackwomen's Creativity*, an anthology of the work of Black women of all sexualities. Sulter has since achieved the distinction of having her art work purchased for the permanent collection of the Victoria and Albert Museum and the Royal Festival Hall. While I was writing this chapter, Zamimass, a Black lesbian political organization, curated the first-ever exhibition in London by Black lesbians only. Although it was regionally based it marked the beginning of sharing our creativity publicly. Zamimass hope its next exhibition will be a national one, bringing together the work of Black lesbian artists from all over Britain.

Our media

We have also contributed to newspapers and magazines. *Outwrite*, an anti-racist, anti-imperialist women's monthly, was set up in 1982 by a group of mainly Black women, some of whom were Black lesbians. It covered stories about women all over the world, including Black lesbians. After seven years it folded, a casualty of a dissipated women's movement, lack of money and worn-out collective members. *Spare Rib*, the longest-running feminist publication and most widely known in the rest of the world, was founded in the 1970s. The collective went through many changes, being initially composed of white middle-class women and ending up as an almost exclusively Black female heterosexual collective. However, during its life Black lesbians were involved in the collective, and continued to contribute articles regularly until the monthly magazine disappeared overnight in 1993.

The first and only magazine to talk about sex and sexuality, *Quim*, was founded by a group of Black and white lesbians in 1989. Despite the fact that it celebrated all lesbian sexuality, it was heralded as a soft porn and sado-masochistic (SM) publication. Although a Black lesbian was involved in the initial concept of the magazine, very few Black lesbians have been published in it. Indeed, this quarterly periodical has predominantly served the white lesbian

SM community. However, in 1994, *Quim* was guest-edited by a Black lesbian performer and writer Leonora Rogers-Wright, and the majority of the magazine was dedicated to Black women speaking out. For the first time in British Black lesbian herstory, women of African and Asian descent modelled in numbers for *Quim* magazine, posing with dildos, handcuffs and ropes, and wrote what could be considered SM and bondage short stories. In 1991 British Black lesbians of Asian descent attended the first Asian lesbian conference in Bangkok, and set up a quarterly publication, *Asian Lesbians Outside of Asia* (ALOA). Although the group still exists, a publication has not been produced during the past year.

In response to the lack of literature about Black women, a new newspaper, *Diaspora*, by and about women of colour was launched on International Women's Day, 8 March 1994. It is run by a collective of Black lesbian and heterosexual women who hope to cover a wide range of issues concerning all Black women.

Expressing our sexuality

Performers and artists have also been a vital source of Black lesbian culture. Through song, poetry, dance and plays, Black lesbian sexuality has been celebrated. The a cappella group Sistahs in Song (active in the 1980s) and performers like Parminder Sekhon and Michelle Asha Warsama are only a few of the many talented women who have been visible through their work. In 1982 the Theatre of Black Women was set up by Black lesbian and heterosexual women, with the aim of giving a voice to the Black female performer. Several of the group's plays were written by Black lesbians, including Jackie Kay. The group disbanded in the latter part of the 1980s due to a loss of funding. Sauda, a group of African-American and African-Caribbean lesbians based in Britain, created prestigious events, featuring all women of African descent, during 1992 and 1993.

Raving

Although poetry events, performance nights, books and other publications have added to the multi-faceted character of Black lesbian life, nightclubbing has also been an important source of our culture. Club nights run by Black lesbians have provided a safe haven for many, especially those who find it alienating in predominantly white clubs. Such clubs are a response to the racism we have experienced on the lesbian and gay scene, from being overtly denied entry into venues, to reggae, calypso and bhangra not being played.

Blues parties originate from the African-Caribbean heterosexual community; in the lesbian community they are run predominantly by women of African-Caribbean descent. These take the form of a party held in a house, where there is a door charge, a sound system with DJs and a bar. They are frequented by lesbians of both African and Asian descent and by a few white women. Blues parties for Black lesbians have existed in Britain since the 1970s, often in cities where there may have been no other Black lesbian groups, poetry events or performances. Although some people think of them as drunken, smoky affairs, they have provided an essential source of networking, a place where Black lesbians could come together and relax. During the early 1990s Paradise, a nightclub which rented out its space to lesbians and gays, introduced a night called 'Asia'. Asia was attended by many lesbians of Asian and African descent, and DJs like Ritu played bhangra, new world and disco music.

Shakti has also provided venues for lesbians and gays of Asian descent, where bhangra and other types of Asian music are provided for the clientele. Lesbians of African and Asian descent have also organized one-off events in women's centres, but sadly such occasions are now few and far between. In London Black lesbian Blues parties are rare – once every four months – and venues are becoming harder to find. DJ Yvonne Taylor, part of the sound system Sistermatic, who were active in the 1980s, believes that because of the lack of Black women-only venues Black lesbians are raving on the mixed Black gay scene.

In 1994, London boasts three venues which are predominantly Black: Shakti and the Pressure Zone are for Black gay men/women and their friends, and Shugs is women-only but predominantly Black. Occasionally groups like the Black Experience will hold parties for Black gay men and women, and female DJs like Sister Culture, Ritu and Levi will organize nights for women. Outside of London, places where many Black lesbians and gay men attend are even harder to find.

Current political organizations

Political organizations almost seem to be a thing of the past. Organizations like OWAAD have disbanded, and although there is still a feminist movement of sorts, many group activities seem to be quite dormant. However, there are two political groups which continue to take an active role in issues relating to Black lesbians and national and international politics.

Wages Due Lesbians

Wages Due Lesbians (WDL), is one of the longest-standing lesbian groups in Britain. It was set up in 1975 by both Black and white lesbians on the platform of anti-racism. Although some of the lesbians belong to Black Women for Wages for Housework (BWWHW), for specific issues, WDL is perhaps one of the most successful examples of Black and white lesbians working together. Although the group is based in London, it has members scattered all over Britain. The organization's aims lie in the roots of the international Black movement: reparations. Hence, it demands that lesbians (and all other women) should be compensated for their unrecognized work.

Since its formation WDL has fought for the Black women not to be torn between her Black and lesbian identity, and has highlighted the link between homophobia, poverty and economic exploitation. It has continued to promote this debate because it believes that these are the concerns of the Black community, and consequently it has tried to bridge the gap between the lesbian, gay and Black movements by pinpointing all our common interests. WDL also believes that by connecting economics and homophobia, Black lesbians will continue campaigning for the issues which Black working-class people have to fight for, namely better housing, health care and wages. In WDL's book, *Policing the Bedroom*, it reports: 'The fact is that greater economic possibilities for women definitely help to overcome the barriers of being lesbian, promoting lesbian visibility and discouraging sexism. Increasing cuts and unemployment make it much harder to come out.'[2] The organization argues that the lesbian movement is actually far bigger than it appears, but because of our lack of economic power Black lesbians are more likely to remain closeted. The organization has spearheaded several campaigns during the past two decades. In particular, it has championed the rights of lesbian mothers and has recently taken a leading role in the campaign against the Child Support Act, highlighting its effects on Black and white mothers, including lesbian mothers. Along with BWWHW, it has worked together to ensure Black women's visibility and to protect them against the effects of the 1991 Child Support Act.

WDL was also active in the Clause 28 campaign against the prevention of promoting lesbian and gay literature; the campaign against Paragraph 16, banning lesbians and gay men from adopting and fostering children; anti-racism movements; international campaigns against, e.g. the Gulf War; and has fought for anti-racist politics to be included at the national lesbian and gay festival, Gay Pride. Today WDL are at the forefront of the campaign to stop genocidal experiments – the testing of AZT on HIV-positive African children – and many other national and global campaigns which concern the Black and lesbian communities. One of its founder members, Wilmette Brown, believes WDL's success in attracting Black lesbians and women lies in its healthy mix of politicizing and socializing. She believes that lesbian cultural activity has often been guilty of racism, by excluding the Black lesbian experience. The organization continues to give Black lesbians an opportunity to network with lesbians from all over the world.

Zamimass

Zamimass is a Black lesbian-only organization which embraces lesbians of African, Asian and Middle Eastern descent, together with lesbians indigenous to the Americas, the Caribbean, Australia and the Pacific nations. It was set up in 1990 after the International Lesbian and Gay People of Colour conference in response to the dissatisfaction of many Black lesbians with the lack of unity between Black lesbians of different ethnic origins and cultural backgrounds. The members define themselves as Black working-class lesbians who experience a multitude of oppressions. The committee is open to all Black lesbians who are committed to working in an unselfish way for the collective liberation and unity of all Black peoples. Zamimass is working towards a classless society which recognizes us for all the work we do, according to our abilities, providing everyone with the basic needs for survival. It demands a society free of racism, with equal opportunities, and an end to the state violence, police brutality and imprisonment of Black people. It works towards creating a society where Black people, and the countries from which we originate, can benefit from the wealth we create, and to establishing an education system which teaches people the truth about Black history. Similarly, it fights for the rights of women, lesbians and gay men, arguing for the end of discrimination, sexism and homophobia. The organization also campaigns for the emancipation of the elderly, families, the unemployed and young people.

Zamimass was instrumental in promoting a Black lesbian and gay section in the annual Gay Pride march, and curated the first ever Black lesbian exhibition. Despite a major split during its early days, the organization has managed to survive. Its immediate aim for the future is to create an all-year-round retreat centre where Black lesbians can escape to. With donations, membership fees and no funding it continues to fight for the cultural upliftment and visibility of all Black lesbians in Britain.

Concluding comments

As we move into the last five years of the twentieth century, the attitude is if you are planning to set up a group, centre, conference, etc., find the capital and finance it yourself. Because Black women, including Black lesbians, make up a disproportionate number of the unemployed, and are in receipt of some of the lowest wages, this familiar ethos presents a daunting and monumental task. Self-determination and self-preservation are familiar concepts in the Black communities, but in the wake of a rise in racist and homophobic attacks, we could quite easily be pushed underground if we were to lose all our institutions.

The choices we have to maintain an active Black lesbian community are few. We can invest in our own communities by putting the money we earn back into Black lesbian businesses, organizations, publications, etc. Another option is to create a community with not only Black lesbians of African and Asian descent, but with other Black lesbians. We could also continue to forge links with Black gay men and pool our resources, or perhaps try again to work together with white lesbians and be part of a community where our issues are prioritized along with everybody elses needs. Whatever happens, at least the foundations of Black lesbian political and cultural activity have been laid, and can be built upon and revitalized at any time by new Black lesbians.

It is important to add that lesbians of African and Asian descent, out or closeted, have all played a role in the Black lesbian movement. It is a political act in itself to have sexual relationships with the same gender, when heterosexuality is considered the norm in both Black and white communities. We have all challenged our communities and families, and all of us are vulnerable to homophobia. Active or passive we all have a role in the Black lesbian struggle. We all have something to be proud of.

Notes

1. Beverley Bryan, Stella Dadzie and Suzanne Scafe, *Heart of the Race*. Virago Press, London, 1985.
2. Wages Due Lesbians, *Policing the Bedroom*. Wages Due Lesbians, London, 1991.

Books

Beverley Bryan, Stella Dadzie and Suzanne Scafe, *Heart of the Race*. Virago Press, London, 1985.

Da Choong, Olivette Cole-Wilson, Bernadine Evaristo and Gabriela Pearse (eds), *Black Women Talk Poetry*. Black Womantalk, London, 1987.

Da Choong *et al.* (eds), *Don't Ask Me Why*. Black Womantalk, London, 1991.

22: *Talking Black*

Peter Fryer, *Staying Power*. Pluto Press, London, 1984.
Valerie Mason-John and Ann Khambatta, *Making Black Waves*. Scarlet Press, London, 1993.
Wages Due Lesbians, *Policing the Bedroom*. Wages Due Lesbians, London, 1991.

Articles

Dorothea Smartt and Valerie Mason-John, 'Black feminist movement on both sides of the Atlantic', *Spare Rib*, 1986.
Brenda Emanus and Valerie Mason-John (under pseudonym Valerie Charles), 'Sisters under the skin', *The Voice*, 1986.
Valerie Mason-John, 'Theatre of Black women', *EveryWoman*, 1986.

Thank you to Wages Due Lesbians (Wilmette Brown, Sara Callaway, Cristal Amiss) and Zamimass (Abena Onomass) for providing me with information, and to Yvonne Taylor for her knowledge of Black lesbian night-life.

Chapter two

A Retrospective: Black Together under One Banner

Savitri Hensman

AMONG lesbians of African and Asian descent in Britain, the term Black is used in widely varying ways. To a large degree this reflects different views of the struggles of lesbians of African and Asian descent in Britain and our hopes for the future. It is sometimes argued that 'Black' cannot properly describe people who are not of African descent. Some Asians regard themselves as Black, although others may strongly reject this identity. Black is sometimes taken to include everyone descended, through one or both parents, from Africa, Asia and Latin America and the original peoples of North America and Australasia: although I recognize the wide variations in culture and experience, this is how I use the term myself. However, a number of people who once referred to themselves as Black now prefer the term used in the USA, 'people of colo(u)r', because they believe it to be inclusive of more people. In the USA Black refers to African-American people only. While the term has become popular among some Black lesbians in Britain, there are many who dislike it because it is reminiscent of the label 'coloured', which was once used to categorize Black people in Britain. There are also other Black lesbians who are fed up with being defined by their colour, and wish to see themselves as African or Asian lesbians, because colour coding has been one of the many ways white people continue to oppress us.

When Black lesbian groups were first established and the first Black lesbian conference was held, the definition of Black was debated several times, sometimes heatedly. Some women assumed that the term Black only referred to African-Caribbean people, others felt it referred to dark-skinned people, and so the issue of who was and was not Black was often on top of the agenda. When the London-based Black Lesbian and Gay project was granted funding to establish a centre in 1985, after much discussion it formulated a policy on the term Black, which has come to be used as the common definition among Black lesbians in Britain. You must be able to trace your descent through one or both parents, to Africa, Asia, the Middle East, China, including the Pacific nations, Latin America, the original inhabitants of Australasia, North America, or the islands of the Atlantic and Indian Ocean. However, despite this model we tended to talk too much in the abstract, without acknowledging the personal experiences which affected how we felt and thought about the matter, and to lecture rather than listen. Again, Black women were meant to be tough: it was easier to express anger than pain. Nevertheless, to our credit, we managed on some occasions to reach a consensus, and on others at least to agree to keep working together.

Tensions still remained, however. Some lesbians of African descent felt, I think, that their hard-won space was being encroached on, and the uniqueness of their experiences denied. A number of Asian and Latin American lesbians, and mixed racial heritage or light-skinned lesbians of African descent, who turned up at Black events (not necessarily for lesbians only) and whose presence was challenged, stopped going to such gatherings to avoid risking the pain of rejection. Some organizations, seeking to encourage a wide range of lesbians to participate, took to printing their definition of Black on their publicity materials. This was partly, but not wholly, effective. Some lesbians of Asian and Latin American descent had learnt to be wary, while others did not want to organize with lesbians of African descent, for a variety of reasons. Some were prejudiced, some were not fluent in English, some assumed that Black suggested a common culture. It is difficult to describe a South Asian culture shared by everyone from rural Nepal to coastal Sri Lanka and others of South Asian descent throughout the world, let alone a broader Black culture.

Sometimes events were publicized as open to all lesbians 'of colour' – the term common in the Americas – because it seemed to have the advantage of being less open to confusion than Black. But as it turned out, 'of colour' could not be relied on to prevent disputes. The International Lesbian and Gay People of Colour conference, previously held in North America, took place in London in 1990. When the women gathered and the organizers asked a light-skinned West Asian lesbian to facilitate the discussion, a British-based African-Caribbean woman objected angrily. What was at issue was not a choice of terms but rather, I think, whether lesbians from such a range of backgrounds had anything in common, and if they did, whether their unity would be founded on mistrust and rivalry. I believe that the debate about what Black means concerns more than a choice of words, important though this is. I do not claim that there is a correct meaning which should be generally accepted by African and Asian Lesbians throughout the world, or even in Britain. I recognize that the experiences which are most meaningful to each of us, and how we interpret and act on them, vary. When looking at how lesbians of African and Asian descent feel about the label Black, it is important to look at our history in Britain. A look at the past can perhaps throw some light on the underlying issues.

A cold climate

Most people of African and Asian descent in Britain occupied menial positions: for example, as slaves (until slavery was abolished), servants and seafarers. Some were treated relatively well, but others faced brutality or summary dismissal. Probably little evidence survives of the relationships of companionship and physical intimacy which they formed, including those between women.

Various words were used to describe the men, women and children whose work helped to underpin British society, but who nevertheless remained easily dispensable. One of these was 'Black', which was applied to Asians as well as Africans. In 1688, for instance, one newspaper offered a reward of a guinea for a 'black boy, an Indian, about thirteen years old, runaway', while in 1786 another criticized families returning from India who 'bring over with them one or more female blacks to take care of the children, under a promise to send them back to their native country free of expense', but who break their word, leaving their former employees 'daily begging for a passage back'. Another term sometimes used was 'coloured'.

However, a minority of those of Asian and African descent, who visited or settled in Britain, were treated with greater respect because of their wealth, aristocratic birth or professional success. One person who won warm public acclaim in the nineteenth century was Mary Seacole from the Caribbean. During the Crimean War, she worked determinedly amidst sordid conditions, using her medical and organizational skills to relieve the suffering of numerous soldiers. Another was Dadabhai Naoroji, an Indian academic, businessman and campaigner for progressive causes. When he was chosen as a Liberal parliamentary candidate, the Tory prime minister declared that 'however far we have advanced in overcoming prejudices, I doubt if we have yet got to that point when a British constituency will take a Black man to represent them'. Naoroji, according to one newspaper, was lighter-skinned than the prime minister: clearly being Black was a matter of more than skin colour. In 1892 he was elected to the House of Commons. Success stories like those of Seacole and Naoroji were, nevertheless, few and far between.

By the middle of the twentieth century, many more Black people had arrived in Britain, often to work in factories and service industries, in poor conditions and for low wages. Facing discrimination by landlords, employers and others, many joined together for mutual assistance and support. Black people from a particular nation or region would often help one another to find accommodation and employment. They shared certain ways of expressing and enjoying themselves, and had a common interest in what was happening 'back home'. Often they lived in the same neighbourhoods, and would work and socialize together.

Racism was taking on a more virulent form: in 1958, racist riots broke out in Nottingham and Notting Hill in London; less than a year later a Caribbean man was murdered. The government, to cope with a labour shortage, had encouraged immigration, but in 1962 a law was passed to restrict entry to Britain. In this climate, Black organizations banded together, and set up federations such as the Coloured People's Progressive Association. In Birmingham the Co-ordinating Committee Against Racial Discrimination was formed after a protest meeting convened by the West Indian Workers' Association and the Indian Youth League in the wake of the killing of one of Africa's most eminent anti-colonialist leaders, Patrice Lumumba. Three days after the People's March on Washington, the London-based Conference of Afro-Asian-Caribbean Organizations organized a march from Notting Hill to the American embassy against racist discrimination in Britain and in support of the civil rights of African-American people. Solidarity with the struggles of oppressed peoples worldwide was an important feature of the Black movement at that time.

The Labour Party initially opposed the 1962 Immigration Act, then changed its position and endorsed it on taking power in 1964, while at the same time introducing anti-discrimination legislation. In that election, the British National Party won 9 per cent of the vote in Southall, and in Smethwick in Birmingham the Tory candidate won, reversing the national swing to Labour, after his supporters waged a crudely racist campaign. It was increasingly accepted by mainstream politicians that immigrants were a 'problem': what was at issue was how humanely this problem would be tackled. Moderate Conservative and Labour MPs helped to prevent a slide into hardened bigotry, but the idea that Black people were undesirable as neighbours, except perhaps in small numbers, had been established.

A sense of personal freedom

I was born in 1962 into a rapidly changing world. Many former colonies in Africa, Asia and Latin America had won independence or were about to do so, often after long and painful struggles. One of the nations which gained independence that year was Jamaica, another was Algeria, at the end of a fiercely fought war against French rule. Each victory over colonialism weakened the old order in which most people could expect to spend their lives as subjects of an occupying power. Unlike my parents and grandparents, who at their birth added to the vast numbers in the British Empire, from my earliest moment I was a citizen of an independent Ceylon. The newly independent nations were now entering the international arena. They were part of neither the Western nor the Eastern bloc, although some aligned themselves with the USA or its rival the Soviet Union. Instead, they were part of a fresh 'Third World' (a phrase adopted by French-speaking anti-colonialists in the 1950s, I think), which posed a challenge to the old order.

It was not just in the field of government that a transformation was taking place. At one time, the cultures of the peoples of these three continents had been widely denigrated as barbaric or at least primitive. The debt of Western culture to those who were supposed to be inferior had been downplayed. Great works of architecture, art, literature and music had been ignored or dismissed by eminent Western scholars, and educated men and women from the colonies had tried to show that they were not like their neighbours but closer to Europeans in their thinking and lifestyle. But this attitude was not universal: some Paris and Oxford graduates had rejected comfort and respectability, using their education to celebrate the past achievements of their peoples and expose the injustices they faced under their colonial rulers. Some white people had treated the 'natives' with respect despite the hostility of other expatriates. By the 1960s, however, languages, religions and artistic traditions which had long been undervalued gained greater respect internationally.

Economically, too, the colonies and ex-colonies were seeking to break free. What was produced, and how, had been heavily influenced by the needs of the traders and industrialists of the colonial powers. It was important to those who had struggled for independence that direct rule should not be replaced by neocolonialism: a different form of economic development was essential. Some sought to modernize along Western lines, while others saw the way forward as co-operation for the common good rather than putting self-interest first. The Chinese and Cuban revolutions had an impact which went further than South-East Asia and the Caribbean. While, in the month I was born, an influential article was published in which Tanzanian leader Julius Nyerere stressed the merits of an African tradition of community, against the acquisitive and competitive outlook brought in under colonialism. He urged that 'the same socialist attitude of mind which, in the tribal days, gave to every individual the security that comes of belonging to a widely extended family' should be preserved and extended beyond the tribe, the nation and even the continent to humankind as a whole. It was a time when people in the three continents inspired one another with their dreams of a better future and their struggles to make them a reality. New opportunities and choices were opening up for those in the former colonies, including women-loving women.

In the meantime it was necessary to get by, in countries where the effects of underdevelopment were often worsened by deep social and economic inequalities. Many migrated. In 1964 I arrived in England with my immediate family. We were most definitely categorized as Black by the state and by the white British people. As a small child, I did not of course follow all the twists and turns of national politics. My parents and older sister and brother tried to protect me, and I was lucky enough to live in a neighbourhood where virulent racism was less common than in nearby Southall. But, as I adjusted to my new surroundings, it became clear through various means, from my treatment in the playground to comments on TV, that people like me were not fully welcome here. White people treated us as inferior to themselves, they spoke down to us and behaved as if we were primitive animals. Like many, perhaps the majority, of Black children, I reacted with a mixture of pride and shame in who I was. Meanwhile racist attacks and Black struggles continued, and in the wake of visits to Britain by African-American activists Martin Luther King and Malcolm X, the Campaign Against Racial Discrimination and the more militant Racial Action Adjustment Society were formed.

If I had been aware of the depth of prejudice against lesbians and gays, and that one day this might be turned against me, I would have found British society less welcoming. Those Black people older than me who were aware that they were attracted to the same sex had good reason to be discreet. Until 1967 all sex between men was illegal. This law was vigorously enforced, and eminent white citizens either found themselves in the dock, their careers brought to an abrupt end, or were forced to pay out large sums to extortionists to keep their private lives secret. Sexual relationships between women were usually regarded with disbelief or strong disapproval.

The widespread distaste for, yet fascination with, 'unnatural' acts and passions was partly the legacy of the imperial past (and to some extent present) when so-called clean-living, God-fearing white men were supposed to bring the benefits of European civilization to the rest of the world, backed by 'their' women who would give birth to and bring up future generations to carry on this work. This concern for upholding traditional values and sex roles, and maintaining racial and cultural purity often came with a fear, and sometimes envy, of those (including not only colonized peoples but Europeans who broke the written or unwritten rules of their society) who were supposedly free from these restraints. For those who did not fit the social norm, the twin temptations of seeking to be accepted by conforming as much as possible and rebelling ostentatiously expressed contempt for these values held by other people. However, by not being altogether free of such attitudes, meant it was hard for some to resist completely. In such conditions, it was an achievement to survive and hold on to the ability to love.

Turbulent times

In 1968, Conservative MP Enoch Powell made a widely publicized speech in which he claimed that immigrants were taking over large areas of the country. Elderly white women were being victimized, he alleged, and in allowing dependants to enter, so that the 'immigrant-descended population' could grow in future, the nation was in effect 'heaping up its own funeral pyre. . . . As I look ahead, I am filled with foreboding. Like the Roman, I seem to see the River Tiber foaming with much blood'. Politicians, he warned, had no right to dismiss the fears of constituents that 'in this country in fifteen or twenty years the Black man will have the whip hand over the white man'. He touched a chord in some white people who not only resented having to come into contact with those whom they considered to be their inferiors, but also were deeply fearful of them. Many felt insecure, sometimes because of rapid change in areas of their lives, such as work and housing, over which they felt they had little control. In addition, they had been brought up to believe that members of different communities could not live together conspicuously, sharing with and learning from one another, without one community or the other losing its freedom or identity. I think that I and many other Black children growing up here were also influenced by this belief, and hostile surroundings reinforced fears of 'outsiders'. Values such as hospitality and tolerance had a certain attraction but seemed out of place, even risky, since those who practised them would be at a disadvantage in dealing with their neighbours. I think this wariness, instilled at an early age, was later to affect the way that Black lesbians who had been brought up here, including me, approached others, in contrast to those who had spent their earliest years in very different societies.

Meanwhile, although it would have been obvious to a detached outsider that Black people were not on the verge of taking over, Powell's speech had a powerful effect. Racial tension rose sharply. Powell was dismissed from the shadow cabinet, but he had the vigorous support of many white people. In London, dockers and meat porters marched to the House of Commons in his support. At the same time over fifty organizations, including the Indian Workers' Association and the West Indian Standing Conference, formed a national body, the Black People's Alliance, 'a militant front for Black Conciousness and against racialism'.

In the USA, the term Black was more often applied to people of African descent, in particular African-American people, who continued to struggle for justice. Many regarded themselves as involved in a wider struggle. Malcolm X said in 1965: 'We are living in an era of revolution, and the revolt of the American Negro is part of the rebellion against the oppression and colonialism which has characterized this era.' International solidarity took a practical form in the opposition to the USA's military involvement in Indochina. Against the arguments of some Black leaders who thought the war offered the opportunity to emphasize their community's usefulness and patriotism, Martin Luther King took a powerful stance against the Indochina war. This was linked with his view that 'The Negro must not allow himself to become a victim of the self-serving philosophy of those who manufacture war that the survival of the world is the white man's business alone.' Black freedom involved a rejection of subservience and helplessness, and an acceptance of responsibility. Some white people, too, opposed the war, arousing fierce debate. Many of society's values, including traditional sexual mores and male domination, were under challenge, and in this atmosphere of questioning and conflict, police harassment of Black and white patrons of a gay bar sparked off the Stonewall riot in 1969.

Black struggles in the USA, non-violent as well as violent, were often met with brutal force by white supremacists and state forces. Many activists were imprisoned or killed. In Britain, the violence was on a smaller scale; nevertheless the Black movement set off strong reactions from some in the establishment. The late 1960s were turbulent times in much of Europe; some hoped, or feared, that revolution was round the corner. In the view of a *Times* news team, the 'ominous lesson' of the Campaign Against Racial Discrimination was that 'the mixture of pro-Chinese communism and American-style Black power on the immigrant scene can be devastating'.

However, no immediate transformation of society took place. Long-term work would be needed if justice was to be won. While differences and divisions among Black people could sometimes be set aside at times of severe threat and intense struggle, they still existed. This was to occur in the Black lesbian movement, resulting in serious damage. For Black people in Britain and elsewhere, to survive and win justice despite the powerful forces ranged against them, unity was vital. But this would rest on shaky foundations unless possible causes of tension were recognized and addressed. Black lesbians, in order to fight the Black struggle, had to remain in the closet. This tension brewed so much that it caused a major division in the Black women's movement in Britain. During 1981 the Organization of Women of African and Asian Descent (OWAAD) organized a conference at a time when tension between the police and the Asian and African-Caribbean communities was coming to a head. Riots occurred throughout England, in all the major cities. Some women at the conference were angry that women should want to discuss such a 'trivial' issue like lesbianism when the country was in total chaos over racism. They believed that sexuality and other women's oppressions should be secondary to the needs of the wider Black communities. The rift was set, OWAAD never recovered from the split, and it collapsed a year later.

Differences and divisions

All Black people in Britain in the late 1960s and early 1970s had some experience of racism, but in differing forms, depending on their occupation, citizenship status and other factors. In colonial societies, which tended to be deeply hierarchical, some had been favoured more than their neighbours, on grounds which varied widely. One of these was ethnicity: the British rulers of Kenya, for instance, had brought in Indians to occupy high-level posts; and in French-controlled Kampuchea, where few people were given the chance of secondary let alone higher education, it was generally Vietnamese who were appointed to administrative jobs. In this way, white people could avoid much of the day-to-day unpleasantness of the relationship between ruler and ruled, deflecting this on to Black people instead. Other grounds for privilege included fluency in the colonizer's language; being of partly European descent; being light-skinned; and practising the same religion or customs as the colonizing nation. Closely tied up with some of these factors was the issue of social and economic class. Traditional hierarchies, of gender or caste for instance, were occasionally challenged but at other times utilized in colonial societies.

In such situations, while the occupying power exerted control over the lives of the 'natives' in general, some convinced themselves they were more civilized than their neighbours, who in turn felt inferior or bitterly resentful, or veered between the two. White attitudes to Black peoples overseas were also sometimes absorbed through the educational system and in other ways: textbooks, stories and films which sought to downplay and justify the atrocities of the slave trade or the near-annihilation of the original inhabitants of North America found their way around the world.

Black solidarity was further weakened by competition for scarce jobs, land and other resources. Anger at the injustices one faced could easily be turned on those who had also been treated unjustly, albeit perhaps in a different way. Some people were acutely aware of the indignities they themselves experienced but oblivious to those of others. My immediate family, partly Tamil, had narrowly survived with the help of Sinhalese neighbours when politicians had stirred up ethnic nationalist violence for their own ends. Religious faith had sustained many people through the humiliations of colonialism, but religious supremacism, too, could see people living in the same localities against one another. Affection and desire could develop across social barriers. But even when Black lesbians from different communities came together as friends, lovers and sisters in struggle, prejudice (often unconscious), memories of past insults and injuries and suspicion of 'outsiders' instilled at an early age sometimes led to mistrust and pain.

In Britain, the way in which Black people were treated depended to some extent on how close they appeared to come to society's cultural and physical ideals, on stereotypes of what 'their kind' were like and, of course, the power they wielded. A wealthy businessman from an oil-rich nation could command some respect even if he happened to be Muslim, had not been educated here and did not wear a collar and tie. Being regarded as 'not like the rest of them' in one way or another offered Black people a welcome respite from some aspect of the racism which day by day ground away at their security and self-esteem. But there was also a risk of finding oneself distanced from others who were Black, and indeed from aspects of oneself, while still remaining on the fringes of white society. This was linked with how people related to the past. White racists sometimes harked back to a golden age of Western culture. This required a distortion of their own complex history – Christianity, for example, was presented as a basically European faith – as a refusal to acknowledge that the West's involvement with other nations and cultures in recent centuries had played a major part in shaping Western society too.

Some Black people also looked back to the 'good old days' before white colonialists arrived. Their history with all its achievements and failures, benevolence and cruelty, was recreated as a seamless whole. The ruthlessness with which Western landowners and industrialists had treated their own people, let alone foreigners, in amassing wealth and power was ignored or dismissed as a defect of the white character: Black leaders, it was assumed, could be trusted not to treat 'their own' so callously. Other Black people took a less clear-cut view of colonialism, but shared an optimistic outlook on the future.

Some Asian people who disliked being called Black were openly prejudiced against anybody of African descent, and were keen to distance themselves from them. Others were more concerned with rejecting a term under which diverse peoples had been dismissively lumped together. Regrettably, in trying to remove the reminders of their colonial past they also risked forgetting their legacy of struggle and solidarity. Those of African descent who denied that people of Asian descent were truly Black (which was to become a controversial issue in the Black lesbian movement) sometimes did so because they believed that Africans, unless of partly European descent, were darker-skinned than Asians (usually but not always the case), and that anyone whose skin colour was lighter would experience less racism. They ignored the fact that fluency in English, residence status and other factors also affected the way people were treated. Others were rightly concerned to insist on the uniqueness of their own identity and experience; but I believe that, in not acknowledging Asians as Black, they risked missing out on the opportunity to unite with others faced with similar questions about the future.

Under colonialism, much that was traditional had been destroyed, left to decay or adapted to suit the convenience of the conquerors. Therefore, it was understandable that many Black people should seek a clear sense of their heritage. The fact that tradition was often made up of widely varying strands and developed throughout the history of each community was sometimes overlooked. Scholars and religious and political leaders, talking and writing about ancient societies, tended to stress the importance of men like themselves. That strong and independent women existed, let alone that some had women lovers, often went without mention; and those historical periods when patriarchy was strongest, power imbalances greatest, tended to get the most attention. So for Black lesbians, in particular, there were risks in being uncritically nostalgic for the 'good old days', before different ethnic and religious communities were violently flung together by colonialism and imperialism.

Similarly, what happened in colonial times and subsequently also helped to shape our current reality. For instance, some colonial powers had made gay sex a criminal offence, and this had influenced the way that many Black people thought of same-sex love. There was no point in simply wishing this had never happened. Instead, in confronting the consequences, we could learn and gain inspiration from many different struggles for justice and examples of societies where lovers of the same sex were not punished, and call on international solidarity in dealing with the forces ranged against us. But it was difficult for us not to be influenced, at least a little, by those who wanted to ignore, or unmake, the network of relationships which had developed across cultural and geographical boundaries.

Differences within the Black movement in Britain were exacerbated by divisions over what the long-term aims of the antiracist struggle were, and how they might be achieved. As in the USA, different people favoured different methods: seeking to persuade people in authority of the need for change; non-violent direct action; violent confrontation with white supremacists and the state. I believe each method had advantages and disadvantages, and which was most appropriate depended to some degree on the situation. What is more, Black people who unite in specific struggles sometimes had different long-term objectives. Some sought integration into the mainstream of society, so that Black people could compete on equal terms at all levels. Some wanted to create parallel structures, where it was Black political leaders and business owners who ran the affairs of the Black community. In the USA some Black nationalists sought a state of their own, on occasion even making common cause with neo-Nazi white separatists, although with a very different motive; in Britain, however, with its much smaller Black population, this seemed less feasible. Some sought a more equal society, free from the extremes of wealth and poverty, where all could contribute and none would be exploited. And some Black people had no clear preference.

37: *Black Together under One Banner*

Debates on the aims and tactics of Black struggles were sometimes extremely intense and heated. This was partly due to the pressure under which they took place and partly, I think, to a certain way of approaching issues which was common in Britain (and maybe other parts of Europe too), and which had influenced English-speaking people in other countries. In this scheme of thinking, if two things differed, one had to be better, the other worse; indeed, if one was good, the other might well be evil. How much of this was rooted in Western philosophy, and how much of it resulted from the fierce struggles which had shaped modern society, I do not know. It was assumed, for instance, that humankind was at odds with nature (although thinkers differed in which side they took), and that, in the field of sexuality, behaviour different from the norm was a sign of moral weakness, wilful perversity or, alternatively, of superiority to ordinary, more conventional people. This dualism was often valuable: it meant that important issues were less likely to be fudged. What was second-rate or actually destructive was less likely to go unchallenged. But it could also be divisive, especially if it was assumed that only certain people, for example philosophers, religious leaders or theoreticians in the vanguard of a radical movement, could fully grasp the absolute truth and communicate it to others. This sometimes led people who differed or disagreed to pin hostile or dismissive labels on one another, or to reject what were in fact valuable insights, because they felt that what they themselves had to offer was not taken seriously.

Black people trying to break free from the effects of racism in their own hearts and minds, as well as in society, sometimes argued that white people, far from being superior beings to be looked up to and imitated, were inferior or even demonic. Black people's individuality had often been denied, and they had been punished for one another's real or supposed misdeeds; white people, in turn, were all to be held to blame for what Black people had suffered. This was perhaps an inevitable stage in shaking off the legacy of the past, but it was a dangerous one in which to remain. For there is a vital difference between insisting that people who benefit from a certain kind of oppression have a particular responsibility to oppose it, and suggesting that people are inevitably trapped by the identity into which they are born. The idea of white collective guilt was sometimes taken further, dividing the Black community; some members believed that the numerous Black people who were of partly European ancestry (such as myself) were contaminated. Such views appeared to suggest that people were shaped by their biology or conditioning and that their own choices counted for little. Nevertheless, although Black people might occasionally be bitingly critical of white people in general, they were often more tolerant in practice; and in any case, Black people, while capable of hurting individuals, did not have the power systematically to oppress their white neighbours.

Not all Black lesbians in Black or women's groups were involved in organizing against racism, some were unable or unwilling to take part in collective struggles. Those who did, gained a valuable grounding in activism, but also often acquired attitudes and ways of dealing with people, whose opinions and experiences were different from their own, which could prove destructive.

Here to stay

What position would Black lesbians have in the future which the Black movement sought to bring about? A number of Black men, some of whom were conservative and others supposedly radical, believed strongly in male domination, as did some women. What mattered to them was that the white man should not reign supreme, but the Black man should either reign alongside or instead of him. This often went with the view that society was basically hierarchical, with people at different levels under obligations to one another. The fact that, in practice, the limited power that Black men had over Black women and children, and sometimes other Black men (for instance, Asian factory owners who employed Asian workers), was frequently ignored and misused. It was attributed to the presence of a racist society or blamed on those at the receiving end who, in supposedly not showing enough respect, provoked their own mistreatment. In such a set-up, there would be no place for any kind of love between women which might threaten male dominance or prevent women from fulfilling their duties to the men in their lives. What is more, if there was rivalry between male leaders, for instance over territory or political influence, those under their leadership would be expected to follow their example. Women would be under pressure to set aside their bonds of sisterhood and love, out of loyalty to men who had little real regard for women. Black lesbians influenced by this ideal, however, subtly, could later find their relationships with one another under strain because of the words and deeds of so-called community leaders.

There were other people who believed that Black women, as well as men, should be treated on the basis of merit in the professions and the world of business. Those who were successful might be respected enough, and have sufficient resources, to explore their sexuality, and to live and love as they chose. Even then, they might risk losing custom from or promotion by those, who because of their own wealth and status, had the power to discriminate. The majority of Black women, heterosexual or lesbian, would be left struggling to survive and usually also to sustain their families in difficult conditions. Their opportunities to take care of their own physical and emotional needs would be limited, and they would have much to lose by offending the men – from employers and landlords to family members – on whom they relied for necessities such as food and shelter. Also, in highly competitive settings, Black women could find themselves jostling with each other in a race to the top, and old grievances and rivalries could easily be revived. Black lesbians who held this view of the way forward might work together to ensure that the rules were fairer, but sooner or later they would come to treat one another competitively.

There were sections of the Black movement, largely socialist, who urged the building of a world where women would be free and equal, no longer weighed down by numerous burdens and injustices. Even these, however, were sometimes organized in such a way that many women – especially those with children to look after – could not participate fully, and the views of those who did take part were not always taken seriously.

As for lesbian and gay sexuality, to the best of my knowledge it was not widely discussed in the Black movement. This is not surprising. In the mid-1970s, as I became aware of my feelings towards other girls and women, I searched the local library for information. At that time, although the acceptance of same-sex relationships in ancient Greece and Rome was quite widely known, I cannot remember reading anything by or about Black lesbians or gays. If I had been more knowledgeable I suppose I might have rooted out some of James Baldwin's work. However, one of the more encouraging books on the shelves, which explained that homosexual people were quite ordinary and not suffering from arrested development and which did not discuss the possibility of aversion therapy (I had no wish to receive electric shocks or be induced to vomit), told me that such people could be found in all sections of society.

Statistically there had to be other Black people who felt as I did. On TV lesbians and gays were few and far between, and generally white. I was lucky enough to know that a couple of my acquaintances were gay, and that the stereotypes of 'queers' were not true, but again these men were white. Some Black lesbians managed to find and draw strength from one another, but there were few positive images around to inspire us to come out in large numbers. What is more, racism was an ever-present threat. Combating it could not be set aside until matters of gender and sexuality had been resolved, nor was it easy to risk damaging links with one's sisters and brothers by forcing them to confront issues which many found painful or just puzzling.

In the turbulent climate of the late 1960s, the women's movement had flourished, and by the 1970s a number of Black lesbians were involved. However, it is important to add that there have always been Black women involved in the feminist movement in Britain, but we have not always been so visible. The women's movement criticised patriarchal dominance in family life, and this was taken up by the more radical part of the gay movement, although in practice lesbians often found it hard to work with gay men because of their sexism. Feminists tried to organize in ways where responsibility for thinking and decision-making was shared, not delegated to a handful of leaders, a common practice in male-dominated radical groups. Politics was not something lofty and outside the sphere of women's everyday lives; instead, the personal was political. Although heterosexism and the influence of a sexist society persisted to some extent, issues of sexuality could be examined in more depth, and in such surroundings many lesbians were able to come out.

However, the women's movement often failed to live up to its own ideals. It sought to uncover the effects of oppression on women's daily lives, but matters of interest to Black women were ignored or dismissed as unimportant unless they coincided with those of an elite group, whose concerns somehow marked out the limits of what were 'women's issues'. Although everyone was supposed to share responsibility, in group discussions the views of white middle-class women were often given more weight. Challenging this was all the more difficult because it was sometimes assumed that women could not oppress each other, or that such oppression was of minor importance compared to that of women by men. Irish and Jewish women, women with disabilities and working-class women in general could also easily find themselves pushed to the margins of the women's movement.

Feminists rightly drew attention to male injustices against women in the community and family. Black lesbians also had to deal with racism, and sometimes found themselves in alliance with their sons, brothers, workmates and other men – sexist though they might be – in struggles together against this. Although the interests of Black women were not always the same as those of Black men, there was some common ground. But putting energy into anti-racist and other struggles was sometimes regarded as being male-identified. And Black lesbians and gays had to be tactful in what they said about 'the family' if they were to avoid defensive reactions from Black people whose family relationships the state refused to respect or sometimes even acknowledge.

Over the years, many predominantly white women's organizations were to recognize, at least to a limited extent, the need to oppose racism. But this was a slow and difficult process. Many Black women who defined themselves as feminists, and others who did not, joined Black women's groups. Black lesbians in such groups took part in intensive struggles on a range of issues. The Immigration Act of 1971 had placed harsh restrictions on entry into Britain by people who were not 'patrials', a category set up to allow people, usually white, whose parents or grandparents had emigrated from Britain to Australia, Rhodesia (now Zimbabwe) or elsewhere to enter the country, while most Black people were excluded. They might be allowed in to do a specific job for a specific period of time. If they were the dependants of people settled here, they could apply to the British authorities where they lived for permission to enter. In practice, this often dragged on for years, as the wives and children of men here tried to convince racist officials that they were really who they claimed to be. Immigration officers subjected people to humiliating interrogations – some brides-to-be were examined vaginally to determine whether they were virgins – until a public outcry (spearheaded by Southall Black Sisters and other Black women's groups) brought an end to such sexual abuse. Homes and workplaces were raided in the hunt for illegal immigrants. Such drastic immigration practices and legislation particularly affected Asians, including numerous people of Indian, Pakistani and Bangladeshi descent, and the issue was taken up by community activists.

Among African-Caribbean people, racism in schools was a major concern. As in other Black communities, education was generally highly valued. So parents were incensed to find that white teachers often assumed that their children lacked intelligence. Many were classified as 'educationally subnormal', those who got bored or angry at their treatment risked being classified as disruptive and banished from the classroom. Black female campaigners exposed and tried to bring an end to such practices, and supplementary schools and educational projects were set up in a number of neighbourhoods.

Police harassment was also a major problem for people of African descent. Young men, and to a lesser extent women, were assumed to have criminal tendencies and were stopped and searched. Those who objected risked being accused of obstructing or even assaulting police officers. Some people were arrested on suspicion of loitering with intent to commit an arrestable offence. This rather nebulous crime was difficult to disprove, and since in those days magistrates tended to believe anything a police officer told them, many were found guilty. Black people convicted of minor offences were likely to be sentenced more severely than their white counterparts. Many found themselves locked up away from their families and friends. Again, organizations such as Brixton Black Women's Group campaigned around these issues, often attempting to bring a feminist perspective to the struggle. Other forms of discrimination besides racism were at work: some white youths in mainly working-class areas also experienced harassment. But in the African-Caribbean community, in particular, the tension between police and public built up to such a level that there were major clashes.

Racist attacks continued, especially against Asians, who were assumed to be relatively passive and so easy targets. The police often refused to act, and when those on the receiving end fought back they were sometimes arrested themselves. The National Front, by then the best-known far-right organization in the country, marched through the streets under police protection, contested elections and tried to build a base in certain community groups, such as the right wing of the Conservative Party and some trade union branches.

While some in the British labour movement opposed racism in the workplace, others colluded with it. Some Black adults, especially from certain Asian communities, were self-employed, but many others ended up in jobs with low pay and poor conditions. Trade unions were often not interested in taking up their concerns. When the Black Mansfield hosiery workers went on strike in 1973 for better pay and conditions, a prominent member of the local Hosiery Workers' Union, a National Front activist, helped to mobilize support for the white workers who colluded with management. The Black women strikers of Grunwick's in London in 1976 managed to win not only the official support of their trade union but also practical assistance; however, after a while this support fizzled out.

Black women often faced indifference, lack of access to interpreters and insulting treatment in housing, health and other fields. Blatant racism in the mass media, especially the press, was common: Black people were a 'flood', and 'invasion'. Vigorous mobilization by the anti-racist movement helped to check the rise of the far right. So, perhaps, did the take-up of its most popular theme by mainstream politicians such as Margaret Thatcher, who in 1978 promised that her party would 'finally see an end to immigration', since 'this country might be rather swamped by people with a different culture'.

The experience of racism varied from locality to locality, community to community, differing according to the situation and the people involved. It could be blatant or subtle; it was not just a matter of prejudiced attitudes on the part of individuals, deeply hurtful as these could be, but was often built into society's institutions. In one way or another, it affected every Black woman in Britain. Some Black lesbians were highly vulnerable if they took part in any kind of activism or even socialized freely, especially those whose residence rights were not secure. Others found that their reserves of time, energy and compassion were exhausted by their own needs and those of their immediate circle. Still others became active in community affairs. Black women's groups were able to strengthen their links through the Organization of Women of African and Asian Descent (OWAAD). In this, and through broad campaigns and acts of solidarity, Black women were able to share and seek to interpret their experiences and discuss controversial issues.

Getting together, moving apart

When Britain entered the 1980s, mistrust of and anger at the police was high. It was fuelled by the mistreatment of Black people in custody and inaction over racist violence. As cited earlier, riots broke out and mainly young people, of African-Caribbean and Asian descent, battled against the police. During this same period at one of OWAAD's conferences, Black lesbians gathered in a workshop, and from this the first black lesbian group in Britain was formed. At around the same time, the Gay Black Group was also founded. I gather, initially, Asian men, fed up with racism in the gay scene and movement, had decided to set up their own group, but almost at once this was broadened. People of both African and Asian descent played a crucial part in the foundation of a Black lesbian and gay movement.

Those involved in this new movement were still active in mixed settings. In fact, I first found out about it during a campaign around Black people's right to self-defence, when I was overwhelmed by the sight of a number of Black men sporting pink triangles and wielding the Gay Black Group banner. It was becoming harder for the Black communities to ignore the lesbians and gays in their midst and for the lesbian and gay movement to play down the issue of racism. One form that this took was the sexual stereotyping of Black gays and lesbians, for instance as 'passive Orientals' or 'sensual Africans'. The stereotypes varied but the principle was the same. In this society Black people were judged mainly by usefulness, as a cheap, mobile and easily discarded source of labour with perhaps some novelty value, and by extension became a backdrop for other people's fears and fantasies. Without great care, this could spill over into intimate relationships.

One effect of the riots of 1980 and 1981 had been to shock the authorities into taking more notice of the Black communities. Genuine concern for their welfare was combined with a fear of further large-scale public disorder. In addition, many years of patient work were paying off and there was increasing recognition that Black people were part of, and contributed much to, modern Britain. There was also a growing willingness on the part of various local authorities to acknowledge that their Black residents had been unfairly treated, and financial grants were one way of improving the situation.

More funding was made available for the areas in which most Black people lived. Accepting funds from the state had long been controversial. Black organizations which did so had at times been labelled as 'collaborators', sometimes quite unfairly: Black people had every right to resources for which they had already paid dearly; there was no automatic loss of integrity in setting up, say, a training workshop or day centre with public funds. Indeed, money raised through private donations, or by selling goods and services to people who could afford them, could also raise conflicts of interest. However, there were negative features. Particular problems would arise when the aims of the group clashed with the needs and desires of the funder. This might involve not criticizing racism too forcefully, or perhaps less commonly, verbally flagellating white liberals seeking to do penance for their own, or others' misdeeds. Again, it was easier to get funding for, say Gujerati language or Caribbean cookery classes than for monitoring police racism, as some projects found to their cost. And getting more funds often meant highlighting differences among communities: why separate African and Asian centres might be needed in the same borough for instance. This encouraged an emphasis on the differences between Black people rather than on a common struggle against racism. Lesbians conscientiously filling in application forms or negotiating with funders on behalf of Black organizations to which they belonged, may have found that what started off as a fundraising tactic in time became a habit.

The mass media was now more interested in what Black people thought and felt about society, and what better way to find out than to ask community leaders. This implied a uniformity of views and interests among people of a particular ethnic or religious community. The newspapers and radio stations set up to appeal to a mainly Black readership or audience generally targeted specific communities. When Black programmes were broadcast by the mainstream media, they were usually aimed at a Black or Asian (generally South Asian) audience, seldom both, although a few enterprising broadcasters were allowed to cross these boundaries, especially after Channel Four was launched in 1982.

Despite the pressures, Black people in Britain had maintained, and continued to develop, their cultures. Through old and new art forms, they celebrated and protested, explored their experiences and forgot the pressures of the outside world for a while. Customs and traditions reinforced their sense of who they were. When the works of Black artistes who had won popularity 'back home' gained outlets here, and those who were British-based were supported in their creativity, this was of value to the whole community. However, this could encourage an emphasis on what was more commercial and less challenging, and a superficial approach to complex and varied cultures. There was pressure to conform, to dress or speak or act in certain ways in order to 'belong', and to stress one's differences from those on the outside.

It was obviously in the interests of the powers-that-be for Black people to channel their energies into relatively safe activities and to be disunited in the face of racism; as in the days of the empire, tactics of divide and rule could prove useful. But it would be wrong to blame the growing divisions among Black people in

Britain entirely on the conscious efforts of the country's leaders, or even on the structures they helped to maintain. Black people who had attained professional or business success, who had been elected on to decision-making bodies or reached the ranks of middle or senior management in the public sector sometimes co-operated with one another and offered Black members of the public a quality of service they had previously been denied. Some, however, were competitive and contemptuous in their attitudes, and when such behaviour was directed against Black people of other communities this could foster resentment. Black lesbians might need one another's support in dealing with the racism, sexism and anti-lesbianism which surrounded us, but trusting one another was not always easy.

The possibility of Black people turning on one another may have been linked with a sense of frustration at the difficulty of achieving major social change. After centuries of struggle, although there had been some achievements, most Black people still experienced racism and other forms of oppression. In Africa, Asia and Latin America, winning true independence had proved extremely difficult. Sri Lanka, to which my parents had returned and of which I was at the time still a citizen, was wrecked by corruption, repression and ethnic tension which had escalated into civil war. Politicians condemned Westernization, but local people and the environment were being sacrificed to attract overseas aid and investment. This was far from unique. The phrase 'Third World' had come to be associated with famine, misery and underdevelopment. Some Black people in the West referred to the three continents by another term, 'First World or First Nations', or argued that no common term could rightly apply to such diverse nations. In fact, they were held in subjection by the same forces. And people across the continents continued to resist, sometimes at great cost. The occasional victory, as in Nicaragua, showed that these forces were not all-powerful.

Ethnic nationalism and religious supremacism, often fuelled by a thinly disguised worship of raw power, did not result in full-scale warfare among Black people in Britain. But they did undermine unity and trust, and make communication among people with different experiences of racism harder. Tension was often greatest among those from the same broad geographical region. To complicate matters further, throughout the 1980s there were few books available in Britain by Black feminists, let alone Black lesbians, and almost all of these were from the USA – where Black applies to people of African descent. Some of these writers were strongly anti-imperialist and expressed a sense of solidarity with other people of colour worldwide. But this probably struck less of a chord in many readers than the explorations of personal identity. Although many had been involved in Black struggles in this country which involved several communities, I do not recall these being talked about much. In any case, in the West, the written word tended to be valued much more highly than the oral tradition. So the definition of Black became a contentious issue among Black lesbians. To put this into perspective, Black lesbians could be sometimes very supportive of those from other communities and sometimes deeply rejecting. Different women's experiences varied. Nor were divisions among Black lesbians originating from different continents the only major divisions, by any means.

Some groups and gatherings were set up for the Black lesbians and gays from particular communities. These have been valuable, allowing people to explore particular aspects of their culture and specific problems. However, even in these groups there was sometimes pressure to conform and to deny certain aspects of one's identity. Many Black lesbians in Britain have never attended a Black lesbian gathering because they prefer mixed settings, are not out enough to attend any type of lesbian gathering, or live too far away from lesbian venues. Some have been denied access due to having a disability, low income or responsibility as a mother. It is easy for those Black lesbians who regularly receive affirmation and support from others to forget that there are many for whom this is not the case. Black lesbians living in the big cities, especially London, are spoilt for choice in comparison to those who live in small towns and isolated areas. In reaching out to us effectively and challenging society's attitudes, co-operation among Black lesbians from different communities has, I think, proved to be very valuable.

Into the future

In the early 1990s, the situation of Black people, especially Black lesbians, in Britain has come to seem quite bleak. A number of private firms and public institutions have lost their earlier enthusiasm for equal opportunities, some because they are now struggling just to survive. Small Black businesses are going broke, community organizations closing for lack of funding. Black women often find themselves out of work, or taking pay cuts. Britain's only Black lesbian and gay centre is constantly under threat of closure, being forced to find its own private funding to remain open.

Restrictions on Black people entering Britain have been getting even tighter. Increasingly, visitors from the Caribbean, Asia and Africa are refused entry, and a law has been passed allowing immigration officers to turn down visitors, with no right of appeal. This affects all Black people with friends or relatives who are not citizens. It is now almost impossible for Black asylum-seekers to settle here. Discrimination in education is now acutely affecting some Asian people, as well as those from the African-Caribbean communities. The far right is on the rise in Britain and other parts of Europe, and Black people from various different communities have been injured or killed. In 1993 a fascist councillor was elected in East London (happily, he lost his seat in May 1994). The need for unity – though not uniformity – among those struggling to survive the rising tide of racism is acute.

Black lesbians are under great pressure. Many former activists are burnt out or demoralized, and there are not always others to take their place in sustaining community groups and campaigns. However, a number of Black lesbian groups and organizations, such as the Black Lesbian and Gay Centre, in which black lesbians are predominant, have so far survived because of co-operation among sisters from many different ethnic, religious and cultural backgrounds, and indeed from various traditions of struggle. Black lesbians have continued to inspire one another to act more boldly, think more deeply, be more creative.

Words change in meaning over the years. What may be acceptable at one time may be insulting or simply outmoded a few decades later. The fact that the word Black has been used in Britain for centuries to describe people of Asian as well as African descent does not necessarily mean that this should continue. Perhaps 'people of colour' will come, in time, to be used more widely. Perhaps some of us will begin to define ourselves by the countries we originate from, or use both Black and African or Asian. It is in the end up to individuals to define themselves in any way they choose, and to take responsibility for their choice of definition. The term Black is one I prefer. I feel it links me with those earlier generations of Black people who survived and struggled in this country through the centuries; that I have learnt and grown through campaigns in which people united under the banner of Black; and – although I have sometimes had my right to call myself Black challenged – that I have also experienced generous support on the part of those believing in solidarity among Black people. But I realize that my personal experience is not universal. And certainly I do not believe that being Black means that we all have the same culture, opinions and interests: unity is not the same as uniformity. One of the things I enjoy about moving in Black lesbian circles is the diversity in background and outlook, which prompts me to rethink my assumptions and gain new insights into my own, quite different, experience.

What matters more than agreeing on terminology, I believe, is that Black lesbians, however we describe ourselves, seek to deepen our understanding of our own and one another's experiences, and develop greater solidarity. We need to talk and listen to one another more attentively, to learn from the successes and failures of earlier struggles, neither to avoid discussing what is problematic nor to allow it to divide us. And, although it will be very difficult to build a world in which our humanity is fully recognized and we are free from all exploitation and oppression, we need to sustain one another in hoping and striving to make this a reality.

Books

Manning Marable, *Race, Reform and Rebellion*. Macmillan, London, 1968.

Julius Nyerere, *Ujamaa: Essays on Socialism*. Oxford University Press, Oxford, 1968.

51: Black Together under One Banner

A. Sivanandan, *From Resistance to Rebellion: Asian and Afro-Caribbean Struggles in Britain*. Institute of Race Relations, London, 1986.
Rozina Visram, *Ayahs, Lascars and Princes*. Pluto Press, London, 1986.
Martin Walker, *The National Front*, Fontana, London, 1977.

I have also drawn on my memory and on what I have learnt over the years through reading and watching and from the various Black people with whom I have lived, worked or socialized. Further reading on this subject can be found in *Making Black Waves* (Scarlet Press, 1993), by Valerie Mason-John and Ann Khambatta, and *Staying Power* (Pluto Press, 1984) by Peter Fryer.

Chapter three

A Vision Back and Forth

Linda Bellos

I HAVE approached the writing of this chapter with some trepidation but also with much excitement. It is an honour and a privilege to be asked to write about the way forward for Black lesbians. I have tried to write honestly and personally, and most of all I have tried to make it clear that there are a range of views among Black lesbians. I cannot do justice to all of those views – in truth I can only reflect my own – but I hope that what I have said rings true for many Black lesbians, if not all.

A personal retrospective

I have been a Black woman since 1950, the year in which I was born, and a lesbian since 1980. These are important facts about who and what I am, but they do not sum up my entirety; they do, however, influence how I see the world. I have been interested in politics since the early 1960s, when I sought a rational explanation to racism. I found *Das Capital* by Karl Marx both difficult and challenging. It was no doubt pretentious of a thirteen-year-old to read one of Marx's most complex and turgid books, but it did offer an insight into the man-made nature of the world.

From an early age I was inspired and motivated by a desire

to change the world. In 1965 I joined the usual youth groups, the Young Socialist League and Leninist Group, and sold copies of the *Daily Worker* (later to become the *Morning Star*) outside the Brixton Woolworth's and to my teachers in school, although not, unfortunately, to my schoolgirl colleagues. I went on the last big Aldermaston march in 1968, and was at the Grosvenor Square rally in the same year and the rally against the Greek coup and the Soviet invasion of Czechoslovakia. I was also reading the emerging writings from the Black Consciousness movement in the USA. Given the political era, my activities were not untypical; like many young people I thought that the world was unfair and unjust and full of inequality, including my own personal experiences. I thought then, as I do now, that the world could be changed, and I have committed myself to contributing to that change.

While I reject some of the naïve strategies that I, like many others, thought would bring about change, such as violent revolution, I do not reject all of the visions and passions of my youth. However, I am now better informed about the ways of the world, its systems and how its people operate than I was in my youth. I discovered feminism long after its first developments in Britain. I had initially rejected it because it seemed to me to question my sexual relationships with men, which at the time was not something I was willing to do. So I looked no further for fear that it would upset my applecart. In reality, I later discovered that feminism was not at that time hostile to heterosexuality. I think that I also accepted the leftist critique of feminism as being bourgeois, even if every other aspect of my own life at that time and that of many other socialists could equally be described as bourgeois. Having become a lesbian and then a feminist, the changes in my life were profound; things I had taken as natural and immutable became subject to question and criticism in ways that they never had before. But I brought to my feminism all of my past and present, including my Marxism and Black consciousness.

When I found the anger and hostility of feminists too much, and when, coincidentally, Margaret Thatcher won her second election victory, I determined to put my political energies into the Labour Party. Ironically, I found it a far friendlier place than the women's liberation movement, despite all the rhetoric about sisterhood. In the Labour Party there was no embarrassment about acquiring power in order to achieve change, while in the women's movement anyone who was given a byline on an article was attacked for wanting to be a star. However, I soon realized that I would not have much of a voice or power if I joined the Labour Party, and it was only the opportunity to get involved in the party's Black Sections, which I thought was a necessary and vital contribution to socialism, that really attracted me. It was through Black Sections that I was nominated to become a councillor in Lambeth, an area where I lived and had been brought up. Shortly after, through a series of unforeseen events, including the disqualification of most of my colleagues, I put myself forward to become Leader of Lambeth Council. I was elected, and remained in office from 1985 to 1987.

Those two years were among the most exciting and dramatic of my life. They involved dealing with the reality of power beyond the theoretical level, and I am grateful for being given the opportunity to experience it. It was not without its difficulties, most of which sprang from the press and government's policy of singling out Lambeth for particular scrutiny. The fact that I was an out lesbian became an issue that the press chose to dwell upon at every opportunity, but I had expected that. What I could not readily accept was that the Labour party leadership was so unsupportive when personal attacks were being made upon me. In the end what finally drove me out was not being adopted as the candidate for the parliamentary seat of Vauxhall, and not the politics of the Labour Party. It was my home territory, and when a white woman from outside the area was adopted, I felt there was no place in the Labour Party for me. After all, if a Black woman cannot get adopted in a overwhelmingly Black area like Vauxhall, where else could we win seats? And if I was unacceptable to the leadership because of being a lesbian, what was the point of being there at all?

The experience of those five years as councillor, two of which were as leader of the council, were very important to me; they gave me an abiding respect for the democratic process of having to listen to people with opposing views, and therefore taking into account their existence. It is something I bring back to my feminism with increased vigour. I find it very difficult to describe a complex set of feelings and layers of experience in words on paper. It seems to me that as Black lesbians we are so marginalized and silenced by almost everyone that it is hard to fight one's way out of the silence. But I have tried. I am an intensely optimistic person, I believe that it is possible for us to remake the world but I do not think that it is an easy task, or that Black lesbians can do it alone. But I do sincerely believe that precisely because of our experience of oppressions we are best placed to offer insights and strategies for a new and better world.

The pros and cons of feminism

It is now nearly seventeen years since the last women's liberation movement conference in Britain. Over fifteen hundred women attended, but only a handful of us were Black. If there was to be another conference this year I am sure that the proportion of Black women would be far greater. It is important to consider both the implications of large numbers of politicized Black women and the reasons why the women's liberation movement ceased to exist.

When I came out as a lesbian in 1980 there were few other Black lesbians who were out. I did not doubt that there were many Black lesbians but, like me, they had found the few lesbian spaces which existed overwhelmingly dominated by white lesbians and very intimidating. My coming out was partly influenced by the politics of feminism, which had made me question the naturalness of the sexuality I had been told was the norm – heterosexuality. When I realized that the feelings I had for another woman were sexual, I had difficulty recognizing them. I knew the word 'lesbian' but I thought it only related to white women.

My image of what a lesbian was had been formed by a lurid and hostile media: I had been led to believe that all lesbians were white, ugly and predatory. However, when I examined my own feelings, I found they were not sordid or unhealthy but loving and sexy. I did not fancy all women, it was just one that I had taken a shine to. In the personal crises that followed, I tried to make sense of those feelings, which involved a lot of processing of my received conditioning. Feminism provided a critical framework for my questions. I can't say that I read many things that were affirming to me; most of the feminist books were by and about white middle-class women. Despite these limitations I found, and continue to find, feminism relevant to all women, even if I do not accept white women's definition of it. I am sure that having children, one of them a boy, made my perspective different from that of other lesbian feminists around me. I later discovered many more Black lesbians, who were mothers and had boys, who did not share the same anti-male politics of many white lesbians.

My coming out was noisy, if not raucous, and I rapidly became aware that I was being viewed by other white lesbians as something exotic. This was at first extremely worrying, although it didn't happen all the time, and I soon learnt to deal with it. However, being viewed as sexually more interesting by white women was, and is, profoundly racist. It was as though all Black women are the same. The myths and stereotypes about Black sexuality in the predominantly heterosexual world were alive and well and living within the lesbian community.

Feminism for me was a new way of looking at the world. I had previously accepted that while it was unfair that my brother did not have to do any housework when I did, there was no system that explained this basic inequality to me until I discovered feminism. Whether it was called patriarchy or sexism, feminists had created a language to explain how men oppressed women. In my early days as a feminist I understood that different strands of feminism had different explanations of the way that our oppression worked, and I thought it was wonderful that no one group had a monopoly on analysis. This was in contrast to the male leftist groups that I was familiar with, each of which was convinced that their version of socialism was the only true socialism and that everyone else was revisionist or vanguardist, or any other term of abuse they could invent to put down those who did not toe the party line. Feminism was, and still is, a broad church of beliefs about the oppression of women. Some feminists still think that our oppression stems from the capitalist system, others from the suppression of the matriarchy, but, equally, many others subscribe to neither of these grand theories. What is unifying about all women who call themselves feminists is the belief that women are oppressed as a group. We tend to disagree on how the oppression affects us, and what the main concerns of feminists should be.

From my initial involvement with feminism it became clear to me that I did not wish to become involved in feminist groups that claimed to be for and about all women but in reality were only catering for the needs of a small section of women. Therefore, groups that ignored race and class as realities of women's lives had no interest for me. At a personal level I felt such groups alien and elitist. They were quick to silence anyone who tried to add a perspective other than a white middle-class one. I doubt that the women who were involved in this narrow approach had any idea how privileged and smug they sounded, and indeed were. They thought that they had a working definition of feminism and it was only about other women like themselves. When white working-class women and Black women were considered and placed on the agenda, it was often accompanied by patronizing statements that working-class and Black women (not mutually exclusive categories) were not interested in feminism, or were too busy with survival to come to meetings. As someone who had been active in socialist groups this all sounded remarkably familiar: middle-class people explaining why they had to lead the revolution because we were either too busy or too disinterested to know what was best for us. They would decide and then tell us.

The groups I rather dismissively describe may not have been typical – I have no way of knowing – but what became increasingly clear to me was that a failure to take on board race and class into a feminist analysis was going to reproduce the very limitations and reasons which made me flee from the male left. I was looking, therefore, for a feminism that was about, and included, all women. If all women are oppressed, how and why are we? I wanted to know the answers, because it was from these answers that strategies could be developed to end our oppression. I did not see any point in merely working for more women lawyers or programme-makers at the BBC, because this would not in itself change the position of all women. I held the view that it was useful to have women in positions of power, but that would not automatically mean change if those women emulated Margaret Thatcher, for example.

I became interested in campaigns and groups that were

fighting against male violence. It seemed to me that all women were affected, in different degrees, by the threat of the reality of men's violence. Unlike some other campaigns this was a unifying issue. I had rejected, for example, the then national abortion campaign, because I saw it as a call from white middle-class women to have control over their bodies. Although it was something I approved of, abortion for Black women was too freely available for the wrong reasons: doctors, apparently couldn't do enough of them. Similarly, Black women would visit the doctor for fibroids, and be told, after only a basic medical examination, that they needed hysterectomies.

The feminist groups I joined were exciting and, I think, productive. I learnt a great deal about organizing and getting things done. I really believed in the notion of sisterhood. However, after a few months it became clear to me that I was being extremely naïve. Sisterhood could not eradicate racism, at least not on its own. Neither could it deal with the other forms of oppression that exist. It was then that I came to the realization that I would have as big a fight against racism within the women's liberation movement as I would outside of it.

Race, sexuality and gender bound up as one

In addition to the usual issues of coming out were the concerns we have as Black women for our families and communities. It was this issue that led me into many arguments and disagreements with white women. They could not understand why we could not reject our communities and religions in ways that they advocated. When we pointed out that we had much in common with Black men on issues of racism, they would try to persuade us how oppressive our cultures and religions were to women.

Within the feminist movement Black women were asked to decide which was more important, being Black or being female. It is an impossible choice to make since we cannot change from being either. White feminists could not see that they were defining gender as a white issue, even while they proclaimed otherwise. For us as

Black lesbians we cannot and should not have to choose. However, sometimes we find ourselves trying to distinguish what is happening to us when we are harassed on the streets. Is it to do with being Black, is it because we are women, or is it to do with the fact that we look like a lesbian? This is not a permanent position to take, instead it is a pragmatic assessment of reality, a necessary shifting and changing dynamic as we negotiate the world. By not understanding this, many white feminists, and some Black ones, have created a false dichotomy. I found it deeply frustrating to have to argue continually against a view that said gender was the only or most important issue we faced. Such a view ignores class and race, it ignores disability and sexuality. As a Black lesbian I was well aware that my gender was a source of my oppression, but it was not the only source.

I am not fully convinced that there is an agreed understanding of the concept of oppression. For example, I suspect that each of us who uses the term means something different by it, or at best adopts a personal response to the term dependent upon who we are. I define oppression as a system which operates to deny individuals (or species) freedom to define their own goals/strategies/objectives. The system does not arise at random but is put, and held in place, by human action that is power. Oppression is therefore about the abuse of power in a systematic way. Philosophy and ethics shore up that system seeking to justify and rationalize it as natural, or if not natural at least better than anything else that could be put in its place. Sometimes the system uses overt and naked force, as with apartheid or Nazism, and other times it exists in a more subtle and less obvious way, as in the oppression by men over women. In my view, it does not follow that if one accepts this definition of oppression, one therefore accepts that all people who are oppressed experience oppression in the same ways, or that the group who benefits from the oppression of others does so to the same extent. This to me is an important point which is sometimes confused. It is certainly used as an excuse by some to exclude themselves from consideration of the systems that they are aware of and belong to, arguing wrongly that because they themselves experience oppression they cannot therefore be responsible for oppressing others.

Although I believe that the concept of oppression is important, it has proved to be so problematic that perhaps it requires re-evaluation. It is after all a negative concept, one that requires individuals to *stop* doing something, but since the system obscures individuals' personal responsibilities it is sometimes unclear what exactly we can do. Instead, a more positive approach to issues is to consider the notion of equality, to try to create a world in which each person is viewed and treated as an equal human being. In my view feminism has come closer than any other movement in its attempts to create something better; it has so far failed for the reasons I outline below, but it has the potential to make a profound impact in the world. Feminism is about changing the world, but while there was a women's liberation movement that change seemed mainly for white women. The movement found it difficult if not impossible to deal with a more complex analysis of who we are as women. For example, there was a definition of feminism which drew on a narrow experience of women – that of the white middle-class heterosexual women who had originally created this wave of feminism – from which it tried to generalize all women's experience. Later, when white lesbians fought against this narrow definition there were ructions. There were even more disputes when Black women, white working-class women and women with disabilities challenged this notion too. In the end the movement fell apart as it tried to accommodate the conflict that erupted. I believe that feminism is still relevant to all women, even if the women's liberation movement is now defunct. But if feminism is still defined in its original terms, it will continue to be seen as irrelevant to the majority of women.

Black out

Being a lesbian is more than about who I sleep with, it is also about the way I see the world and the way the world sees me. The politics of the Black communities has often been vehement in its condemnation of any sexuality other than heterosexuality. I recall much contempt and hostility around lesbian sexuality at a conference held by the Organization of Women of African and Asian Descent (OWAAD). It was adamantly and clearly stated that lesbianism was a white women's disease. Much has moved on since that time, with many Black newspapers giving space and support to Black lesbians and gay men, although it would be complacent to exaggerate the shift.

Black lesbians and gay men have had to fight for our right to exist within the Black communities, but it is a fight many of us have taken up because being Black remains an important part of our whole identities, and we could no more be silent about our race within the lesbian and gay community than we could about our sexuality within the Black communities. I am not suggesting that it is always easy, or that we can and should come out on all and every occasion, but many of us do assert our sexuality when others around us assume that everyone is heterosexual and we know that this is not the case.

It has always angered me that white people, particularly white liberals, are very quick to label Black communities as more homophobic than their own. Many white people have said to me: 'It must be harder to come out in the Black community than it is within the white one.' I cannot imagine on what grounds such a view is formed; I believe white people must perceive themselves as better and more enlightened than us. However, the prehistoric views about sexuality expressed by the Tory Family Group as well as in such popular tabloids as the *Daily Mail*, *Express* and the *Sun* would seem to undermine this perception. But this ability to see faults in us while ignoring their own is not confined to issues of sexuality alone.

For some time I have held the view that many white people in Britain, including feminists, do not see themselves as having a culture. We have a culture, something that is exotic and different, but theirs just is, it does not need to be named, it is simply the norm against which everything else is judged. It is within this context that much of the argument about difference among feminists has been waged. White women have tolerated the difference of Black women, but can only understand that difference as a threat. They would listen to our arguments from a position of whiteness. There were of course exceptions: white women who recognized that they were different from the norm and who were open to hearing other differences without feeling threatened. These were white women who could respect difference and even celebrate it, and they were also somewhat rare. In the main there has existed a hierarchical environment in which Black women and Black lesbians are deemed to be doubly or triply oppressed.

While it is true that experiencing sexism and racism appears to be a double dose of oppression, it is not helpful to view the issues in this limited way. Not only is it impossible to measure, but it stimulates the tendency to view Black women as victims. This would not be a problem if the white women who adopted this approach would acknowledge their own oppression at the same time. But what they tend to do is argue, 'I'm alright Jill', while other women, in this case Black ones, are oppressed. Racism is not tackled by this approach. Instead, a hierarchy of oppression is created but not dealt with. It is as though naming the problem means that no more needs to be done; it lets them off the hook and removes the need for further discussion. This may be unfair to those white women who are genuinely trying to acknowledge the realities of racism, but by the existence of a hierarchy in which they themselves are not oppressed, such women can and often do resort to an impotant response of guilt.

Looking at oppression

Western thought seems to me dominated by the notions of 'either' and 'or'. One is either wholly good or wholly evil, Black or white and male or female. Values are attached to each and there is little space for grey. All men are bad, all women are good. These moral certainties may be enough for many people, but they are not enough for me. I think that truth lies beyond these simplistic notions. We can say with some degree of certainty that there are systems of oppression, but we need to look at the detail of how those systems operate, and on whom.

In Britain, all people benefit from the debt of the Third World, but some people benefit more than others. Likewise, we can say that all men benefit from the oppression of women, but white men benefit more than most Black men do. Such a view only helps us to distinguish between men when we come to develop strategies to overcome the oppression of all women by men. Surely a failure to distinguish between the different ways that men benefit, or are affected by the oppression of women, means that the solutions to our oppression will be flawed and potentially discriminatory? For example, in the early 1980s some women involved in anti-violence campaigns and Reclaim the Night marches advocated a demand for more police on the streets. They failed to take into account the impact it would have on Black men who were then subject to the Suspect Under Suspicion (SUS) laws, where they could be stopped and searched at random by any police officer. There was no guarantee that police officers would necessarily 'protect' women even if they stopped harassing Black men. By calling for one solution without considering the consequences for other oppressed groups, we do not succeed in ending oppression, we merely shift it on to another group. But this is part of the pattern of British politics, one group competing with another or being forced to compete.

The term used to describe the growth of aspirations and groups struggling to claim and name an experience of sexism other than the narrow white one was 'identity politics'. It developed out of the need to assert our specific differences as women, a need in my view that still exists. However, there are distinct limitations to the politics of identity. In essence, identity politics can become a marginalizing move to score points over other women, by talking about how differently and more oppressed we are. This is not inevitable, but in the context of the liberal, guilt-ridden climate of this society it is often exploited by those who feel excluded, and perceive themselves as helpless to do anything about the fact that they are, say, able-bodied, white and middle-class. Identity politics does not apparently extend to such people because they do not feel they have an identity to claim. Instead, they seem both to deny who and what they are and at the same time feel guilty for the privileges they enjoy.

There is a simple point about oppression that is rarely understood by the liberals, which is that we as Black women can also be oppressors. By this I mean that while we are subject to racism, sexism and homophobia we may also be members of larger groups that are oppressive to others. For example, there are no doubt some Nigerian lesbians who were supporters of the Yoruba position against Biafrans, and some lesbians of African and Asian descent living in Britain who share the divisive views of elements of the Black communities against each other. There are anti-Asian views held by some people of African descent, and anti-African views held by some Asians. There are class and social distinctions which we may adhere to because we have not questioned our received learning. What I am trying to say is that just because we are subject to oppression and discrimination ourselves, it does not automatically follow that we will be sensitive to the oppression of others. It always surprises me that there is such shock about the treatment of Palestinian people by the Jewish State of Israel. The assumption that the experience of the Holocaust would make the Israeli Jews more sensitive to other people's needs and rights is flawed, as is the assumption that Black men will not oppress Black women because of their knowledge and experience of oppression.

In a similar way, Black lesbians can, do, and will oppress others, unless we recognize the existence of the power that we possess. To deny that one has any power because one is oneself the subject of other people's power is damaging and ultimately dangerous. And yet in the narrow and almost competitive way that oppression is often considered, this approach is encouraged. A world of either/or. If you are a woman you can't be oppressive to others. As this defies reality it leads to disillusion and frustration from those who experience oppression at the hands of those who are also oppressed, but in different ways. In the case of many white liberals it leads to political paralysis: 'The world's in such a mess there is no point in me doing anything about my own conduct and power relations.' Or, 'I'm part of the oppressive dominant culture and there is nothing I can do about it but feel guilty.' This classic way of dealing with power leads of course to its maintenance, and we are awash with guilt.

Within this climate those of us who experience denial and rejection by the movements of liberation that claim to include us are left harbouring our shared grudges, and make few inroads into the real power that is exercised by the minority, regardless of whether it is the minority of men or the minority of white women. Identity politics have therefore become a space into which the concerns of the majority are sidelined. How do we overcome this dilemma, one in which we need to work with others who share a common experience of race/class/religion/disability/sexuality, and yet not allow these identity groups to become cut off from each other? It has been observed before that all the minority groups added together constitute a majority, but mass politics tends to be about an undifferentiated whole. So we are left with isolated special-interest groups and dehumanized mass politics. If the women's liberation movement failed to acknowledge real differences between women, it does not follow that we can build a politics out of our differences. What we can do, perhaps, is to learn the lessons of past and present struggles and celebrate our differences while we work together on our common experience.

Out of the closet

Now that there are so many more Black lesbians – thousands instead of hundreds – the impact of Black lesbians within feminist politics has grown. Black lesbians continue to be active in the organizations and campaigns that are the mainstay of feminism, but there is not much in the way of explicit politics. That is not the fault of Black feminists, but it is a situation that we can do something about. Black lesbians have long been exploring the differences between us. Women of African and Asian descent have continued to work together, sometimes successfully sometimes not. There was, for example, a very painful episode at the first Black lesbian conference, Zami 1 in London in 1985, when Asian women were effectively marginalized by an assumption and assertion that Black meant of African descent only. Despite this failure to clarify or agree definitions from the outset, there has been a remarkable degree of unanimity between Black lesbians on our shared experience of race and racism, and a willingness to listen and understand our differences.

Black lesbians are in my view best placed to contribute to a reformulation of feminism. The old order was restricted to those who originally conceived it. It was therefore inevitable that it was narrow and restricted. But the contribution that Black lesbians make is to bring a broader perspective to the definitions of what it means to be a woman. However, this is not in itself sufficient, when even among Black lesbians there are significant differences of class, religion, culture and disability. But as we have continued to negotiate over differences, and have not been destroyed by dealing with it, we can perhaps take that process to a wider struggle.

There are many Black lesbians who no longer, or never, defined themselves as feminists. Their reasons are many and varied, but mainly arise from some very negative interactions with white feminists. I myself continue to define myself as a lesbian feminist, partly because feminism gave me the space to come out and partly because I refuse to allow a small group of white women to hold a monopoly on feminism. Black lesbians, whether they define themselves as feminists or not, do continue to debate and challenge issues of race and sexuality.

Thoughts on sado-masochism

It is particularly interesting for me to talk with other Black lesbians about sex, and find that I am not alone in feeling annoyed at the assumption many white lesbian feminists make that all Black lesbians automatically oppose sado-masochism (SM), on the grounds that it is inevitably racist. This assumption is also prevalent in the Black lesbian community, and therefore it is rarely, if ever, discussed among us through fear of a verbal attack. My recent discussions with other Black lesbians have included the questioning of our sexual relationships with white women and the issues this throws up for us. Negotiating power and the contradictions of being powerless at the hands of another woman are intriguing when you are Black and she is white. The issues that power and sex throw up for Black lesbians are not often publicly talked about, but they are, in my view, central to any real debate about what it means to be a Black lesbian in Britain today. I do not mean that there is one answer, since all of us are different, but I do mean that as Black lesbians, whether or not we were born in Britain, our sexual identities are to a great extent influenced by the dynamics and debates that surround us. Power and powerlessness are features of racism. We respond to the dynamics of racism in different ways, each adopting strategies that seem appropriate and effective for us. We are also influenced by the sexual stereotypes of ourselves that a racist society produces. Even if we fully reject those stereotypes, they do have an influence, because even to reject them is to acknowledge that they exist.

So we have our individual reactions to sexual stereotyping, whether we are of Asian or African descent, and we have a knowledge and investment in looking at power and powerlessness. Those Black lesbians, such as myself, who have started or continued to look at sex and desire have had to confront some of the issues that the debate over SM has thrown up. Our conclusions are not necessarily straightforward or predictable. Some Black lesbians do explore dominance and submission within their sexual practice, and some do not. Most of us, whatever our views on SM, reject the use of master and slave role-playing as part of the scenarios. It maybe convenient for many white lesbians to identify this aspect of SM and so to condemn the practice outright, because it has an appeal that is almost incontestable. But as I understand it, SM has been the only area to consider issues of desire, pleasure and fun, and to that extent I do not think that any lesbian can afford to reject out of hand what it is saying.

There are profound problems in a sexual practice that says anything goes, and because I desire to do something then I should do it. I may desire to steal or kill, that does not mean that I am censoring myself if I do not do these things. Nonetheless, advocates of SM have asked some important questions about what we do desire, and they are very emphatic in their need for mutual consent and trust within SM relationships. That does not eliminate the issue that sadism and masochism have their problems for each of us as lesbians and as women in this society, but I do accept that no one coerces anyone into SM. Most lesbians who participate in SM choose to do so freely.

We have not been very honest about the role of power in the sexual activities we enjoy, and Black lesbians are no better or worse than white lesbians on this issue. For many of us there have been far more pressing and immediate issues to consider than our own sexual practices, but I am increasingly of the view that if there is to be any political movement of Black and/or white lesbians then one thing we have to talk about, if only to get it out of the way, is that we are lesbians and we do have sex with other women. Being a lesbian is not incidental to me, and it does not mean only solidarity with other women, although it includes that. It also means that I acknowledge myself as a sexual being. In the face of a world that hardly recognizes the existence of white lesbians, it seems to me even more important as a Black lesbian that I name myself, and that we as Black lesbians do talk about the sexual aspect of being lesbian.

Feminism does seem on the surface at odds with SM. On the one hand feminism says it is about equality for women, while on the other SM advocates the eroticizing of inequality. But to reduce the contradiction to these simplistic notions ignores the need to re-evaluate both. Feminism has provided some important insights into our position as women in society, and in criticizing male power and the use and role of sex in our oppression it has also taken on board some very repressive notions of sexuality. From reading the thoughts on sex of such outspoken women as Pat Califia and Susie Bright, it seems that they react as much to the restrictiveness of feminism as to the restrictiveness of men. So far few lesbians who do not associate with SM or anti-censorship campaigns have written or spoken publicly about lesbian sexual practice. I believe it is important to do so because 'the personal is political', that is to say, what we do in our private lives has a bearing on how we operate in the outside world.

As Black lesbians many of us are involved in community politics, whether they are the politics of our Black communities or the lesbian and gay community, and as such we are negotiating with contradictions and tensions. More than this, we are challenging existing models of what it means to be Black and what it means to be lesbian. I believe that we also have to contribute what it means to be sexual. If we strive for equality and the end of oppression, as all of us do, why does sex stand outside our critical framework? And if we allow the narrow anti-sex position of some white lesbian feminists to determine our responses to a critical look at sex, we are in danger of subscribing to repressive and/or guilt-ridden practices. Black lesbians are confronting power issues on a daily basis, perhaps therefore we are in a good position to look at the power dynamics entrenched in sex, in an open and enlightened way.

What I have in mind is the open, questioning exploration of

ideas that was once used to characterize feminism. All ideas were up for grabs, we did not accept that just because men had more physical power than most women that meant they were superior to women. And equally, we need not accept that something is automatically right or wrong just because the Tory Family Group or Mary Whitehouse says so. As Black lesbians most of us have had to pick our way through ideas and ideologies which we partly agree with and partly reject, omitted as we are from most Black and lesbian and gay considerations. Individually, therefore, we have had to plot our own course. Now is perhaps the time to bring it all together.

Thoughts on the future

The way ahead for Black lesbians remains in Black lesbian groups, but it also includes those of us who want to be part of a wider movement for liberation from all forms of oppression. At present no such movement exists. Black politics is as separated and disparate as it always was. Socialist politics has almost disappeared. Ecology politics has been split by ideological differences and the lesbian and gay agenda seems to be about 'the pink pound'. Black lesbians, as always, continue to be involved in these movements and many more, but there are few ways of bringing together the complementary strands of these movements while they are presented as a choice between either/or.

Because we deal with more than one oppression at a time we as Black lesbians are well aware that it is possible and necessary to tackle more than one form of oppression at a time. We cannot afford to wait until the socialist or feminist revolutions succeed in tackling sexism or racism. I have never subscribed to the view that first we deal with the big issue (whatever that means), and then we can deal with the other problems. In my view the means by which we seek change are as important as the ends we seek to achieve. What this means for me is that we have to try to describe and envisage a world that we want to see, one that is free from the oppression of women, Black people, of lesbians and gay men, of people with disabilities and of all forms of oppression.

This simple idealist view is not impossible to achieve, it has never been tried. We have seen in history many attempts to eliminate one form of oppression, but this has sometimes led to another form being put in its place. So when the yoke of imperialism has been thrown off, nationalism or communism will replace it. When, in 1917, the Bolsheviks succeeded in the revolt against Tsarism, the oppression of women did not end. It was taken for granted that women within the revolution would still be nurturers and homemakers even if this was combined with heavy factory labour. The problem as seen by Russian revolutionaries was capitalism, and like many a latter-day feminist they would allow no incursion on to their single-issue agenda. It seems to me that history has shown that if we do not deal with the real issues that arise between people, as they arise, we may replace one known form of oppression with another.

Our approach, therefore, has to be multifaceted. If we want a world in which we can be free as Black lesbians we have to have a world in which all people are free. To do that we need to create systems that allow everyone to achieve their full potential, and not be subject to other arbitrary power and prejudice. Such a world is far from the one in which we live. White men have made up the rules and have asserted the naturalness of them. It is as oppressive as anything that the Soviet Union ever came up with, but coated with the gloss of individual freedom so long as we subscribe to its very limited definition.

Black lesbians may not have all of the answers, we may not even have any of them, but what seems clear to me is that we have to ensure that we contribute to the answers. Our personal experience of discrimination allows us to see the many ways that it operates. It also enables us to envisage a world in which we are not merely tolerated but respected for the contributions we can and do make. This in part must entail a reduction in our invisibility. For example, we need to confront the way that lesbian and gay men's politics is dominated by white men, the way that some Black men ignore and marginalize the experience of Black women, and the way that white women exclude the experience and existence of Black women, especially Black women in Britain. Identity politics has become the politics of exclusion and is not a model that serves the growing numbers of Black lesbians. Instead, we need to draw upon our shared struggles to be heard and recognized, and go out into the world to change it. It will not be enough merely to have more Black lesbian groups and social activities, although I think we need those too. What is essential, in my view, is that we set the agenda for change, making radical demands about our own needs and those of others who are also denied freedoms and liberty. Relative to some countries we do have freedoms, but compared with what is possible, most people have few freedoms. We, however, can show that it is possible to acknowledge differences, and even celebrate them, without making different the means by which we judge and oppress others. This perhaps is the key to freedom for all, including ourselves. We need the power to do this, not power over others but power to achieve change. If we stop being made to feel embarrassed about the ownership of power, we can make effective use of the power we already have and the power we need to acquire.

Chapter four

A Minefield in the Garden: Black Lesbian Sexuality

Valerie Mason-John and Adowa Okorrowa

The minefield

BLACK lesbian sexuality is influenced by the colonization of Africa and Asia, the atrocities of slavery and by today's racism, sexism and homophobia. However, despite the oppressions Black women face in British society many of us have managed to come out as lesbians, develop our individual identities and celebrate our sexuality. Our lives cannot be defined simply by what we do in bed; sexuality includes how we think, dress, socialize, speak, move, express ourselves and by who and what we prioritize. Our sexual identities are also shaped by the cultural traditions which survived colonization and were passed down through the centuries from generation to generation. In Britain there are communities of lesbians of African and Asian descent with diverse social and political expressions. Individually, we confirm and celebrate our success in surviving the different forces of oppression designed to silence us or make us resort to heterosexuality in fear.

The 1990s backlash in conservative Britain has attempted to

deprive many ordinary people of their equal rights. It has eroded the gains made in the area of sexuality, ensuring that single-parent women, lesbians and gays, Black people and young people become targets of abuse. Women's centres, lesbian and gay centres and groups for Black people funded by local government have disappeared due to the economic and social depression of the last decade. As a result, the expression of love by Black women for women has been pushed underground. As Black lesbians our identities do not separate into any single category, we can experience simultaneously all the oppressions of being poor, Black, female and lesbian. Many people find it hard to accept that we exist, yet we do. The problems that we have with our sexuality come from other people's fears or rejection of us. Such people try to deny our right to exist and target us as scapegoats for society's present self-destructive crisis. Therefore, it is important that we define ourselves. Regardless of where we live, it is crucial that we name ourselves, in our own minds, among friends and within our support networks.

At the moment there is very little information about women-loving women in traditional Black cultures. Much of our ancestral history is documented in the oral tradition. The historical evidence which exists through the oral, written or artistic documentation reveals that sexual relationships between women are, and always were, part of everyday life. However, much of the information was suppressed when white men absconded with much of our cultural heritage. Homosexuality was expressed more freely before colonizers came and suppressed it. 'There are, and always will be, lesbians in Africa and Asia. We have a long rich tradition.'[1] Woman-to-woman marriages were commonly practised among the Yoruba, Yagoba, Akoko, Nupe and Gana Gana communities in northern Nigeria, and among the Kamba in East Africa. Women of the Kuriar tribe, in south-west Kenya and north-west Tanzania, who are unable to conceive children can marry a surrogate mother. The mother chooses a man to father her child, and then brings up the child with her wife. Such marriages have been practised for centuries, and are still carried out in various parts of Africa. 'Woman to woman marriages are much more widespread than history wishes to acknowledge ... lesbian bonding by African women does herstorically exist.'[2] There were also communities in

Asia where women denied men access. In India and China there existed societies of women ruled by female monarchs until the seventh century. Also harems – where several wives belonged to one husband – were described as hotbeds of lesbianism by writers in AD 500. 'There are, always have been, an always will be lesbians in India and in fact we have quite a long and rich history and tradition of lesbianism and homosexuality.'[3]

The lifestyles and structures of ancient, so-called primitive or lost civilizations which featured practices of mutual love and respect for sameness and difference have been replaced by the force of cultures based on respect for violence, extreme individualism and power over others. Since the invention of individual male ownership and institutions of abusive behaviour such as slavery and the rape of women and children, sexuality has become inhibited, the expression of which has been forced behind closed doors. In contrast, sexuality in Africa and Asia was something which you interpreted through dance and celebration. There were initiation rites of male and female sexuality, where each gender celebrated among themselves. Often, homosexuality was common in these coming-of-age rituals. Today, in these two continents, many people still celebrate their sexual identities through many different rituals.

The corruption of our history and traditions has meant that sexuality as a whole is perceived only in relation to men. From the earliest times of patriarchy to now, lesbian lifestyles have been attacked, because of the threat we pose to the emotional and physical control of women by men. Black women who love women today have become a thorn in the side of normality when we have stepped outside the prescribed role which was forced upon us by slavery. Black women and men had to conform to the white norm, to the white religions, and had to forget their cultural practices if they were to escape death, flogging and other atrocities. The genocide of Black people has meant that many Black women have had increasing pressure on them to produce children and maintain the Black family. Therefore, it is inevitable that many lesbian relationships existing in Africa and Asia today are between women who live in the marital home and conduct their lesbian affairs outside this arrangement. Alternatively, they will move their female lovers in when their husbands are away working. In the Caribbean these women are called *zami*, *mati mati* and *wicca*. In some countries in Asia, Africa and the Caribbean homosexuality is punishable by death, pushing lesbian activity completely underground. In Britain, Black women have often been forced into the role of subservient wives, mothers, servants, slaves, big mammas, survivors and prostitutes. All of which fulfil male desires and represent the legacy of colonization.

As the hierarchy of white male power became a reality so the practice of women-loving women went underground. Therefore, it has been important for Black lesbians and gays to research into our ancestors' position prior to colonization, and to discover that we were tolerated, and even celebrated, in some cultures and in many of the countries from which we originate. Such affirming information is crucial to Black lesbian sexuality; there are many of us who have a nagging doubt that perhaps if Africa, Asia and the Caribbean had not been colonized we would be heterosexual and 'normal'. Hence today's Black communities often level the attack that homosexuality is a white disease. Whether this attack is from the fear of further oppression if homosexuality is attached to our communities, or ignorance, it has inevitably stifled the overt expression of Black lesbians living in Britain.

This is the scenario that we as Black women are supposed to follow. With our history of slavery and indentured labour, we have been educated to see white men as the gateway to salvation and to treat Black men with suspicion. The belief in our own individual and collective power has been undermined. The fact is that white men took our land and gave us the Bible. It is this doctrine which many Black people cite when they declare that homosexuality did not exist in Africa, Asia and the Caribbean. Colonization has denied Black women and their children the true expression of their sexuality. Women of African and Asian descent were raped by white men, stolen from their families to work as servants, slaves and prostitutes in white households, and transported to the Caribbean, the USA and Britain as slaves. Instead of rejoicing in their own sexuality, and celebrating the birth of their children, they were forcibly removed to look after white women's children.

This divide-and-rule attitude to Black women, coupled with apartheid, caste systems, segregation and all other forms of racism, has inevitably created distrust of and between ourselves. The products of slavery – rape, sexual, physical and emotional abuse, low self-esteem and the survivor syndrome – have been passed down the generations of Black women. Black lesbians today are also products of this system. Black lesbians still have to survive racism and the homophobic onslaught from both the Black and white communities. Therefore, our sexuality is expressed out of these oppressive atrocities. Just as a survivor of sexual abuse has to develop defence mechanisms to cope, Black lesbians have also to develop coping mechanisms to deal with their herstories and today's racism. All of which contribute to shaping our sexual identities.

MIS-EDUCATION

It says here . . .
I am too black
too tall
too fat
too ugly
too loud
too horny

hair too frizzy
lips too full
bum too big
feet too wide
brain too dumb

as I read from babylon
schools books, they say, I must learn

I'm told
I am too black
too tall
too fat
too ugly
too loud
too horny

hair too frizzy
lips too full
bum too big

feet too wide
brain too dumb

as I listen to the babylon teachers
telling me to learn
Learn to blame myself
learn to change myself
learn to say black with apology
learn to despise me.

Kemi Omodiagbe

Mis-education

The contemporary media and education system often undermine our sexuality. We live in a society that blatantly names Black and female as evil and dirty. From a young age we are taught that, rather than feel proud of our bodies and who we are, we should feel shame. We are also influenced to take on the slave mentality of Black women as submissive, obedient and obliging, in contrast to our countries of origin where women are powerful and often the head of the family. Black girls have a hard and painful time growing up in Britain. In school we listen to stories of Hansel and Gretel, Rapunzel and Snow White. Many of the fairy-tales we listen to are about beautiful and vulnerable young white girls, wicked black witches and handsome white princes who come to the rescue. This image of the beautiful white woman and the handsome white prince has influenced some Black women to long secretly for a white husband and for a white fair skin. Between the 1950s and 1970s, some Black women used household bleach to lighten their skins, and since the 1980s many have bought skin-lightening creams to achieve the same effect.

We are taught that Black is dirty and white is clean and pure, that Black is ugly and white is beautiful. Similarly, we are told that white is synonymous with all things bright and beautiful, good and right, while Black is equated with all things dull, dark and ugly, bad and wrong. These labels are often used to describe everyday human experience, and insidious messages like these have been strongly reinforced by the British educational system. Today's language and imagery are often based around good and bad, right and wrong. Black children's heads are filled with these attitudes, through nursery rhymes, songs and stories. Young Black girls grow up to learn that the ideal of beautiful woman is Marilyn Monroe, Brigitte Bardot, Elizabeth Taylor, Pauline Collins, Twiggy or Madonna, all of whom are white. Grace Jones, one of the first Black women to challenge the white beauty myth in the media, has been portrayed and packaged as an un-tamed animal and wild woman. In the 1990s we now have the Black British model Naomi Campbell, portrayed in the media as the angry, aggressive woman with a chip on her shoulder. Asian women are either exoticized or considered too dowdy and coy to enter the league of stereotypical beautiful woman. Such propaganda has meant that self-love and loving other Black women must be re-learnt. There are no positive role models in British society against whom we can affirm ourselves as beautiful Black women.

Therefore the conditioning of our younger years and adulthood teaches us that the epitome of badness is blackness. Coupled with this, young Black women are labelled from the moment they attend school. Teachers often have the prejudiced opinion that Asian girls are passive, inhibited and frigid, and African/Caribbean girls are aggressive, troublesome and a threat. The soulless denial of who we really are stems from Christian labelling of Black female icons, such as Lilith or Isis, mythical and evil. The morals of Christian society, constructed by men, label us as sexually deviant because of their own fear and hatred of sexuality.

Loving ourselves and our bodies is essential for a strong sense of well-being. It has been an uphill struggle to challenge those negative notions in the media which undermine us. The 'Black is Beautiful' slogan of the 1960s and 1970s, coupled with feminism, was the main instigator for such changes. Feminism offered another alternative to the stereotyped heterosexual woman. However, Black women saw the limits of a political movement mainly dominated by white middle-class women. Although they were involved from the beginning in the 1960s, issues specific to them were rarely addressed. Consequently, a Black feminist model soon developed, and Black women placed racism, sexism, classism, sexual oppression and poverty side-by-side on the agenda.

Although other Black liberation movements saw feminism as an unwelcome distraction from the real struggle and a divisive element among Black men and women, for many Black women second-wave feminism was a recognition of their self-worth. Through rediscovering our common herstories in the Black Power movements, and the love of ourselves, Black women were able to move on and develop our own sexual identities. Hence, feminism initiated debate and discussion among Black women on a national level. Conferences and groups helped some Black women to summon the courage to begin to heal from the effects of a colonized past, and gave many the strength to come out as lesbians and love other Black women.

Classified stereotypes

One can assume that loving our bodies comes from knowing ourselves through discovery, unbiased education and acceptance of what we are. However, we need to overthrow the myths that aim to keep all women in one controllable corner. It is a fact that men have always been scared of female sexuality, to the extent that violence against women is taken for granted in many societies. Men have classified female sexuality as passive and subservient. Bad women are those who are sexually active, who choose to have sex with women and speak about it.

Contemporary society produces volumes of material about sex, and most of it reinforces the European body shape and look. The pornographic industry is characterized by male dominance or other fantasies of unequal power relations. Heterosexual pornography rarely depicts women in actual sexual roles; they take what they're given and enjoy it, no questions asked and no demands made. They are portrayed as naughty schoolgirls or kinky maids, and it is assumed that penetration is the ultimate for female satisfaction. A woman sees a penis, and therefore she must want it and devour it. Rarely is any other sexual stimulation involved, and it is even rarer to see a white man fucking a Black woman. White men want white women to fuck and Black women to whip or be whipped by. It is no surprise that the majority of Black women working in the sex industry offer a bondage service, because this is the market where they can earn a living. Black women are pushed into their stereotyped role of kinky, dominating, but not desirable enough to be passive. Many Black lesbians who work in the sex industry often work as bondage sex-workers, in peep-shows and as hostesses, because they rarely involve penetrative sex.

Many women find pornography humiliating, degrading and violent and yearn for sex material which is realistic and educational. There have been erotic films and literature which describe the possibilities of sexual exploration and enjoyment between two women, while taking account of those real situations in everyday life that can create real pleasure. However, these usually explore white women's sexuality. The 1994 Lesbian and Gay Film Festival was the first time that more than two films exploring Black lesbian sexuality had been screened. Sexuality is such an everyday thing, involving the widest range of feelings that let us know that we are human, and yet Black women are often invisible in this area of life. Because so little is known about our sexuality, many white people refer to the stereotyped images of Black women in the porn industry. The belief that Black men are better in bed is mirrored in the lesbian community. Hence, many Black lesbians have been picked up by white women purely for sex.

The idea that Black women are dominating, insatiable animals and undesirable can stay with us throughout adulthood. We are often pushed into these roles by both the white heterosexual and lesbian and gay communities. Coupled with this, Black women are perceived as inferior to white women, and many Black women and men have colluded with this by wanting to be with a white woman for all the wrong reasons. Taking a white woman as a long-term partner may be the nearest they will get to being accepted as an honorary white. Some Black lesbians, gay and heterosexual men have fallen into the trap of thinking that only white women are beautiful. However, there are many relationships between Black and white people which are founded on the basis of true and healthy love, honesty and awareness. It is inevitable, living in a white society, that when we first fall in love with another Black woman that we may have high expectations of her sexual performance and may even be afraid. The reflection of ourselves can be very painful. It is going against everything which has been fed to us through the media and other institutions.

Out of the closet

Many Black lesbians born or living in England come from families which have struggled to protect themselves from the onslaught of racism. As a result, many members of the Black communities have in some areas become insular and highly conservative in order to maintain respectability. Black people have sometimes clung on to their religions to 'maintain a sense of community in the face of racism'.[4] Sadly many of these religions are entrenched with homophobic contempt. In order to maintain the face of respectability, the Black communities have tended to criticize anybody who steps outside their stereotypical role. Therefore, Black women who are lesbians, feminists or both are called traitors, coconuts or white-minded, and are accused of having a white disease. Black women must fulfil their roles as obedient wives and mothers, and not embarrass their communities. A taboo like homosexuality is perceived as dragging the African, Asian and Caribbean communities further into the gutter. Therefore, coming out can be a scary and traumatic experience for Black lesbians. The possibility of losing our families and communities can mean cultural bereavement. There is certainly very little in the lesbian and gay scene which reflects a Black woman's culture. The choice is between homophobia from the Black and white heterosexual communities and racism from the lesbian and gay community.

Women who are physically and emotionally attracted to other women are told by bigoted heterosexuals that we are in need of purification to make us well. This fascistic attitude can lead to mental health treatments such as torture, rituals of exorcism, enforced psychiatric interrogation and drug programmes. Some Black women who have been subject to these abuses have pretended to conform. However, after such horrific experiences they have found it difficult to relate to women and have lacked confidence in their choice of lifestyle. Our identity comes from the ability to name and recognize ourselves for ourselves. Coming out to ourselves is part of the process of this recognition. Some Black lesbians initially call themselves bisexual before they are confident enough to say that they love women. Society is more tolerant of bisexuality, as it is perceived as a state of confusion and illness from which women will return to the accepted norm of heterosexuality. There are Black women who are bisexual because they are married to men, have children and cannot afford to lose the family structure in which they live because of financial, emotional or racial factors.

Some Black lesbians have become aware of their sexuality without the fear of punishment or guilt of older generations. Once we are able to celebrate our feelings towards other women, we can define our own needs and decide whether to maintain the links with those close to us if they are only prepared to accept us on their terms. Coming out is an important part of our sexual identities, and living a lie is stressful and draining. For many Black lesbians, coming out has empowered them, it has been a relief, ensuring sanity and peace of mind. Some of us are unable to come out, because it would perhaps mean being sent home to our countries of origin, forced into arranged marriages or even death. Indeed, there are Black lesbians who come from countries like Iran, where homosexuals are still legally put to death.

Self-acceptance of Black lesbianism can be approached by looking at our history, which many of us have done through political and personal work. It is important that we talk about the issues that interest and concern us in an atmosphere of safety. Friendships are invaluable among Black lesbians, because between us we can keep sight of our cultural and sexual identities. However, preconceptions of relationships between women can lead us into vulnerable situations. Yes, we can be nurturing and supportive, but this is a stereotype and not all women are like that. Through friendships that recognize individual differences as well as mutual support, we can maintain a sense of dignity and pride. There is so little space where Black lesbians can meet and talk about friendships, our pain, denial and anger, that it makes it hard for our interactions to move beyond superficial levels of communication that are not about the power of one person over another. Often we carry the pain and guilt of letting our communities down, punishing ourselves for being who we are. Through discussion and support on the Black lesbian scene, there are opportunities for the expression of our Blackness, womanhood and sexuality without prioritizing or negating any one part of our identity. This is all part of the process of coming out.

Coming out is about shaping and healing our sexual identities. It involves rising above the threat of physical and verbal attacks from our Black communities and the wider society. The isolation and sense of estrangement imposed on us by heterosexuals can make it hard for us to go beyond satisfying our own immediate needs. Such pressures of racism, sexism and homophobia give Black lesbians very little time to be intimate and enjoy each other. Similarly, Black lesbians often feel estranged from the lesbian and gay community because of its racism. Whenever we come together as a group, racism is almost always on the agenda. Rather than celebrate being with other Black lesbians, our time is taken up challenging the racist attitudes we encounter.

Lifestyles

In order for many Black lesbians to heal from society's oppressions and feel strong, proud and safe about their sexuality, we have created spaces for ourselves. Here, Black women have the opportunity to self-heal, instil energy into other Black lesbians and develop their sexuality away from the hostile world. 'Black lesbian separatism should be recommended for all Black lesbians at some stage. Being with people like you for a while gives you room to find out who you are. It's important to get away from racism and heterosexism. Separatism is about personal growth, strength, common identity and support.'[5] Some Black women have chosen to be Black lesbian separatists so that they can develop themselves. They have chosen to relate emotionally, intimately and politically with Black lesbians or women. This choice of lifestyle hopes to redress power imbalances, and confirm their identities. Those women who practise Black lesbian separatism have relationships only with Black women and live and work with them wherever possible. Some may have contact with their male relatives, while others choose to have nothing to do with them. These women consider it to be an invaluable political strategy and a permanent way of life.

However, while many Black lesbians take advantage of this community, it is not necessarily something that they would feel comfortable with for the rest of their lives. Relating to other Black lesbians does remove the issue of racism among ourselves, but there are still many other forms of prejudices that we must deal with. Because the term 'Black' can encompass so many different racial and cultural groups, it is inevitable that there will be some friction and differences of opinions. African, Caribbean and Asian women only make up part of the Black lesbian community, and even among ourselves there are numerous different racial and class groupings. From our communities of origin we bring with us the prejudices between African and Caribbean women, Chinese and Indian, Indian and Pakistani, Asian and African-Caribbean: the list is endless. Despite our common experiences as Black women, intimate relationships, socializing and discussion can be difficult, painful and sometimes disastrous. The fact is we are not one big happy family.

As I mentioned earlier, some Black lesbians have chosen to have white women as lovers, and as intimate friends. This can and does arouse extreme suspicion, as it is believed that such women are colluding in racist ideas. Accused of betraying their Black sisters and of selling out on their culture, they are labelled as confused and out of touch with their Black identities. This philosophy echoes the politics of the Black Power movement in the 1960s and 1970s, which advocated the adoption of complete 'Blackness' through lifestyle and appearance. Some Black lesbians have experienced the isolation from those who have disagreed with their choice of partner or intimate friends: 'I was ostracised for leaving a Black lover and having a relationship with a white woman. I was told I had let the side down and was accused of selling out.'[6] Relationships between Black and white women can be just as healthy or unhealthy as they are among ourselves. Sometimes Black women have no choice between Black or white lovers, because they live in communities where they are the only out Black lesbians. Whether Black lesbians have relationships with Black or white women the majority of us have Black women in our lives on an intimate level.

Our ability to express and explore who we are depends on our environment and how much freedom we have to create it for ourselves. On an intimate level, our needs are varied, depending on our priorities. As in any other social group in Britain the main way of meeting people is through clubs and bars, where the agenda is already set: mainly drink, drugs, music and sex. It is often hard to talk to other Black lesbians in such contexts, and it can be very isolating. As a result discovering each other can be extremely difficult. For Black lesbians, once we do make friends the main places we meet and talk are at cultural events and blues parties organized by other Black women, where there is the least possible restriction on our sexual expression. We can look at one another, dance and touch each other and define our space. Some Black lesbians socialize with Black gay men: the fact that men often have access to more money than lesbians means that there are many more nightclubs aimed specifically at them.

Some Black women are mothers before they come out as lesbians, and therefore their lifestyles are affected in different ways to those of us who do not have children. The lesbian community is so anti-children that many lesbian mothers, Black and white, often turn to heterosexual women for help. Some may have to live closeted lives through fear of losing their children, or to protect their children from experiencing homophobic attacks at school. The law and morals of this society only officially recognize the nuclear family unit. All lesbian mothers live in constant fear of losing custody of their children, and of intimidation through threats of exposure. Few men rarely want the child(ren), but often take their ex-partner to court out of spite or to have revenge for the fact that their partner is living as a lesbian. Some Black lesbians, who choose to be mothers after they have come out, have children by sleeping with a man or by inseminating themselves with donated sperm. As Black lesbian mothers, however our children are conceived, there is always the threat that social services may interfere or decide to remove the child. Society already believes that Black women are neglectful, African-Caribbean mothers are child beaters, and that Asian mothers are too overbearing and restrictive.

Relationships

Our most important relationship should be with ourselves and our self-image, which needs to be positive in order to live fuller lives. The process of self-discovery is particularly difficult in a society which deliberately undermines Black women. Fighting this continual debasement involves rediscovering and reaffirming the conviction that we are inherently valuable and have the right to exist and live our lives. Sometimes we only know our bodies in terms of attracting a partner, and we give it value only if we can keep the partner interested. Re-evaluating ourselves as whole beings – mind, body and spirit, with specific cultural, gender, political, racial, sexual herstories – is essential for nourishing and fulfilling relationships with ourselves and with others. By looking in the mirror and really seeing what is there, by caring for our bodies, taking the right food and drink, by doing physical activities, we can move towards this goal. Because of our common experiences of oppression and shared cultural expression, friendships have grown up among women of African and Asian descent, and we have created communities together along with other Black women living in Britain.

Our relationships with lovers can be monogamous or non-monogamous. Many Black lesbians choose to be 'married', some live with their partners and share a bedroom, while others choose to have separate bedrooms and lives. Some of us don't live with our lovers, choose not to see them every day, and have our own friends. Such independence can cause problems, even though we may agree on these rules before starting a relationship. Sometimes we can delude ourselves that we are better at conducting non-monogamy than white lesbians, because some of us originate from polygamous and polyandrous societies. All societies practised polygamy and polyandry at one stage, and in a society which advocates marriage till death do us part, and condemns adultery, non-monogamy is not an innate norm for anyone. Some of us claim to manage it successfully, while others have horror stories to tell. Black lesbians also practise serial monogamy, entering one relationship after another without allowing a break for the healing process.

In view of the racist and homophobic society in which we live it is a great feat when Black lesbians can create harmonious relationships among themselves. Even if we split up with a lover, the fact that we can develop a new relationship as friends is a success in itself.

Myths

Within the Black lesbian community there are several myths about our sexual identities. For example, it is assumed that we do not call ourselves feminists because the word feminism alludes to a white experience only. However, there are many of us who have participated in the feminist struggle and have changed the agenda to include our issues. The feminist movement has often failed to take on the issues of race and racism, but Black feminists have made it clear that feminism means something to each individual woman, and therefore our voices should be heard and listened to. Although Alice Walker's term 'womanist' (a woman who loves other women sexually or non-sexually, and prefers female culture) is an alternative term for Black feminists to use, most Black women in Britain prefer to use the term feminist and add the prefix Black.

It is also assumed that because we are lesbians originating from Africa and Asia that we have different expressions to define our sexuality. It is true that there are words like *khush*, *zami*, *wicca* and *mati mati* which all mean either gay or women who love women. But few of us are familiar with these terms. Most of us are comfortable with lesbian if Black precedes it, while some of us are happy with stating that we are Black women who love other women.

The political voice of Black lesbianism has stated that Black women do not practise sado-masochistic sexual behaviour, because of its connotations of slavery, racism, fascism and Nazism. Sado-masochism has been the subject of a long and heated debate between Black and white lesbians, and in the lesbian political community. Although it is rare to see a Black woman dressed in chains, handcuffs and on the end of a dog collar, this cannot be taken as proof that we don't participate in sado-masochistic sex. A questionnaire survey and interviews conducted for the research of *Making Black Waves*, in 1992–93, highlighted the opinion among Black lesbians that what we did behind closed doors was up to us. Opinions ranged from 'SM is tearing the community apart' to 'SM is about consenting adults exploring power dynamics within a sexual relationship. I believe Black lesbians practise it' to 'I don't think SM is necessarily racist. SM exists in all communities.' The questionnaire and interviews marked perhaps the first time that Black lesbians on a national level could express their opinions about SM without the fear of attack. What some of the respondents disliked was the total inequality of power in SM practised between Black and white lesbians. Black lesbians in San Francisco have tried to challenge this inequality of power by developing a community for Black SM lesbians only.

The white lesbian and gay community have also created myths. They assume that lesbians of African descent are butch (adopting stereotypical masculine attributes), because society has deemed us as aggressive, dominating and physical. Asian women on the other hand are seen as femme (taking on the stereotypical feminine attributes), as they have been classified as weak, fragile and vulnerable. Black lesbians of African or Asian descent can be butch or femme, and Black women have to challenge the homosexual and heterosexual communities for the right to choose their role. While white lesbians push us into the butch/femme trap, heterosexuals also try to trap us by imposing their ignorant belief that women who have sexual relationships with women must emulate the male/female marriage roles. This stereotype of all lesbians as the butch/superdyke, who acts like a man and preys on other women, can be damaging. Who would want to identify with such a monster? However, there is always a certain amount of truth in every stereotype. Black women have had to be strong and fight for their rights, in order to survive past and present racist atrocities. Even before the 1950s and 1960s, in Britain and the USA lesbian couples dressed in butch/femme attire so that they could pass as men and women on the streets. It was a protection against homophobic attacks. Similarly, in other parts of the world women have, and continue to, dress as butch and femme. There are folk stories about girls in India who from a young age dressed as boys because their fathers wanted male children. Once they became women they continued to dress as men, marrying women and living happily ever after.

The flower garden – sex, masturbation and celibacy

When it comes to talking about what we do in bed, Black lesbians are no different from any other women living in Britain. Some of us are repressed about this subject, or are too scared to talk about it openly through fear of being judged, criticized and ostracized from the community. Most Black lesbians have sex for love, recreation or cathartic release. Some of us enjoy sex and some of us don't. Our attitudes about sex have inevitably been influenced by the repressed British mentality. Most sex education informs us only about heterosexual sex, and often implies that even this is dirty, shameful and wrong unless it occurs within the context of love and marriage. Christianity and many other religions also have negative attitudes about sex. Because of the emphasis on sex as a private and secret activity, and the perception that lesbian sex is dirty and evil, it is rarely talked about in a positive way. Even among friends it can be a struggle to talk openly about what we like. Heterosexuals assume that we are lesbians because we have not had sex with the right man, or that we are too ugly or unruly to keep a man. All these factors can inhibit our sexuality. Similarly, sexual, physical and emotional abuse in childhood and adolescence can affect the way we express ourselves sexually.

Sex can include numerous activities, ranging from cruising; holding or observing hands; kissing; looking; stroking; teasing; rubbing; fucking; fisting; making love; using sex toys; lubricants; using food; role-playing; threesomes and group sex. What we do in bed and how we enjoy sex and our sexuality is as varied and diverse as are our personalities. Sex and expressing our sexuality can take place anywhere we choose. Sexual intimacy is most definitely part of the ambience in Black women's Blues parties. Perhaps this is where we differ from white lesbians; rather than dance ourselves to death in nightclubs to techno music, Black women organize dances where women, wall to wall, can wind and grind in uncompromising and sexually intimate positions with each other all night long.

Lesbians are often denied pleasurable sex because of the lack of real information we receive about women and our bodies. We have to discover for ourselves that our sexuality is linked to clitoris stimulation and that sex is an emotional and physical experience. The clitoris was only recently included in biological descriptions, because it was thought, by men, to have no function. Awareness of our genitals enables us to think about and continually choose our sexual preferences. Masturbation can be a key to understanding our own needs as Black lesbians, without the internalized pressure to 'get it right'. We can learn what pleases us and satisfy ourselves, with or without a love, as well as have more of an idea of what can please other women. Some women have always masturbated, but there are taboos against it in patriarchal society, as women are supposed to be dependent on their male partners for pleasure. Fantasy can be another form of satisfaction. It allows us to play out our most wonderful desires and dreams in our heads, while safe in the knowledge that we will not be criticized, taken advantage of or let down. It provides us with a safe way to use our minds for emotional and physical pleasure. Sometimes we act out these fantasies and sometimes we don't; the fantasy can often be better than having actual sex. Many lesbians who enter a period of celibacy achieve total sexual satisfaction through masturbation, while others refrain from all forms of sex. Some of us enter celibacy to improve our enjoyment of sex by healing the wounds of childhood, while others choose it as a means of redistributing energy into other creative activities. Celibacy can be a beautiful time for rebuilding strength, for reassessing and concentrating all that energy into other areas of our lives.

Becoming aware of our sexuality is often scary, especially as this can take place at different times in our lives. Like all peoples, Black lesbians use sex as an emotional outlet: to release pressure, express affection, get revenge, feel good, heal an argument or to create intimacy. Sexuality, sensuality and sex do not begin or end in bed. These are, in reality, primarily about self-esteem, self-image and identity. If you can be honest, open, display trust and feel safe, there is more chance of having enjoyable sex. There is no right or wrong way to be a Black lesbian, or right and wrong way for adults to have consenting sex. This is the same for relationships, it is up to us to create and develop our own sexualities. Despite all the shit that we have to put up with, we have managed to find the beauty in each other, and enjoy healthy and fulfilling sexual relationships.

Black lesbian chic

Since Black lesbians have been visible on the lesbian and gay scene in Britain, many of us have always been chic. Being chic, or sassy and smart, is something which is intrinsic to the African, Caribbean and Asian communities. However, interestingly enough, the face of lesbian chic has been credited to white lesbians. Since 1993, the media has been raving about the emergence of lesbian chic as if it is a new phenomenon. Typically, every image of lesbian chic has always portrayed white women. For white lesbians, being chic may be new, but most Black lesbians have always taken pride in their physical appearance, whether butch, femme or just camp. We come from communities which have always taken pride in the way you dress. Style is highly valued. In fact, our appearance has been one of the many conflicts between Black and white lesbians. Long hair, dresses, jewellery, classy clothes and make-up were not previously the face of white lesbian sexuality. Indeed, if you emulated this style, you could be accused of colluding with patriarchy, selling out or even of being a pseudo-lesbian. Some Black lesbians have turned up at lesbian venues looking glamorous and been quizzed about their sexuality. Others have been politely told they are the best-dressed lesbian on a demonstration.

Many lesbians of African descent in their thirties grew up in the era of wig-head girls, rebels, casual girls and soul heads. Each group had its specific style, which included the clothes you wore, how you styled your hair, the accessories you chose, and what type of music you liked. Lesbians of African and Asian descent under thirty have grown up with the styles linked to bhangra, new world, rare groove, reggae and swing music. The images of all these cults have been chic.

Hair has also been a status symbol in the Black community; long hair is always encouraged and a source of pride. Black lesbians have always worn anything from headwraps and African clothing, to saris, punjabi suits, dashikis and European dress styles. Noticeably many lesbians of African descent have broken boundaries by wearing dreadlocks uncovered, or shaving their heads bald. Both styles are sacrilege in the Black heterosexual community: you should either wear your hair long, in braids or cover it up. Dreadlocks have become a symbol of trouble, and members of the wider community can be quite hostile. With the Rastafarian religion, women should never show their hair in public.

Often our fashions become even more chic when we mingle Western fashions with Asian/Caribbean/African fashions: 'Mixing traditional African/Asian dress with male western attire, she shatters the expectation of herself as a Black woman. Each time the onlooker tries to place her by her colour and her headwrap, the fantasy around her identity will be disrupted by her DM boots.'[7]

Whether chic or sassy, *afrekeke* (wearing traditional African cloth) or *asiakeke* (wearing traditional Asian cloth), Black lesbians have definitely influenced the way white lesbians dress. Instead of emulating their stereotype of bleached-blonde cropped hair, leather jackets, jeans and DMs, we have forced white lesbians to explore the way they look. It is no surprise that when Black lesbians emerged on the scene in large numbers, coupled with the explosion of British and American Black youth culture during the mid- to late 1980s, white lesbians soon began to experiment with growing their hair and wearing more sophisticated and femme clothes. The presence of Black lesbians has most definitely contributed to the changing face of the lesbian community. By virtue of our race, culture and our styles, we can and do leave our mark.

Notes

1. Valerie Mason-John and Ann Khambatta, *Making Black Waves.* Scarlet Press, London, 1993.
2. Vickie M. Mays, *I Hear Voices But See No Faces: Reflections on Racism and Woman Identified Relationships of Afro-American Women.* 1981.
3. Radio interview on WBAI, New York, 29 April 1984.
4. Mason-John and Khambatta, *Black Waves.*
5. *Ibid.*
6. *Ibid.*
7. Inge Blackman and Kathryn Perry, 'Skirting the issue: lesbian fashion for the 1990s', *Feminist Review,* No. 34, Spring 1990.

Books

Sara Bennett and Joan Gibbs, *Top Ranking: A Collection of Articles on Racism and Classism in the Lesbian Community*. February Third Press, New York, 1980.
Valerie Mason-John and Ann Khambatta, *Making Black Waves*. Scarlet Press, London, 1993.

Article

Laura Bohannan, 'Dahomean marriage: a revaluation', *Africa*, vol. 19, no. 4, 1949.

Personal archive material, oral histories and memories were also used in compiling this chapter. Thank you to all the Black lesbians who contributed to discussions around sex and sexuality.

Chapter five

Some of Us Are Younger

Sakthi Suriyaprakasam

IN trying to discuss the experiences of young Black lesbians, several problems immediately became apparent. Firstly, although there are several studies about young lesbians, these have not covered the experiences of young *Black* lesbians. The London Gay Teenage Group Survey report states: 'The survey population was therefore predominantly white, and the results which form the basis of this report will reflect most strongly the social, economic and cultural values of young white homosexuals. There has been little opportunity in this report to consider the question of race and racism. It is an area which deserves further consideration in subsequent studies.' Predictably there have been no subsequent studies that have attempted to include young Black lesbian voices. Secondly, there are very few young Black lesbians who attend youth groups, and fewer still under the age of twenty-one. There may be several reasons for this, and by looking at other young Black lesbians' experiences of school and youth groups, it is possible to discover what may prevent young Black lesbians coming out.

However, it is important to stress that the number of young Black lesbians coming out on to the scene, and making visible statements about their sexuality, has increased enormously over the past five years. Ten years ago a Black lesbian who came out vocally about her sexuality was rare. Many Black lesbians remained in the closet until their mid-twenties, and many more came out when they attended 'We Are Here' in 1984, the first conference for Black women which was overtly labelled feminist. Two Black lesbian conferences followed this in 1985 and 1989, allowing more Black lesbians to come out, and giving young Black lesbians a chance to redefine their sexuality.

During the 1980s most Black lesbians living in large cities knew each other, because so few of us were out and about. Even in London the number of visible Black lesbians were so few that you knew everybody whenever you attended a Black lesbian event. Since the early 1980s there have been helplines, a Black lesbian and gay centre, and a variety of events and groups which have been set up to provide Black lesbians with resources. Therefore, it is no surprise that since a network of Black lesbian groups has sprung up in the major cities of Britain, Black lesbians have come out in their hundreds. The Black lesbian groups and organizations which have survived the Thatcherite hatchet, provide a resource for young lesbians coming out today.

Despite the existence of these groups, lesbians of African and Asian descent still have difficulties coming out. One young lesbian of Asian descent, aged eighteen, explained:

> If I told my parents, they would ask, 'how would I have babies?' Then they would say it's against the religion of Islam, and therefore homosexuality will make me unsuitable for a husband. They would call me dirty, a pervert, prostitute, a corrupting influence on my younger sister and her friends, and accuse me of being HIV-positive. They would accuse all my friends of being gay, before trying to murder me.

Young Black lesbians have very little affirming literature or imagery of themselves which they can show their parents, even if they want to. Practically all the publications and films about lesbians and gay men document white lifestyles, portraying white lesbians with cropped or bleached hair, dressed in leather, jeans and big boots. Journalist Valerie Mason-John, when reporting on Black lesbians between the ages of fifteen and eighteen, quoted the women as saying: 'We are not trendy feminists who wear Doctor Marten boots and lots of badges, we are women who enjoy dressing up and keeping in touch with current fashions.'[1]

I interviewed seven Black lesbians, four of whom were Asian and three African, who explore the issues which concern young black lesbians. I have also used my personal experience of the Black lesbian scene for women under twenty-one and the experiences of friends and acquaintances. This is therefore not meant to be representative of all groups of young Black lesbians, but rather an attempt to give an insight into how we perceive the wider community, the pressures we face in coming out, and what our experiences and expectations are. In doing this I have covered the areas of school, coming out to oneself, identity, our relationships with family, our experiences of the scene and of the Black lesbian and gay community.

School

School is still one of the greatest institutions that is based on heterosexual assumptions. Sex education focuses on reproduction and heterosexual lifestyles. Discussion of homosexual content in literature is suppressed, and any attempts to present alternative lifestyles have created a lot of controversy (for example, books like *Jenny Lives with Eric and Martin*, about a gay male couple, by Susanne Bosche, Gay Men's Press, 1983). The passing of Section 28 has increased the difficulty of presenting homosexuality in any positive way at school. This, coupled with the general myths about the corrupting influences of homosexuality on young people at school, has meant that lesbian teachers who could act as role models for young lesbians, providing an avenue for them to talk about their sexuality, have had to be closeted and hidden in schools. Although some youth agencies have made efforts to provide vital information to initiate discussion with young people around sexism, racism and heterosexism, this has not been taken up by schools. The lack of positive images and role models can make coming out an isolating and painful experience for young Black lesbians.

There are other factors which put a great deal of pressure on young lesbians. Most young lesbians grow up with such a negative image of homosexuality that they distance themselves from it. This can lead to conflict as young lesbians begin to identify their sexuality. Having to accept your sexuality, then, often means taking on pervasive negative images as well. In this atmosphere, the knowledge that their sexuality is a large part of their identity which should remain hidden is something most young lesbians learn early on. The effects of this can be wide-ranging, but at the most obvious level, young lesbians can feel quite isolated from their peers, especially as most meeting places for the young people (discos, youth clubs, etc.) are overtly heterosexual.

For young Black lesbians this is compounded by having to deal with racism. Most young Black lesbians face racism at school to some degree, whether institutionalized or on a day-to-day basis. Although experiences of school tend to differ widely, this added pressure means that few young Black lesbians feel empowered enough to come out or even question their sexuality while at school. Mason-John recounts the experiences of two Black lesbians who came out at school. One of them was told by her teachers that 'if she wore trousers all the time she would look odd, and the other was treated like one of the boys. She could remember a girl at school who was placed in a mental hospital because she was a lesbian.'[2] The following examples document the experiences of some of the Black lesbians I interviewed:

> I had a difficult time in school because I came from a country where the English they taught me was very different from the English they teach here. Because I couldn't learn English as fast, they sent me to a special school for six to seven years. I think this really set me back. I feel I could have done a lot better, there was no need for them to do that . . . (African descent)

> I didn't have a bad time at school because I was tough, so no one would mess with me. (African descent)

> At school I kept myself very much to myself. I found the girls around me pretty much immature. I had crushes on at least

half my female teachers. But I didn't feel comfortable in school. It was an all-girls' school and the girls were always chatting about boys. It used to piss me off a bit, but it didn't bother me seriously because I hadn't recognized myself as a lesbian then. (African descent)

I can't remember thinking much about my sexuality at school, mostly because I was always so angry about the racism I was facing. I came to this country when I was fourteen, and it was a real shock to come to an environment where people were constantly calling you racist names and making fun of your accent. It was quite dehumanizing, I found it hard to think of myself as a normal person who could fancy someone. (Asian descent)

I went to a predominantly Asian school in a predominantly Asian area. A lot of the other girls were from the same community, so I was surrounded by the culture and some of the traditional expectations of an Asian girl who grows up in Britain. It felt like I couldn't get away from that, even at school. (Asian descent)

Whatever the experience of Black lesbians in school, the need to constantly juggle different demands and deal with different pressures can lead to a shelving of issues around sexuality.

Coming out

Given the lack of images of Black lesbians in the media and elsewhere, coming out for young Black lesbians quite often involves identifying initially with the white lesbian images that we are more likely to discover. The recognition and acknowledgement of oneself as Black as well as lesbian can be a much longer process. The ways we learn usually involve educating ourselves through books, joining groups, and perhaps calling a help line. But it invariably involves experiencing racism from the very community that we have chosen to identify with, namely white lesbians. Their racism and ignorance of Black people means going to a group and feeling vulnerable as the only Black lesbian there, or going to a club and feeling invisible and ignored with unwelcome hostile vibes or outright racism. The way to a positive self-identity for young Black lesbians is more often a negative than positive process. Mason-John reported the words of one Black lesbian:

> It is a lot harder to be out in the Black community because the adults call homosexuality a white disease. My dad would kill me if he knew, his culture has strict principles and has never had to cope with overt homosexuality. My mother accepts that I am a lesbian, I take her to a Lesbian and Gay centre – but she is white.[3]

The women I interviewed recalled the following experiences:

> When I was coming out, the first book I ever read that mentioned lesbians was some awful thing by Judith Krantz. It was a very negative portrayal. But in the book it mentioned *The Well of Loneliness*, so I got that from the library, and in the introduction it mentioned another book, and others. Obviously they were all books about white women, but I still felt really excited by finding them. I felt like I was reading something that was about me. It wasn't until a lot later that I started to question why I was suppressing my Blackness every time I read these books. I soon realized it was because nothing in them related to my experience as a Black or Asian woman. That's why *The Color Purple* was such a brilliant book for me. It was the first I ever read with Black lesbians in it. (Asian descent)

> The first time I really knew about Black lesbians was when my Dad bought this book called *Home Girls* when I was eighteen. He gave up reading it after a couple of pages and I started to read it. I can't remember who the character was but she was talking about being a Black lesbian. It was the first time I realized that there were Black lesbians. I didn't identify as lesbian then. . . . It's only been in the last couple of years that I've felt comfortable with the term Black lesbian. (African descent)

> I've been to some women's dos where white women have said to me 'Why do there have to be Black-women-only dos?' You can't be bothered to challenge them, you just think, shit, this woman should know better, but then you think, no, she doesn't know any better. We're all brought up in a certain way and it's up to us to educate ourselves, because we don't change overnight. The only thing we change is our sexuality, but our ideology and the way we think can stay the same. We've got to challenge that. (African descent)

Discovering groups and places to go can be a matter of chance for young Black lesbians. Although youth groups are now giving more thought to the needs of young Black lesbians, information about the resources that exist is not easily accessible to most, unless the individual has already tapped into the Black lesbian network. For a young Black lesbian just coming out, this can intensify the feelings of isolation and helplessness. Very few young Black lesbians attend youth groups or continue to attend after the first few visits. Therefore, issues of how best to target young Black lesbians and how to make them feel welcome within a group environment need to be addressed. A typical opinion of the young Black lesbians I interviewed was:

> I would have never gone to this youth group if I hadn't met this woman. She was the first Black lesbian I met. I was in Gay's the Word and she was there as well. She finally came up and spoke to me, we started chatting, and she told me about this youth group. ... When I first went there I felt out of place. I felt everybody was more eloquent than me. I thought I needed to feel more confident and assertive before going back. So I stopped going for a while, and then when I felt I'd gained some confidence, I joined this other group. (African descent)

The family

Families are very important to most young Black lesbians. They affirm our cultural identity which can be threatened at school, within mainstream white society or even among the lesbian and gay community. For many of us families also serve as filters, interpreting the culture of our homeland. So, although we may choose to distance ourselves from our families, they serve as an important resource for our emotional needs. Coming out to parents and family can result in the loss of this resource. Young Black lesbians will therefore more often assess the importance of coming out, weighing the possible losses against the gains. There is a prevalent perception that it is much harder for Black communities to accept homosexuality; in fact, almost the opposite is true when the situation involves young people within the family. Black communities have had to face racism, adapting and modifying their cultural values to fit into a changing environment. This can give us more flexibility within our families to deal with all kinds of issues, including lesbianism. Some Black lesbians find that families are accepting of their lifestyles and their differences, but are reluctant to discuss the issue in terms of lesbianism. This again leads us to question the value of coming out to our families:

> I've never understood people who have to tell their family. My family don't know. The only thing they know is that I'm different – not different because they think I'm lesbian, but because I speak differently, I dress differently, have different ideas. I don't have my hair straightened, that's what they mean by different, and that's fine, I'm happy with that, because they accept me with all my differences. (African descent)

> My parents don't live here, but I see them once a year or so. But I have really good boundaries with them about my personal life, so they know what they can and can't ask me about. (Asian descent)

> When I did tell my family, I was on the verge of moving out because of the problems we were having. When my dad realized I was definitely going to move out, he said to me, 'You're my daughter, I love you, as long as you don't get pregnant or become a lesbian or something . . .' And I said,

'as a matter of fact I am a lesbian.' He didn't take it seriously at first, and then he went ape-shit. But it made things easier in the end because I was less secretive and could be more open about where I was going, etc. On his part, he couldn't acknowledge it, it wasn't real, it didn't exist, so he couldn't challenge me, and that makes things easier somehow. I told my mum because my dad threatened to, and she said she knew, I'd always been a tomboy. . . . I came out to my family because I was already moving out, but I was really fearful of my father's reaction. I was expecting the worst, so it was a relief that it's reached a compromise in the end. But I know a friend who told her family and got kicked out. So I'd never advise people just to tell their family. I'd say probe around to see what their reactions would be, and only tell them if that'll be OK. (African descent)

God no. My family don't know. It's bad enough being the youngest one in the family and the only unmarried one. I get more and more pressure now to get married every time I visit my family. Even though I'm independent from them, and have my own place, it's like when I have to speak with them I regress back to being really young. I can't argue with them properly about it. Also it's a language problem, I don't know if I could sufficiently explain being lesbian in our language, I don't know the vocabulary. I do feel like I'm living two different realities. At the same time though there's this acceptance of my girlfriend. For instance, when I broke up with her, my mother kept saying: 'You can't not speak to her, call her up and make up, you'll feel better,' and I wanted to tell her she couldn't possibly understand, even though she was really concerned for me. (Asian descent)

I haven't told my parents, even though my father probably knows and my mother suspects. I keep wondering what I really want out of telling them, how it would change things. I do get pissed off with people assuming that as an Asian lesbian it must be harder for me to come out to my parents. (Asian descent)

The scene

Young Black lesbians turn to the scene as a way of meeting other lesbians, Black and white, as a way of keeping in touch with what may be going on, and simply as a way of breaking out of their isolation. Theoretically, the scene encompasses everything from lesbian/gay cafes, bars, other meeting places and nightclubs. In practice, however, the scene tends to comprise of nightclubs, few of which are particularly welcoming to young Black lesbians. There are many reasons for this:

> My perception of the scene is basically nightclubs, places to hang out with friends. But there is a problem with the scene. If you're into following fashion it's OK, but if you're very much into yourself, it's more difficult. You always have these people telling you what to wear, what you should look like, and if you don't fit these criteria, forget it. My reaction to them is, fuck off, don't tell me what to do, you have no idea where I'm coming from ... (African descent)
>
> I've always felt as an Asian woman, invisible on the scene. Whether it's because I have long hair, or what, I don't know, but I do feel excluded. (Asian descent)
>
> I hate the lesbian scene, the atmosphere, and the unfriendliness of it. People either ignore you or look at you like you're exotic or something, especially when you wear something more traditional. (Asian descent)
>
> I don't really rate the scene. I go to a few places, but I don't feel comfortable with them straightaway. When I was first going out, and I was desperate to get to places with gay people, I went to this lesbian pub and sat down on my own with my glass of wine ... from that experience, I've gained confidence enough to go to other places. (African descent)

If young Black lesbians approach the scene with a need to feel part of a community, they are often disappointed and angered by how hard it is to feel included, and by the racism, both overt and covert, which they experience on the scene:

> I really don't like going to the mainstream lesbian nightclubs because of the music they play. It all tends to be techno, maybe with five minutes of soul thrown in. They never play anything different. I did once get really excited because I was standing outside this club and someone handed me a flyer to fill in. You had to fill your name on one side, and on the other it listed all the different kinds of music you might like to hear played. I was filling this in and the person at the door told me not to bother with that side, it was only the name and address that was important. That really showed me how much commitment they had to changing the kind of music they played ... (Asian descent)

Another common problem faced by Black lesbians concerns the stereotypes of lesbians as butch or boyish. Although some Black lesbians may fit this stereotype, many others do not. Young Black lesbians often have the assumption made about them that they are straight, simply because they do not fit this stereotype. This can make young Black lesbians feel alienated and excluded. The cruisiness of the scene can also be off-putting to many young lesbians, some of whom might be visiting a club for the first time:

> I don't mind that a club is cruisy, if it would be friendly as well. But it is always so unfriendly. The only people I get good vibes from in a club are the other Black women. And there's a few of us. (Asian descent)

For many young lesbians, the scene seems to cater for a small proportion of people, mainly white lesbians, with very little attempt to attract Black lesbians or make them feel welcome. Going to nightclubs can also prove to be expensive, and this again excludes many young Black lesbians. All of these barriers can be frustrating for many, as there is very little alternative to the club scene in the lesbian and gay community.

The Black lesbian community

There is a general disillusionment about the fact that the Black lesbian community is based around the scene, that there is no longer the same sense of community, of working together politically. Valerie Mason-John and Ann Khambatta recounted the opinions of two Black lesbians:

> There seemed to be much more going on in the eighties, everywhere was new, things were possible. There was so much dialogue and political theorizing. Today there are just parties and literary events. (Araba Mercer)
>
> There were more women's centres and Black groups around to support women when I came out. Today there is only a social scene for new dykes out. There is no political debate, I believe we have become fragmented, people are into enjoying their sexuality through parties.[4]

Although this can be attributed to the many economic and political changes that have affected the feeling of optimism and possibility of real political change, there is also the fact that many young Black lesbians do not identify themselves as part of a Black lesbian community. Young Black lesbians have had little access to the history of the Black lesbian movement, and to the discussion and debates that were part of this process. There is a very real generation gap, not necessarily in terms of years but in experience, between those who have been involved in creating a community and the young Black lesbians on the scene today. There has been very little dialogue between these groups. Young Black lesbians are forced, from the moment of first coming out, to educate themselves and create their own political agenda, without reference to the history of the Black lesbian movement and in isolation. It is no wonder that the community seems fragmented. And yet young Black lesbians are politically active and form their own communities:

> Among my friends, I can say every one of them is into Black politics, women's politics, stuff around sexuality. They do

go on marches like the anti-British National Party march, they're predominantly active. (African descent)

I tend to go out with my friends now a lot. There's a lot of dykes round where we live, and there's quite a strong sense of community. We have our own events, parties. I don't go out on the scene that much any more. (African descent)

Many young Black lesbians have shown a great deal of strength in coming out, approaching people, going out on the scene and creating networks, both creative and political, for themselves. However, many more have to deal with isolation and fear, and with racism from the lesbian and gay community when they do come out. It is important that these young Black lesbians are made to feel part of the community, and this can only happen if the community itself becomes more truly representative.

Young Black lesbians today seem to be forging links much more with Black gay men than their predecessors. Perhaps this is because of the lack of facilities for Black lesbians, or perhaps it is the new way forward: building a community alongside Black gay men, to protect ourselves from racism and reaffirm our varied cultural identities. Coalition politicizing and socializing (lesbians and gay men, black and white, coming together) seems to be the current trend of the 1990s in Britain.

Notes

1. Valerie Mason-John, 'Challenging heterosexism', *GEN*, March 1987.
2. *Ibid.*
3. *Ibid.*
4. Valerie Mason-John and Ann Khambatta, *Making Black Waves*. Scarlet Press, London, 1993.

Books

Gilbert Herdt (ed.), *Gay and Lesbian Youth*. Harrington Park Press, New York, 1989.

Valerie Mason-John and Ann Khambatta, *Making Black Waves*. Scarlet Press, London, 1993.

107: Some of Us Are Younger

Lorraine Trenchard, *Young Lesbians.* London Gay Teenage Group, London, 1984.

Articles

Valerie Mason-John, 'Challenging heterosexism', *GEN*, March 1987. Published by the Women's Educational Group (WEDG).

Chapter six

. . . *and Some of Us Are Older*

Seni Seneviratne

AGEING lesbians of African and Asian descent are perhaps a new phenomenon, because it has only been during the past ten years that Black lesbians have come out *en masse* and made public statements about their sexuality. Role models are difficult to find when so few of us are visible.

Whether we belong in Britain or not, many of us are now settled here as a result of the colonizing of Africa, Asia and the Caribbean. Our Black grandparents have always belonged to another world, another place far away from here, and now we are entering a time in our lives when we, and our contemporaries, are becoming grandmothers. Those of us over forty and out about our sexuality are the first generation of visible, ageing Black lesbians living in Britain. As the situation for Black people has gradually improved (with images in the media, acceptance in professional jobs, etc.), it has paved the way for some Black lesbians to come out. Therefore, the fact that there are few visible Black lesbians over sixty does not mean we don't exist. It is a symptom of racism, colonialism and the struggle for positive affirmation of our Black identities. Many groups set up by white women for older lesbians have stipulated that you must be over fifty, therefore Black lesbians have been missing from such groups.

Although Black lesbians have been living, ageing and dying in Britain for centuries, our coming out has been hampered by our oppressions, which other chapters in this book refer to. Hopefully, in twenty years' time, there will be so many visible, ageing Black lesbians that we will laugh among ourselves when we speak of older Black lesbians being over forty. However, because there are so few around, at forty many of us are faced with the reality of ageing in a country which has few facilities for older Black people, and even fewer for older Black lesbians. Through the voices of four older Black lesbians (including myself), ranging in age from forty-two to fifty-eight, I explore some of the aspects of living in Britain.

Am I older?

Am I an older Black lesbian? Does the fact that I am now over forty add another label to my list? I've always hated labels. I was once asked to write an article as a Black lesbian mother; something about the way these three words were trotted out made me cringe, and I wrote this poem:

Don't call me
Black Lesbian Mother
three labels
neatly tied together.
They box me off
imprison me
in someone else's
preconceptions.
Don't get me wrong
Black I am
claimed through years
of confusion and struggle.
Lesbian I am
risked through years
of fear of rejection.
Mother I am
lived through years
of my daughter's growing.
Look at me

I am more than
these three words
that stick to me
like badges
for you to
define me by.

Well, now I'm over forty, do I need to write another verse? My first reaction when I was asked to write this piece was, 'Do I qualify? Am I old enough.' I'm barely over forty, and I'm only just entering that thirty- or forty-year span when I could be classified as older. What does it mean? What issues do Black lesbians across that span of years have in common? Has my life changed significantly since I entered it? I decided this time to accept the label and then look at it more closely. I interviewed three other Black lesbians who were older than myself, to help me. Mumtaz, like me, in her early forties, was born in Bombay and grew up in Tanzania. She is South Asian and came to England in 1961. Kameedea, just about to enter her fifties, was born in Britain, although she grew up in Ghana with her Ghanaian mother and Jamaican father, returning to England in the 1950s. Dorothy, preparing for her sixties, was born in Jamaica, and moved to England in 1957. I was born in Yorkshire in 1951, to an English mother and Sri Lankan father.

They say 'life begins at forty'. Whether or not it's to do with societal pressure, I think it's true that when you reach forty you take a look at your life, assess what you've done, what you're doing, and begin to wonder how much time you have left to fulfil the rest of your dreams.

The year that I turned forty was very significant for me. It was a time when I was forced to take a look at my life, my health and my future. I fell sick with a virus and this turned into a post-viral illness which lasted for six months. In that time I was forced into a kind of retreat, where I began to take stock of how much I had misused my body over the years and, in particular, how much stress I had expected it to absorb without the benefit of very much help and support. I had survived the trauma of the death of my father and the breakdown of a long-term relationship by literally pushing myself through the emotional upheaval of both. I had continued to devote a lot of energy to my child, my work, my political activity and my friends, leaving very few reserves for myself. During the many hours I spent alone in my sickbed I was forced to rethink my priorities and look for ways to change my lifestyle. I knew many women who had been suffering from myalgic encephalomyelitis (ME) for years and this was my biggest dread, that I had left it too late to change and that from now on I would be severely immobilized. I resolved to get better and take more care of myself.

In the same year I heard news from a very dear friend of mine that she had bone cancer metastasized from breast cancer, with a very poor prognosis. I was shocked and very sad. She was close to my age, and suddenly we were faced with how little time she had left. In the following year I spent several weeks with her while she underwent drastic chemotherapy, and together we followed the Bristol Diet. It was during this period, spent caring for her and myself and looking back on our lives and our friendship, that I began to return to a state of normal health and energy.

During the two years since then, I feel I have made more sense of my life, come to know myself better and rethought my priorities. Dealing with my friend's eventual death has in some ways helped me to value myself. I have been able to maintain many of my political commitments, but with a more realistic sense of my energies and limitations. So, I guess when I was forty I did have the personal life crisis that is always predicted. But I didn't really see myself as being older, and in lots of ways I needed to think that my new life was just beginning.

The first question I asked Mumtaz, Dorothy and Kameedea was whether they saw themselves as older:

MUMTAZ: 'I do see myself as older now. It's been a gradual process over the last two or three years. When I had my fortieth birthday I didn't feel like I'd suddenly become old, but I have over the last two or three years.'

KAMEEDEA: 'I feel as if I've been pushed into thinking about myself as an older lesbian. As soon as I was forty it started and I'd never even thought about it, because I'd always felt that life begins at forty.'

DOROTHY: 'When I was forty I'm not sure I would have classified myself as old, I was fit, playing badminton and volley ball practically every day, and then I had a coronary in my forties. I would even have liked to say I didn't think fifty was old.'

At forty, we didn't suddenly begin to see ourselves as older, but maybe a process started. Something to do with how others began to perceive us, and also about moving into a different phase of our lives. I asked Kameedea whether she defined this as older:

KAMEEDEA: '... and then all of a sudden everyone was looking at me as an older lesbian, and people were asking me for interviews, films, radio ... that started when I was forty ... and more and more I feel that when I go out. I've had people getting up and giving me their seats, and I find that a bit shocking ... perhaps I should dye my hair or something ... perhaps it's all to do with grey hair when people don't actually know how old they are.'

Whether or not the grey hairs appeared at forty, we became more and more conscious of our age and began to identify with women who were possibly dealing with similar issues. I asked Dorothy how she sees me over forty yet still sixteen years younger than her:

DOROTHY: 'I've always seen you as this young woman, because you are younger than I am and you used to say to me in those days "you know I'm not as young as you think I am." I still see you as a young woman. Now you've said you are forty-two I suppose I suddenly realize that although you're younger than I am you are moving into an age range that means you're nearer to me than I thought you were.'

So when did we actually start to identify as older lesbians? For Dorothy the process began when she reached fifty. She began to think about age when her daughters started having children. Suddenly she realized that she was going to become a grandmother:

DOROTHY: 'Since I've become fifty I actually have to recognize that I am older even if I don't call myself old, I am older. I do sometimes have to recognize that being older has created differences in values, in leisure time and how one sees the world.'

For Dorothy, taking early retirement added another dimension to her ageing process:

DOROTHY: 'Ten years ago I didn't think age was important but this year, when I've taken early retirement, I suddenly realize that I'm near to retirement age and moving into a new phase, a new period of my life that does recognize the ageing process . . .'

Combined too with a period of time when her daughters started to have children of their own. It isn't a simple matter of what particular age you reach. Circumstances affect the way we see ourselves. Being healthy and active makes a big difference, as well as the ages of our lovers and friends. Kameedea doesn't really feel older at all:

KAMEEDEA: '. . . probably because I'm having a relationship with someone who is fifteen years younger than me . . . I feel that stamina-wise and energy-wise I sort of keep up with her . . . so I don't feel any different from that point of view.'

But even in our early forties Mumtaz and I have times when we feel older than a lot of the women we socialize with. For both of us a lot of what is connected to our political histories, and sense that we have been involved in a whole variety of things that the younger women haven't experienced. For one thing, there are the enormous changes that have occurred since that time and, in particular, the rapid decline of optimism amongst political activists:

MUMTAZ: '. . . in the early 1980s, when we had the GLC in London and periods when there was an incredible amount of activity going on, I know what I was personally hoping for, was that through that kind of activity and our common interests I would be able to build networks of people I would be close to. So it could be more than just working together. For whatever reasons that hasn't worked, and I feel as though it's one of my sadnesses and one of my griefs about that period and about what's happened since then – because of all the cuts, and all the changes in the infrastructures. It has also meant we've been pushed to cope by ourselves . . . and we are all struggling so hard individually and spreading ourselves so thinly, if we've got the energy left.'

All four of us shared the opinion that there was a sense that things were radically changing for the worse. We all had nostalgic, fond memories of those days when struggle held out more hope of change:

KAMEEDEA: 'You notice how things take so much longer than you thought they were going to take to get anywhere. Things are really slow ... when I was younger I thought that things would change fast and I was there ready to help it change ... now it's almost as if we'll never see change in our lifetime. ... It feels like things are much more laid back than they were in the 1970s and 1980s. Women now are not so intense as we were about trying to change things ... and in a way it feels like things are going to move even slower because there isn't that push to change.'

DOROTHY: '... everyone is struggling not to be identified as a Marxist, socialist or communist, just as everyone doesn't want to call themselves a feminist. ... I still pride myself on saying that I follow a Marxist road ... for me true Marxism is about flexibility, is about changing according to the climate and the economic situation. It's not something static ... where people have made it static, they have destroyed what Marxism is. But yes, I get a feeling of total despair ... everything we've fought for seems to be driven back. I get very depressed.'

We also shared a very strong feeling that the periods when we had been politically active in this country – the 1960s, 1970s and 1980s – were exciting and optimistic times, and that now, in contrast, we have to work very hard to retain some of that optimism. For me, in recent years this has also connected to issues around my health. When I was younger the world seemed to be changing fast and I ran to keep up with it. Twenty years later I was still running and hadn't stopped long enough to see how much the process of change had slowed down, or even begun to turn backwards. I had to face up to the fact that sacrificing my health and sanity to 'the cause' would not change that. In some ways it might not have mattered to have given up so much for the struggle, if we could feel today that we had arrived at a better situation because of it. But we never got to the end. It has been like an endless labour with no baby to reward our efforts. Now it all seems to have gone into reverse, and we have started to look at our own lives and analyze how it has affected us. In reality we failed to change the world and in the process have driven ourselves into the ground. I continually ask myself, all for what? Mumtaz recited a poem that seemed to reflect something of how we were feeling:

MUMTAZ: 'It's written by a woman of our generation, the generation of the cultural revolution. I feel that this poem, in particular, expresses much of what I'm dealing with, and have been dealing with for quite a while, in trying to come to terms with radical change – when all one's frames of reference are turned upside down.'

> Perhaps our thoughts
> Will never be read
> Perhaps the road wrong from the start
> Is still a mistake
> Perhaps the lanterns lit one at a time
> The gale blows out one at a time
> Perhaps burning out a lifetime to illuminate darkness
> Means to have no warm fire at our side
>
> Perhaps tears that flow till they are dry
> Leave the soil more fertile
> Perhaps we sing in praise of the sun
> Perhaps the sun sings in praise of us
> Perhaps the heavier the burden
> The loftier the faith
> Perhaps crying out about all suffering
> Means to be silent about personal misfortune
>
> Perhaps
> the irresistible summons
> Leaves us with no choice[1]

Ageing and health

Getting older, for all of us, seems to have involved beginning to take more care of ourselves. Whether previous neglect was due to intense political activity or heavy work commitments, we all seem to have come to a point where we feel more in control of, and in touch, with our bodies. This does not minimize our concerns, especially in view of the squeeze being applied to state benefits, and increasing anxieties about who will care for us in old age and sickness. Some of us have given up on the National Health Service at a point where it seems to be giving up on us anyway. We are looking to alternative forms of healthcare, but there are worries about how this can be maintained given the cost:

KAMEEDEA: 'I eat better quality food now than I did . . . I remember, when I was younger, going through a period when I couldn't afford to take time off and told myself, that's it, there's no time off. I wouldn't do that now.'

MUMTAZ: 'I became chronically ill in the mid 1970s, and it wasn't till 1989 that I stopped and said, no more, I can't keep going on like this. Before that I was prepared to put that energy in, but now I think what for? When you say, "No more", that's when you find out what kind of support structures you have . . . it's really important to know that there are people around you when you are ill, who are prepared to come and help out.

'I feel anxious in some ways because now I feel more in control of my body. I know I have to do certain things like Yoga, or I mustn't do certain things. So in that sense I feel more in control. . . . But my lack of confidence in the health structures and their future makes me feel anxious in other ways about my health. When my father was older he was able to get home-help support, but that doesn't seem likely any more.

'The choice I made was to give up on the National Health Service because I wasn't getting anywhere. I chose to go into alternative medicines . . . I made that choice and it was an expensive choice, and it meant that for a lot of the time I couldn't do other things.'

The issue of health for all of us was closely linked with work, relationships and living situations. We all, too, expressed concerns about 'being a burden' to lovers or friends, even though for some of us this was an issue that seemed to be in the future:

DOROTHY: 'You don't want to be a burden. One of the things about being a lesbian, even if you have children, you become more lonely. You feel more alone because you are worried about things like weight problems getting worse as you get older, and about how are you going to manage in old age. Often the desire of wanting to live near other people arises as you get older, because of not wanting to be alone. When I first came here, my one ambition was to live in a rural area; as I'm getting older I've changed my mind totally. I've realized how inconvenient that is as a lesbian and as a Black woman, it's just not practical. Those things worry me. It worries me with the changes in the health service and the changes the government is contemplating about state pensions ... you wonder if you are going to be able to survive in old age.'

KAMEEDEA: 'I think about living with my lover who is fifteen years younger, and God I don't want to be sick, or have to be looked after, but that is a thing about the future ... I feel reasonably healthy with a lot of stamina and can put up with a lot.'

DOROTHY: 'One of the things about ageing that is quite significant is your partner and what age she is. At present, I'm relating to someone I've been with for the last eight years as a long-term commitment. For her, there's concern that at the same time as she's relating to a woman who is older, she also has older parents. Her concern is just when she should be enjoying her career she's going to have the responsibility of looking after ageing parents and no doubt a lover who may not be as mobile. So I panic now, that I must get and keep myself fit because I don't want to be a burden to my lover.'

Providing for the future

We are all beginning to think about where and how we'll be living when we get to our sixties and seventies, even though that time is nearer to some of us than others. Maybe we are thinking about it at an earlier age because there is more of a recognition among most lesbians that we do get older and that our lives may change quite significantly because of it. Maybe also there is more anxiety about the future generally: the world seems to be in such a mess, and the welfare state is rapidly disappearing in this country. Maybe we are being pushed into making individual choices and solutions because there is so little collective discussion of the issues. The fact that society is geared towards heterosexual people means that institutions set up to cater for its ageing population have not taken on board the needs of lesbian and gay people. The idea of older lesbians spending their last years in an old people's home is not appealing, and especially not if you are Black. Dorothy is beginning to think about buying a house, to give her some security in her old age:

DOROTHY: 'I'm in the process of buying a house now after being mobile most of my life ... it's about putting roots down and also about safety as you're getting older.'

Mumtaz is also considering whether to move out of a big city to a more accessible place:

MUMTAZ: '... for the first time in my life it feels possible that I might move out of London ... to live in a more physically practical way and nearer to women I could get support from.'

Kameedea has already made this move and is dealing with the implications that has for a Black woman in particular:

KAMEEDEA: 'One of the things that made me think twice about moving was where I was going to live and whether I was going to live in an area that was predominantly white, especially having the kids as well. ... That still feels a bit of an issue living near Hebden Bridge ... there's just a handful of Black people around here ... I can go days without seeing any Black people at all ... I've always got in mind how I can afford to get to Ghana and down to London ... I just love going down to London and wandering through Brixton market, it gives me a complete buzz, it feels so good ... I do miss that and I think about the kids.'

I have just moved into a small house with my daughter, after living collectively for most of my adult life. This is not to say that I regret the ways I have lived in the past, nor that I have given up on any idea of collective living for the future. It is, however, a reflection of the ways in which, as I get older, I have become clearer about doing what makes sense for me and my life, even if it means changing old patterns. We have all been lucky enough to lead very active and physically mobile lives, and are now beginning to face the implications of a future time when this may not be possible. We all agreed that irrespective of the individual decisions we were making now, some collective ways of looking at the future for older Black lesbians, in terms of housing and support, are necessary:

DOROTHY: 'I would like a few of us to sit down and think about housing in the context of – communal housing, a place where you all have your own room – because it is going to be a problem . . . who is going to care for us?'

Financial concerns

It is very worrying that we are being pushed into making individual solutions, because these are not practical, especially for women who don't have a secure job or own a house, for instance. Anyone who has to rely on a government state pension is not going to be able to survive, let alone have any quality of life. This concern about our financial situation as we get older had raised many issues for all of us. For those of us in secure and fairly long-term jobs there was the worry about moving out of that at a time when we should be consolidating our service record and securing a decent pension. Added to that is the concern about sick pay, and the increasing probability of needing to take time off as we get older. For those of us doing freelance work there is the panic that we are not going to be able to take on enough work as we get older, and also that the employment situation is getting more risky. It seems that once you are over forty you are over the hill, employers know there are plenty of younger people who will work for them, for longer hours and less money:

DOROTHY: 'I've always worked, never been unemployed in my life. Last year I really started to think about early retirement because of the pressure in the local authority where I worked . . . I hadn't planned it, but you suddenly feel they're offering you all these things and you're sitting there and not taking it. It was a concern . . .

how am I going to survive until I reach the ripe old age of seventy, if I do? I lived a nomadic life for years, so it's about security, about your pension fund, but I was very lucky because I did pay superannuation and, when I did decide to take early retirement I was able to get thirty-something years. It is a concern – about how you survive, and what standard of living you will end up with.'

KAMEEDEA: 'When I was younger I was dead keen about work, loved teaching, being out there and doing it ... now I feel life's too short to be bogged down by anything as stressful ... that's why I'm trying to just do my own thing. ... I made a decision about five years ago that I definitely wanted to give up teaching and perhaps do other things. ... I felt like I'd worked really hard for twenty years and I needed time. ... I felt like time just goes so quickly ... I didn't want to be stuck in a job which I hated in the end. ... I wanted to do something creative and that's what I've been trying to do. ... Money and how you're going to survive is always a worry. I still think about how I am going to manage and I'm always sitting there trying to work out a budget for coping with this and that. ... One of the things I thought was, I've got to get out of London ... where I had a mortgage which meant I had to work ... and I did just that. I got this house which I don't have to pay a mortgage on, and not having to pay rent or a mortgage has made such a difference ... we were very lucky, we sold a house in London before everything plummeted down to rock bottom and the prices here hadn't gone up.'

MUMTAZ: 'The nature of the photographic work I was doing when I started working in the early 1980s seemed to me to be striving towards working collectively with women to produce pieces of work, and now I feel like I've been pushed more and more into working personally. That is what I want to do, but it isn't just what I want to do. ... A year ago a friend and I worked on a tape/slide show on child sexual abuse. We applied for a grant but it was turned down. I finally got the opportunity to produce it through Autograph [the national organization of Black photographers based in London], but there was only money to cover materials. Although we had no money to pay anybody, a friend of ours produced original music for the show. I didn't like not being able to pay her. I don't like being asked continuously to do things for free, and it's not to do with not wanting to give anything. It's to do with survival and how much energy you've got.'

I have reached a point in my work situation where I feel a need for a change, and in lots of ways I need to change direction, concentrate more on my creative work and maybe do more free-lance work. But it feels too risky, not only because of the economic climate but also because of my age. I feel a need for a secure income much more than I did when I was younger. The prospect of losing this, losing my chance to get sick pay, losing my chance to get early retirement with a reasonable income, is hard to face up to. I'll probably make some sort of compromise, and I know that age is an important factor in any decision I might make.

Relationships and sex

Do we have different expectations from relationships as we get older? It seems to be something that differs according to our experience and personal choices. On the one hand, Mumtaz was struggling against the pressure from outside to make sex and sexual relationships the most important focus in her life, in contrast to her own desire to build meaningful friendships either with an ex-lover or with other women:

MUMTAZ: 'There's an enormous pressure from the outside world to make sex *very, very, very,* important. I don't know whether there are various ways of working that out so that we deal with our own sexuality and our own sexual life differently . . . what I'm finding at the moment is that there are very few models for the kind of relationship that I have at the moment with my ex-lover. Although we are not lovers, I consider her to be my family more than I consider my blood family to be my family. We try and make it clear to people that we're not in a kind of monogamous relationship, but we work together . . . if she's in trouble or if I'm in trouble, I know that I'll be a priority for her and she'll be a priority for me. It feels like I've got to the stage in my life where I don't have lots of people around me but I have one or two very important relationships, of which this is one. . . . What we have in common is our age . . . we have very different experiences, but we seem to have an understanding that comes through growing up through a similar historical period.'

On the other hand, Dorothy was fighting against the pressure to make sex less important in older age. She is also acknowledging the variety of factors that make up relationships, especially long-term ones:

DOROTHY: 'As you get older, sex is still important. I would hate to think that when you reach fifty it isn't, but I suppose the sex in a relationship, especially a long-term one, does change. ... What I want out of a relationship is about sex, is about loving, is about caring, is about somebody to be on the same political lines as me, with a consciousness of what is happening in the world. I want somebody who I can talk to, who likes the things I like, like books and the arts. I'd like to spend more time enjoying the arts as I get older, and feel that I've got more time and more flexibility with money. I want to share that with someone.'

Two of the women I spoke to were in committed long-term sexual relationships, and the one who wasn't had an equally strong commitment to an ex-lover. Although my current relationship is in its early days, I know what I am looking for, and have an expectation of something more long-term. Whether these factors are affected by my age is too difficult to say. I would like to think that there is infinite variety in our choices as Black lesbians, and that we'll still be open to making new relationships into our seventies, eighties and nineties, if that is what we want.

Children

It is when we look at our children, or the children of our friends, that we get a sense of the years passing by. All four of us had different experiences in relation to children, and they touched on many of the issues that will affect older Black lesbians. I can remember lesbians of thirty panicking that they had to make urgent decisions about getting pregnant before it was too late. That age limit has been pushed back to forty now, but the issues are still the same. For older lesbians who don't have children there has to be a conscious choice about not only if, but when and how. Recent development, such as the outrage at single women using artificial insemination by donor (AID) are also limiting their choices. For those of us who had children before we came out, we live our lives as lesbians with children, sometimes facing custody battles, sometimes facing prejudice, and having to deal with its effect on our children. Those who want to adopt or foster are also confronted by the prejudice among social workers. Although the official attitude of many social services departments has tipped in favour of single lesbians being allowed to adopt, there is still no recognition of the value of lesbian couples as adoptive parents. Indeed, the recent government white paper on adoption seems to confirm this. As older lesbians we may not face prejudices against older women adopting, but there are still constant threats to our rights as lesbians to adopt. Mumtaz made a decision not to have children, and spoke of her feelings about this:

MUMTAZ: 'I never wanted to have children and I haven't had a lot of contact with children ... I made a decision that I didn't want the responsibility that children bring. I recognize I might have missed out on some of the joy that they also bring, but I don't have any regrets.'

Dorothy is currently experiencing being a grandmother, but in the past has also had to deal with the difficult process of coming out to her daughters when they were both young women:

DOROTHY: 'The biggest trouble about this ageing thing was being first a mother-in-law and being then a grandmother. ... I was determined I wasn't going to be called Granny, the children call me Grandma. I knew I didn't want to be called by my first name. I felt it was important to the children that their grandmother was special to them. I didn't want to confuse them. Being a grandmother was very significant in accepting that I was entering into a phase of getting older. My struggle with that was what was expected of me as a grandmother, because I was still active, still working, still playing badminton when my first grandchild was born. Suddenly people expect you to be at home sporting a blue rinse – or a black rinse in my case – when your family comes for tea Sunday afternoon. I was determined that wasn't the role I was going to take. I was able to handle that ageing part of being the grandmother for years until my daughter moved to Sheffield, where I live. Therefore, being a grandmother became a living reality because it was on my doorstep. I found that very difficult. That's where my lesbianism came in too ... being a grandmother, being a lesbian and how to handle it.

'There are lots of issues to do with children. Although I've always known I was a lesbian from being at school, being brought up in the Caribbean, things happen, certain things are expected of you. For example, you get married and have children and you live this lie, this closeted lie for years. It was late in life when I came out of the closet – I was in my late forties and fifties. I decided that enough was enough and I wanted to be much more open and clear about my lesbianism, especially with people who meant something to me. I had to break this news to my children, because a relationship I had been in for a long time with a man had to come to an end. They had known him from when they were young. I had met my current lover and wanted to be open with the kids. The thing is they had known a long time. They had an idea that their mother was a lesbian, so when I actually did break it to them it wasn't so traumatic for them. It was much more traumatic for me having to face this, because normally it's children who tell mothers, not mothers who tell children. Once I told them, it was like a burden off my shoulders. I had been really worried how they would handle it. But it's worked out OK with the children. My problem now is two other areas of being a mother – their children (i.e. being a grandmother), and the in-laws, their partners' families. It's not my responsibility to tell them, it's theirs. Their partners have accepted me, their families don't know, I don't think. Again, through one's entire life, even at this age, you have this Jekyll and Hyde sort of state, where you live one life here and the other life there. It is just like a mask, you're continually wearing this mask all your life.

'My grandchildren are coming to a stage where I will have to tell them ... one of them does observe, ask questions and he asked my daughter recently, what is a lesbian? And is that what grandma is? Because she sleeps with ...? She just didn't know how to handle it and bypassed it. I think one day I may need to say quite clearly I am a lesbian, because I want him to pick up positive things about it . . . and he's very fond of my partner so that won't be a problem.

'I'm lucky, I know other lesbian mothers haven't found it so easy. My children have always looked on me as the eccentric mother – different – and I'm lucky that neither they nor their partners have excluded their grandchildren from me, because that would have hurt. Summing it all up as regards to my relationships with my children and my grandchildren, I'm very lucky.'

Kameedea is fostering a four- and a five-year-old, and has had to deal with the problem of people assuming she is their grandmother, and wondering whether she should contradict this:

KAMEEDEA: 'With the children now, people always think I'm the grandmother. . . . My lover is thinking of having a child and I want her to do it in the next year because I feel like I'm too old to cope with babies and put up with them . . . I was wondering if she does have one what will my relationship be? Had I just better say I'm the grandmother, or what? . . . I won't be able to say I'm the mum because no one will believe me.'

Listening to these different experiences made me reflect on my relationship with my own daughter, who is fifteen. I came out when she was two, and she has lived with my lesbianism as an everyday positive thing in her life since then. She was six when I consciously discussed it with her, as a way of preparing her for other people's prejudice. I have maintained an openness with her, which means she can discuss my relationships with me quite comfortably. I am becoming more and more conscious of the relatively short time that is left before she flies the nest and looks for her own independence in the world. Although this makes me sad in some ways, it also gives me a feeling of anticipation and excitement about being able to live my life differently. Maybe I will be able to do more of the things I have dreamt of doing but couldn't because of my responsibilities to her. I could go travelling to different countries or maybe live somewhere else for a while. My anxiety about this is that I won't be healthy or active long enough to do everything I want to when the time comes, which is why it has been so positive for me to talk to older lesbians who are still pursuing their dreams.

Coming out in the Black community when you get older

Coming out to our children is one thing, but how have we dealt with coming out within the Black communities that we relate to? And does it get easier as we get older? There is a sense in which the older I've become the more confident I feel about myself generally and, therefore, about my sexual choices. I don't feel so worried any more about how other Black people will react: they either take me as I am or leave me. I used to feel very nervous about the implications of coming out for my work or political activity. Now I feel stronger and more confident about dealing with it. The fact that there are more Black lesbians around today than ten years ago gives me a much clearer sense of support and confidence.

I can remember a time in the 1980s when I was trying to find out where I fitted into the Black community and struggling to be part of a movement of Asian women, that I thought I was the only Black lesbian in the world. Hence, I often felt that I must keep my lesbianism a secret. It feels so different now. Young Black women who are coming out have a community to identify with. It's not so easy for Black people to point a finger and say: 'You are too Westernized, lesbianism is a white thing.' And even if they do, there are now support networks ready to challenge them. That's not to deny there are still a lot of young, isolated Black lesbians out there, dealing with prejudice and thinking they are the 'only one.' But at least now, once they begin to make contacts, there are networks where they can get support and where most of all they can meet other Black lesbians. Such a structure just didn't seem to exist among Black lesbians ten years ago. There is also more material available about lesbians living in our countries of origin, so it has become easier to challenge the notion that lesbianism is only a white phenomenon:

DOROTHY: '... as a Black lesbian my sexuality has had to take second place to my Black politics, and it's only now that I've got older that I have the luxury of actually owning my sexuality and doing something about it. ... It's easier now. ... When I was in my teens back home, and even in my twenties and thirties in England, I don't think as a Black woman it was as easy to fight about our sexuality. And I don't think many of us did ... we fought about other things. So I think the very fact that I recently participated in the video about older lesbians, for the lesbian and gay TV series *Out*, on Channel Four, shows how things have changed. ... We have been given the opportunity to use many more public platforms. When we as Black lesbians and gay men keep control of some of those public arenas that we go into, then I think it can only be good. But we have to keep control ... what bothers me is when we allow other people to guide us.

'For years I felt that there was no one else like me ... I didn't feel like that at home in Jamaica, because I knew there were quite a few of us. There were lots. You met them at school, in the nursing profession, university, etc., but when I came to England I didn't meet any Black lesbians for a long time. The first time I did, it was nice to feel that here is someone else who recognizes me, and she is Black. It made quite a difference. I can remember struggling, especially when I came to Sheffield, to find older women and older Black lesbians.'

KAMEEDEA: '... there's so much more support now from other Black lesbians that it must be easier. ... You need that support and that understanding, there's such a big difference in terms of cultural acceptance ... there's more awareness generally now. There was always this idea that it didn't happen to Black people.'

The other side of this is the contrast between how visible we can be now – as women between the ages of forty and sixty – compared to those who are older than us. Such women, who may have been forced to lead more traditional, closeted lives, keeping their lesbianism a secret, would perhaps now find it impossible to change. This may explain why it's so hard to identify many Black lesbians over sixty:

DOROTHY: 'The lack of many visible older Black lesbians could be about not wanting anyone else to know, not feeling safe about it.

For a lot of us especially the older ones, most of our relationships have been with white women. We felt safe to be with white lesbians because then we are not taking it back into the community. Maybe that has a part to play, that our coming out and socializing has happened more in a white structure than a Black structure . . . so the Black friends you make who are your age are not lesbians.

'Yes, I'm almost certain there are lots of us who have had to lead a double life. . . .Yes, I think there are lots of us who are married and have children, and still want the acceptance of family. At the end of the day you're not going to run very far from the safety of your own community into a white community that might accept your sexuality but not accept your race.'

The need for Black lesbian role models who are older than us was something we all wanted. Providing inspiration, ideas and support, they would help us look to the future with confidence:

DOROTHY: 'You may ask, why do I feel I want to find anyone who is older? . . . I think sometimes as you're getting older in a society like this it would be nice to meet up with older women, because there are so many things you need to talk about, so many things you need to share, as well as the things you won't share. It depends on where you live, when you acknowledged your lesbianism, what was your way of life. So, for instance, you might be my age but not aware of your lesbian identity until you were forty, so your experience is going to be different from those women who recognize their sexuality at the age of fifteen.

'I was watching a programme on TV some years ago about a group of older American Black women in their seventies and eighties in the jazz world. There they were for years, as dykey as they came, older Black women, and it was nice to see that.'

MUMTAZ: 'That's why it's good to be able to have older people around you who can be role models and can show you that things are possible. If there's a positive image, a role model for me of an older woman, it's Chamunda, the Hindu goddess, the crone, the death goddess, the goddess of ageing.'

Whenever I meet Black lesbians who are older than me and still have progressive, challenging lives and ideas, it makes me feel more optimistic about my own possibilities. Maybe I too can carry on being who I am, that I don't have to conform to preconceptions of a fifty-, sixty- or seventy-year-old woman. Which brings me back to the question of labels. The fact that I agreed in the end to write this chapter means I've accepted 'older' as another possible definition of myself. The process of interviewing three other older black lesbians has, however, made it much more than a label. We have opened up a discussion which is long overdue. We have explored a whole range of issues which are of common concern to us all and, more importantly, have defined our differences. There is no typical older black lesbian, but there is a common thread that runs through all our lives and will continue into our old age, namely the determination not to be defined by anyone else's assumptions, and to carry our commitment to growth and change throughout the rest of our lives.

Note

1. Untitled poem, perhaps by Shu Ting. Trans. by Mumtaz Karimjee, copyright with Mumtaz Karimjee.

Chapter seven

Shooting the Shots: Lesbians of African and Asian Descent in the Media

Maya Chowdhry

The beginning point

IN researching this chapter I gathered a lot of my information from informal chats with African- and Asian-descent lesbian film-makers and photographers who didn't want to participate in the actual interview process. In reaching out for film-makers and photographers I answered some of the questions I was interested in exploring. Are they visible? It was difficult to locate women to interview, and much of this information was collected through word of mouth. I was greeted with comments like 'she's straight now', 'I don't think she's made a lesbian film', 'she's in the closet'. These comments – this process – are all part of the society in which we exist as Black lesbians: a society which is racist, that has strict labels for sexuality; a society which tries to confine and contain female sexuality.

Closet or confining labels

Some women chose not to be interviewed for this piece, either because they defined themselves as bisexual or they were in the process of redefining their sexuality and didn't want to be seen as a Black lesbian film-maker/photographer. One Black lesbian photographer was not happy to discuss her work in the context of her sexuality in such a public way, because the lesbian focus made her feel vulnerable, exposing light on her work from an unwelcome angle. For another Black lesbian, a career in the film industry meant that she had to keep her lesbian face in the closet; she felt she was fighting a white male industry as a Black woman and didn't want her sexuality used as another point of misrecognition – she wasn't prepared to take the risk. An unwillingness to discuss the construction of images also surfaced as another reason for the women's refusal to speak to me. Refusing to define yourself is also a definition: partly it's a matter of language and partly it's an unwillingness to compromise yourself in terms of this label. Nevertheless, whatever reasons are given for sidestepping the debate, it still rages on in the wider world.

The context

African/Asian-descent lesbians exist in a racist and homophobic society, and their concerns are viewed as marginal by the mainstream film and photography industry. It seems that if the work appears in its own right, as a documentary film or a photographic exhibition, it's acceptable, but if it capitalizes on its African/Asian lesbian message, it's considered 'too hot to handle'. Some images seem explicitly lesbian, but it's important to distinguish who is defining these images.

In search of a Black lesbian image

Maya Chowdhry is a South Asian film-maker, writer, photographer and performance artist.

'I was born in Scotland; my mother is of Scottish and English heritage, and my father is Indian, from the north-west frontier province of Pakistan. In my work as a film-maker and photographer I portray the numerous concerns which affect me as an artist, including my identity and my sexuality. Sometimes the images are seen as subtly lesbian: in "Signs", a photographic installation exhibited at the Pavilion Gallery in Leeds, there were several specifically lesbian images in a piece which deals with women's work in India using image and text. The images make a point that lesbians' work is important and shouldn't be forgotten; that lesbians are often invisible, as women's sexuality isn't always obvious.

'In "Running Gay", a programme for Channel Four's documentary series *Out*, I dealt with the issues surrounding lesbians and gays in sport. While researching the programme I was faced with a dilemma about inclusion: if there were to be three main interviewees, then what should the mix of Black/white, lesbian/gay be? I resolved this by having a lesbian, a gay man and a Black lesbian. Should I have included three Black lesbians? The remit of the programme didn't stretch that far. It was important for me to find an articulate Black lesbian, because I knew that whatever she said would be held in tablets of stone by the lesbian and gay community.'

Mumtaz Karimjee is a South Asian photographer.

'I started working as a photographer ten years ago because of the need to challenge stereotypes, but one of the things I feel has happened in the process of these ten years is that I've found it's very difficult to challenge stereotypes without creating other images. In the creation of other images, whose images and what images we use becomes incredibly important. In the mid-1980s I was working in a photojournalistic or social documentary style, which was extremely problematic, because I felt I was challenged quite often on my right to take photographs of other women. I think this is a problem which has never been resolved. I think that as far as social documentary/photojournalism is concerned, it's based on the fact that photographs are taken of other people in different situations, and I think the problem for those of us who are actually doing the taking or the making of those photographs is, how can we be responsible. I think this debate was never taken up in the Black women's community, let alone the Black lesbian community.

'I feel I've circumvented this debate by moving into much more constructed imagery, and have stopped trying to work in a photojournalist/social documentary style. I still get asked for free photographs, and I have to say no, otherwise I wouldn't be able to earn my living.'

Tanya Syed is a South Asian film-maker.

'My mother is from Wales, my father is from India, and I was brought up in Scotland. I work with film and sound, and I've made a number of films over the last few years. My most recent, *Salamander*, is set at a local take-away in London and is about people occupying different spaces. It discusses the private and personal space in a public space. I filmed people in the take-away, and it's also about my experience of going in there. There's a lesbian relationship built up within the film between a woman who goes in the take-away and an Asian lesbian lorry-driver. This is the one I deal with in a more experimental way.'

Isiling Mack-Nath (pseudonym Zak) is an African-American lesbian film-maker. In 1986 she made *The Mark of Lilith* for her degree film.

'I came here eleven years ago to study European cinema. I think people are really excited about seeing Black lesbian characters on the screen, because there are so few, which is encouraging. With *The Mark of Lilith* there's a certain amount of exposure around racism, and I think it let off steam in a way. It gave people a starting point for a dialogue.'

Pratibha Parmar is an Asian lesbian film-maker. She has produced work funded by the Arts Council and Channel Four, particularly for Channel Four's lesbian and gay series, *Out*. In her documentary work she is seen as the most visibly out Asian lesbian working in a fairly mainstream part of the film industry.

Sherlee Mitchell is African-Caribbean, and became a photographer by default.

> 'I happened to be teaching literacy in a project that had a photography element as well, and I was interested in it for my students' sake. I started teaching very basic photography to them and I did a City and Guilds in black-and-white and other photography. I really spent most of my learning teaching. I started in 1993, I hadn't picked up a camera before then, I never had one as a child.'

Identity and context

I asked each of the women if they could define a Black lesbian image, and what were the points of recognition we look for as image-makers and audience.

PRATIBHA: 'It's the understanding and awareness of what role images play in how you are perceived by other people, and how you see yourself. How the process of the creation of images informs your identity.'

ISILING: 'For me, my own personal obsession is about not necessarily coming to fixed definitions of identities of what is a lesbian or what it is to be African or Asian, but to constantly push the limits of that and show the diversity and hybridizations, the mixtures.

'I see my work more and more in a queer context, not just lesbian, but very strongly addressing a lesbian audience. A lesbian audience is more than likely to be predominantly white, which is fine, so I'm addressing a lesbian audience with points of entry for African women or women of colour.'

MUMTAZ: 'Because we're talking about such small numbers, it's also difficult for me to talk specifically about myself as a lesbian photographer within a lesbian community. What I feel at the moment is, yes, I'm a lesbian, but that's not all of who I am. I have all sorts of separate identities, and a lesbian identity is part of that. I have an identity as a South Asian woman, and there are all the class identities that inform us as well. I also feel there's my identity as a survivor of child sexual abuse. And there are different periods and different times when I seem to be focusing on different parts of myself. Sexuality is also something that I feel is going through its changes, and I know women who have identified as lesbian who are no longer in relationships with women, and it feels like a whole fluidity. And yes, that's not to deny that we desperately need a lesbian community in order to feel alright, just like we've needed a Black community to find a stronger voice.

'If you're a Black photographer you are always trying to produce a Black lesbian image, and work out where and how they meet. As for me, I also want to be able to photograph stones on the ground, kids playing and whatever else. I have to accept my identity as a Black lesbian, but I don't have any specific image of myself. There are so many of us and we're all different in different ways. I'm trying to say I'm me, I'm a Black lesbian. Where do we look for an image of ourselves when there are so few images out there?'

SHERLEE: 'I generally don't like going around telling people that I'm a lesbian. That's not because I'm ashamed about being a lesbian, I just feel that it's not necessary to do so, and that also I don't think anyone needs to know. Heterosexual people don't go around telling me that they're heterosexual, and I don't go round telling them that I'm a homosexual.

'As a photographer, generally I don't think I'm known as a lesbian photographer, I'm known as Sherlee Mitchell, a woman who produces photographs. Obviously, there's a core of people who know that I'm a lesbian, but that's not how I bill myself. My race and my culture (and that's from the heritage point of view, not what my sexuality is) are more important to me. My sexuality is me, but it's not the be all and end all. If I wasn't a lesbian – like tomorrow, let's say I'm no longer a lesbian, I've changed my spots – I'm still a Black woman. I feel that having to live in this society I'm still someone who would be fighting for women's rights whether I was a lesbian or not, because of my make-up and the person that I am. So I don't think that being visible, in the sense of being vocal about my sexuality, is important to me as I know it's important to lots of other people. I wouldn't judge them for that. I think that it's their personal choice. I personally don't think I'm in the closet, but other people would say that I am because they shout it "out the houses". Whereas I'm a very private person and my business is my business, and that includes everything in my life.'

TANYA: 'I make experimental films which fall into a particular aesthetic in that type of film-making. You're not always going to say in a direct way what your identity is, because you quite often don't express it in a direct way. With my first film, *Chameleon*, I did feel invisible at the beginning, probably because I wasn't out myself, but I was pleased when it was picked up and shown in a lesbian context.

'I wouldn't say *Salamander* is a lesbian film, because there are other elements in it. It's difficult, because how do you define lesbian? Lesbians are interested in all sorts of things, and do all sorts of things. Usually, when people define something as being lesbian they are expecting a particular kind of story line, and they're expecting you to discuss yourself in relation to your sexuality, but it goes beyond that. For people's understanding of how you use language, I would say *Salamander* has got a lesbian context, which is important in the film. A lot of people describe it as a subplot; I wouldn't say it's a subplot. The expression of female sexuality would probably be more acceptable than defining it as lesbian. It's to do with popular understanding of female sexuality. A couple of gay men have seen the film and thought that the two women were men. In a sense, I've left it open. If I'd gone out there thinking that I really wanted to make this overtly lesbian film and a gay man came along and thought they were all blokes, then all my intentions fall away, but that's interesting to me. I don't mind being misconceived sometimes, but if I didn't feel quite strong about myself I'd find it quite destructive.

'I've been brought up in this country and a lot of my experiences are from this country. If I'd been brought up in India, I'd probably have a different aesthetic. I don't think my identity stands still, but in discussion that sometimes doesn't get taken on. Basically, it's not just what you show it's who you are that puts it into a particular category.'

PRATIBHA: 'One of the first things that we have to address is the notion of Black art itself – what it actually is. Some Black artists feel that there is something innately and essentially unique to Black artists themselves, because of particular experiences and sensibilities which they share both racially and culturally. But then there are others who argue that you can't really talk about Black art as something very distinct from art in general. We have to be mindful of this debate, because it's very easy to start talking about Black art as an homogenous response to something.'

In contrasting the work of these film-makers and photographers, the question of what is a Black lesbian image is answered by each of them. It is all of the images which they are creating, and more: the Asian lesbian lorry-driver and the gender/cultural boundary-crossing woman in Syed's *Salamander*; the Black lesbian footballer in my documentary 'Running Gay'; the Black lesbian seeking desire in Mack-Nath's *The Mark of Lilith*; the strong erotic 'Blackwoman' self-portraits of Mitchell; the Asian woman in the sea who seeks her lost spirituality and a way home, in my film *Monsoon*; the erotic centre of a flower in Karimjee's images.

Defining definitions

ISILING: 'A Black lesbian image for me is very much about an African or Asian lesbian's personal vision or personal aesthetic, and their concerns from their point of view. Also, it addresses specifically an African or Asian lesbian audience, which doesn't exclude a white audience or a European audience. They may or may not have ethnic references or influences. It doesn't pin it down into any one definition.'

SHERLEE: 'I don't personally like to say that a Black lesbian image is one single thing. It either comes from someone who is not a Black lesbian, who constructs something and gives us an idea that they feel this is what an image is. It's then for us as Black lesbians to say, as far as we're concerned it's not. The other comes from Black lesbians who are producing the images themselves, who actually say that this is what we feel, these are the images we want to put out. But at the end of the day, they are still individuals and cannot speak for the whole of the Black lesbian population.

'In the context of producing images, I used to believe that a Black image was obviously of the person who was producing it. So, if the person wanted to produce images of trees or a landscape – and they were Black and lesbian – that was an image from that context. I still believe in that up to a point. Now it's to do with seeing more images around of what is supposed to be lesbianism, and actually recognizing that some images don't represent me, whether they are images of Black women or white women – predominantly white women usually. In the context of what it means for me, it goes on to other questions about the sort of images I create. I didn't exhibit as much as I would have liked, primarily because I was teaching photography. I went through this whole dilemma of whether I was a photographer or a person who took photographs? Some would say it's the same thing. Anyone can take a photograph if you give them a camera, that's been my whole ethos of teaching. Anyone can produce an image, it's very easy, but it's about creating an image in your head first, seeing that image, constructing it, and that's where the artist comes in.

'If someone says, that is an image of an African-Caribbean/Asian lesbian, then obviously I see that and I question it. If it's not of a particular person but is of a concept, then I also have to believe what that person has said.'

TANYA: 'A Black lesbian image is something that's either made by a Black lesbian or can be identified by another Black lesbian. Other people will put those definitions on them. I've made them, I'm a mixed-race lesbian, so my cultural background is going to go into them in some way, although I might not be aware of just how it's going in. I'm looking at my own identity every day, it's not something fixed. My experience of identity is that it can change, but I know lots of people don't have that experience. Maybe it's something to do with being mixed-race, that you can fit into one or the other, but my experience is that you fit into neither.'

MUMTAZ: 'I can't define any particular image as a Black lesbian image. If I see two Black women together in a particular sexual way, you might be able to say clearly those are two Black lesbians, but for me there's nothing essentialist about it. My work, "In Search of an Image", was particularly about searching for a lesbian image, it was self-portraiture. I don't know, if the text had been missing whether somebody would define it as lesbian imagery. For me, it's a lot to do with the image being defined by the context in which the image is used or has been made. Taken out of that context the image can almost have all kinds of meanings.'

Creating images

Both Mumtaz and Sherlee have constructed self-portraits in the search for a Black lesbian self. Tanya, Isiling and I have all appeared in at least one film, either as the main character or antagonist. While searching for a Black lesbian identity we have sometimes used ourselves as the starting point:

ISILING: 'Because the place of the vision is from the subject, it's really, really important not to be the object. I've got this thing about objectification and eroticism as having a place and being important, but that's different from being an object – which women and Black people very often are – of someone else's discourse. Being the subject, putting yourself in the centre of it, offering yourself and your own vision of the world is very critical. I often star myself because I've seen so few images that seem to mirror me. So the only way I know how to do it is to put myself there first, and then find other stories or other connections that are out there but that haven't been pictured or represented yet. Not that there are no representations, but they seem very limited and quite contained. They have the lid put on them quite quickly, and they don't seem to grow into themselves.'

TANYA: 'It's to do with who's looking at you, how far you want to take on board their own awareness and visual capacity and how far you want to take on board stereotypes. I think I work against that from the particular type of images I want to put into my films, because they're not fitting into something that's expected.'

Current work

MUMTAZ: 'The work I'm doing in exploring erotic imagery is very abstract and it's not even based on human form. So yes, within the context of the lesbian postcards that I've done recently, somebody could say, well, that's taken by me and I'm an out lesbian so it's a lesbian image. Taken out of that context it could be seen as an image made by somebody else. It's a photo of close-ups of flowers, which I think are extremely erotic. They were to do with reconstructions of sexuality and meanings of sexuality which can be defined, and they have, for me a personal meaning. However, for other people they could have a different meaning. Sometimes I feel it's safer to do it that way, without images of people, whether the model is oneself or someone else. If you interpret it in that way, you can say it's my work on Black lesbian imagery, but for me it's my work on sexuality and I happen to be a lesbian who's making it. I think it contains a bit of both the image-maker and the content, I don't think it can be either one or the other.

'There's also the issue that there might be images of lesbians – Black lesbian images – that have been made that don't say anything about us. Does that mean that the person making them is not a lesbian, and that they aren't part of lesbian imagery? I was recently invited to submit a sampler for a book cover for a book about Black women and health (in this particular case it was women of African descent). The woman that I eventually photographed was certainly not a lesbian. I think the publishers of the book would be very cross if I went around saying this is a lesbian image, and I don't feel that it's a lesbian image.

'If you take my work on child sexual abuse, that was about me being a survivor of child sexual abuse. Now, I also happen to be a lesbian, but not all survivors of child sexual abuse are lesbians. It wasn't specifically about my story or anyone else's story, it was looking at violence in the context of our survival. It's important to my portfolio as a lesbian photographer, but again is it clearly lesbian imagery?'

PRATIBHA: 'As an artist I would assert that my territory is as broad as I define it, and that it's not going to be defined for me by my different identities, or by the colour of my skin, or by my genitalia, or by who I sleep with. But there are many different issues tied to this, like the notion of an Asian aesthetic – that just by virtue of the fact that we're Asians we produce a particular kind of work.

'There are going to be a lot of people who are very surprised that as an Asian woman I've made a film which is looking at AIDS, and has not just Black women's voices but white gay men and white women talking as well. I want to challenge the whole notion of what we as Black lesbian film-makers are supposed to make by definition of who we are, our identities. People have expectation boundaries of your identity. But we've got other things to say, we live in a much broader scenario. Our territory should be as broad as possible. And what does it mean to be experimental, anyway? I'll give an example that I used in *Khush* [a TV documentary about South-East Asian lesbians and gay men]. I took a scene from a black-and-white Indian film made in 1942, *Chandralokha*, in which the woman dancer is being watched by a man. The whole sequence is constructed around the male gaze. I edited out the male viewpoint and substituted it, quite unashamedly, with a lesbian gaze. So I had two women performers who became the viewers and who take pleasure in this. For me that was very much about reappropriating and subverting particular dominant heterosexual codes that exist in Indian films, and substituting them with a lesbian gaze.'

SHERLEE: '... in Black imagery – and I'm not just talking from an African-Caribbean perspective but even an Asian one as well (in the sense of "from the British point of view") – the images that we see are very deliberate, deliberate to the point of making us apart from the rest of society. In the context of documentation, we document Black people in a riot, on a march, a woman who's crying over her child – we're always apart from the rest of Britain. What I wanted to do, in some ways, was actually use that in the context of what I also see as a Black person, not necessarily as a lesbian. I see Black people, Asian people, white people making love, being very kind and gentle to one another, having families, being ordinary (whatever ordinary is). I also want to construct a fantasy, which, OK, we can say is a stereotype because of the idea of Black women/Asian women being exotic, but we can also use those images to speak for ourselves and give ourselves a voice. I'm making images of people, and if those people happen to be lesbian or gay, that isn't the main emphasis, that isn't the issue. The issue for me is to produce images primarily of Black women, and that's because generally we don't see images of Black women. Of course we do see them, but in anthropological representations or modern-day anthropological contexts (which is documentary). I want to take us out of that and put us into different settings: on a beach; in the countryside with the sheep; Black farmers; swimming in a swimming pool; Black older women; that sort of thing, regular stuff that we know goes on in our communities every single day, but which is not seen by the wider community. That's what I do ... what I want to produce, because I think that photography as a medium – just pictures as a medium – is so important. It's so powerful. I want to change things, I don't believe I can do it by myself, but I want to be part of that change.'

ISILING: 'I'm working on a short feature, *In Search of the Ideal Orgasm*. It's anti-narrative, and the main character is very autobiographical again. It looks at the ways in which she begins to perceive what is erotic, what is lesbian desire. She keeps these video diaries on interactive video disc, and begins to feed in images which obsessively take over her life. She's in a hip-hop punk band and does sexual cabaret performances, so there's an SM element present. An anarchist, nihilist kind of philosophy prevails, as she unpacks and deconstructs what her Blackness is, what her lesbianism is, what her gender is, in order to get to some zero place to see if there's a consciousness, an identity, a subjectivity beyond cultural conditioning. And she's also creating an image of lesbian orgasm.

'I have problems with narrative – with Hollywood in particular – with narrative as just reinforcing certain positions and places for people, especially around gender. And where things are either completely marginized or contained in such a way that they're not a threat to the status quo. Narrative always represents that for me. I'm quite attracted to it, because people want stories and they want characters as well, and that makes sense in terms of getting access to ideas. It's always best through people and through their stories and lives, so I always in a way go back to narrative as long as I can expand it and not be trying to get to some status quo. I'm always trying to disrupt that and open things out and challenge people with it.

'I'm completely committed to experimental work and multimedia work, because I think it does have a political force. I also think that if it's elitist it's a bit like preaching to the converted, so I think narrative does have a place.'

SHERLEE: 'Most of the concepts of photography, film-making, have already been set out. There isn't anything new even in the computer and video age, especially the fact that living in Britain we are very Westernized. No matter how much we empathize, use our heritage and culture we are still extremely Westernized. The way that we use our imagery in many cases is also very Westernized. Just looking at image-making, at what photography has been doing over the last two hundred years, what we're producing now isn't really that much different, but I suppose we're doing it from a different moral viewpoint and background.'

Difficulties

ISILING: 'In creating Black lesbian images, audience expectations are the biggest problem. There's such a demand for positive images, but for images that go beyond the stereotypes, beyond the two-dimensional images, and beyond the victim. Audiences put quite a lot of pressure on image-makers to show this positive image, which can be just as deadening a stereotype as any other. There's also the question of what you can and cannot represent; I think there are fears sometimes of being exposed as a community, being made vulnerable as a community, having our dirty laundry washed in public, that can be quite self-censoring. But then on the other hand, funders will say things like, well that's not realistic, I've never seen a Black lesbian who does that or thinks that. So there are stereotypes from a lot of different sources. With funding and exhibitions, Black women have become a genre or a theme for which an audience has been cultivated. You get to be cultivated for those kinds of images and themes now, but only if they fit within certain prescribed and recognizable forms. It's what is acceptable and what is believable and what is positive.'

SHERLEE: 'In this society we're invisible, we're not seen as lesbians, we're not seen as home-makers, we're not seen as people who go out to work, we're just not part of the society. It's slowly changing, but it's only changing because Black men and women are going out with white men and women, so there's that visibility. But you're only visible with a white partner: you see that on TV that's like the "in" thing.'

MUMTAZ: 'The problems in creating Black lesbian images come when we try to create images that basically try to speak for everyone – I don't think that you can do that. I can create an image, but I cannot assume that the image will speak for everyone. I think that the big shift in myself over the last year is that when I started working with imagery, I felt I could challenge these huge stereotypes that had been created. But I actually think that you can't just go head on and challenge a huge stereotype without considering who you are speaking for and what you are speaking about. I can't claim to be speaking for every Black lesbian, so when I create a Black lesbian image I create a Black lesbian image which speaks for me, because I am a Black lesbian, but again I'm one of many.'

Underneath Black

ISILING: 'I think there are a lot of parallels and similarities. I think there are different ways that African women and Asian women are seen, there are different types of stereotypes that have to be overcome – the supposed passivity of Asian women, the supposed aggression of African women – which might require different ways of working. So, for example, showing a butch Asian dyke is a way of dealing with that stereotype. It really depends how involved people are in their own ethnic cultures as well, how much of those influences and imagery they bring to their work. For an African-American, I think Africa does exert a strong and positive influence which is essential, but at the same time it's also quite mythic and distant and so some of the West African imagery may or may not be there.'

SHERLEE: 'The Asian images that I've seen are very "Asian", in the sense that the African, as in the Caribbean/British images that I've seen, are very Eurocentric (and that's controversial to even say that). The majority of the Asian lesbian images that I've seen are very much of a society and culture that I know I'm not a part of. I understand to a point, obviously, because quite a lot of the time they do speak English in the film or they have English words underneath the photographic images. The language obviously sets me apart, because I'm not always able to interpret what I feel I see (I'm not just talking about vocal language, I'm talking about heritage and cultural language, too). This is because I haven't been brought up with a lot of Asian people, although I know what I know within the context of what I see in Britain. I think a lot of the Asian images that I've seen aren't always about the context of what's in Britain. Those are some of the differences. Obviously there are similarities, and obviously there are things I can identify with. I feel that I'm more in tune with the African lesbian images I've seen. A lot of them are Eurocentric and that's just recognizing the whole process of colonialism in its entirety really.'

PRATIBHA: 'I don't want to remain silent around certain areas which are seen to be perpetuating certain racist stereotypes ... I want to reappropriate those images for myself as an Asian lesbian. ... In Suniti's [Suniti Namjoshi is an Asian lesbian writer] work, she's got this poem to the Goddess. The goddess is an icon and symbol that comes up quite often in her poetry and prose. I wanted to pick up on that particular icon because Suniti, as an Indian lesbian, is using a part of her own cultural heritage, but she's using it in a very lesbian way, with a lesbian consciousness and sensibility.'

Making a living out of images, or just making images

SHERLEE: 'I'm working as a health worker. I've always had a job with my photography. I think that's always been the reason I don't have time to do my photography work. A couple of years ago

I was freelancing as a photographer and doing some work, but I just couldn't deal with the rat race. It was driving me nuts, I don't like conforming at the best of times, and I really felt that it was not me to be chasing people and being very greedy about money and how much people were going to pay me, and all that crap.'

MUMTAZ: 'I've not been able to earn my living out of my creative work, and I've always had to do other jobs to subsidize that, so in the end who am I working for?'

Our visibility

MUMTAZ: 'My images have been seen in publications like *Fabled Territories*, *Fine Material for a Dream*, *Stolen Glances*, *Misrepresentations*, in various magazines like *Ten 8* and at the Women Artists' Slide Library. It's not possible any more just to be creating your work, you've actually to think about money, and that restricts how much work, and as Black lesbians there's a great big hole there. If they have any kind of influence, I'd like them to say that there isn't just one type of image, and break down that stereotype of Black people, Black women, Black lesbians. I'm part of a wider identity and therefore a wider work.'

SHERLEE: 'My exhibitions have been at the Black Art Gallery, Pyramid Arts, Peckham Leisure Centre, Centerprise, and most are very community based. But I'm very much into community images, I'm not really into art galleries, I'm very much into immediacy.'

TANYA: 'My work is seen in film festivals, which are predominantly for experimental films from Europe, the USA, the UK, and in art galleries as well. My films are art-based and a lot of people who look at them are probably from a similar background and also are already involved in film-making. They don't get seen by people who would not normally look at that kind of work. Both of the films I've made have been shown to people who are not lesbian, not Asian, but who look at them and get something from them. I don't make films for a particular group of people, but at the same time I do work from my own experience.'

ISILING: '*The Mark of Lilith* has been quite well seen, in festivals, universities and at all-night raves where other vampire films are screened. I feel that it was quite a visible film, that I was visible as a Black film-maker with it and as a lesbian.'

MUMTAZ: 'I feel that I was certainly, up until the late 1980s and early 1990s, really highly visible. I think that visibility has retreated because I've retreated. I sometimes think that visibility creates a pressure of continually having to produce, and I can't just produce because people want me to produce. Another problem for me is sometimes the expectations that people have. I sometimes feel quite vulnerable about them in the context of lesbian imagery.'

SHERLEE: 'I don't think the gay community sees my images as gay images, because they're not like the regular images that we generally see of lesbians and gay people. Generally, the Black lesbians that I see do not look like the stereotype of lesbians, so if I pick out two black lesbians that I know and I photograph them, everyone else assumes that they're two Black women really into their Africanness. Even if they're together, it's still not seen. That's not my worry, at the end of the day I've produced what I wanted to produce. I'm not that precious about the visibility and the idea that people have to like my photographs. I'm more concerned about what I'm doing and how that feels. I think at the end of the day I produce images for myself, I don't produce images for an audience.'

TANYA: 'I wasn't instantly recognized or classified when I started making films, it's only happened recently, probably because there are a lot of Asian lesbian film-makers. Having your work put in a programme that describes/titles that it's something to do with lesbianism or Asianness gives you a visibility which is harder to get if your work is programmed with other film-makers who are not of the same, or similar, cultural background. In such a situation you might get into a more stereotyped category, and are more likely to be misrepresented.'

Future images

As Black lesbian film-makers and photographers we take our own image as an African/Asian out into the world and receive messages about what sort of an image it is; these messages interact with our work, which may be modified, and then reassess and continue our work:

SHERLEE: 'I want Black images, of whatever shape or form, to be seen anywhere and everywhere, and I don't think they should just be in galleries. The assumption is that all lesbians and gays (Black, white, whatever) are arty people and will go to a gallery just to see images that represent themselves. But a lot of people aren't interested in going into galleries, so for me it's important that images go out in magazines, in books, in shopping centres, in launderettes, on billboards, using all forms of media, and not just on a white wall.'

PRATIBHA: 'It's the whole question of language – visual languages and literary languages – and how you actually use the dominant codes of particular languages; how you disrupt them, or appropriate them, deconstruct them and then actually reformulate them to say what you want to say, informed by your own particular sensibilities. ... We are not saying, "This is what's happening in the centre, that we're at the margin creating our own visual representation and our own modes of expressions", but actually that the dominant modes are being changed by what we're doing.'

SHERLEE: 'In some ways what is happening is that photography in itself is actually dying, the art of photography is dying, because now you put an image on a computer and you can change an image to whatever you like, you can reconstruct an image in a studio.'

ISILING: 'My biggest obsession at the moment is computer-generated and interactive video disc-type imagery using databases and cyberpunk kinds of influences – generating and creating images from nothing – where no images exist. I think being a Black lesbian means you create yourself, you make yourself up as you go along, and I'm transferring that to the technology. I'm quite interested in hybrids of images, bringing things together, creating things from fantasy or putting things in the world that people would not have imagined possible – and doing that from a Black perspective, from a lesbian perspective. I think it gives lesbians a future, a stake in the future way of representing ourselves and visualizing our ideas and fantasies where it might not have existed before. Just putting those things together opens up ways of thinking about things that you haven't thought about before. I'm drawing parallels between three characters sharing the same universe and interacting with each other. This is very similar to having three different images, a pornographic image, an advertising image and an anthropological image, maybe, on the screen at the same time – they have similar kinds of effects.

'While generating images, how do you picture lesbian orgasm? What would that look like? Would it look like a medical image? Would it look like a virtual reality image? Would it be more like a pornographic image? It's creating things that we don't see, that's what I'd like to see: the technology from a Black lesbian perspective, anyway. That doesn't necessarily have anything to do with Black lesbianism, but it's informed by that always.

'We just don't see a lot of deeper stuff. For example, what we as African and Asian lesbians are thinking about and talking about, we don't see that on the screen. . . . I think it's necessary to see those things, whether people agree with them or not. There's such a limit to what we've seen, it often seems two- or even one-dimensional, that all you have to do is put a Black face on the screen and somehow you understand something about who they are. There has to be some delving and there have to be contradictions. I think that it's OK that things aren't always clear or easy, or fit within prescriptive ideas of what it is, whatever identity people are labelling you with.'

SHERLEE: 'I'm saying that Black lesbian images are not being shown, and I don't actually like what the rest of the whole lesbian image cartel – because I think it's a cartel at the moment – is doing. I have to be prepared to actually change people's concepts and perceptions of what they see.'

TANYA: 'I'm not really interested in making images of Asian or Black lesbians in isolation. I want people to be able to express their identities, but after that I feel quite strongly about people being able to cross borders with each other and cross different cultures – being able to interact with each other. On one level I'm not a separatist like that. Although Black/Asian images are important to me, I'm more interested in debating identity in a wider context.'

MUMTAZ: 'When I first started working I felt I had to rigidly define the context in which my images were seen. Now I am feeling constrained by rigid definitions and I want to be free of them, I want to have the freedom and the confidence to say here's the image I've made, take it or leave it.'

I believe that there is a thriving Black lesbian film and photography culture in this country. I also believe that Black lesbian image-makers are now working in a wider context, that we are part of the wider film/photography industry. This industry needs to recognize that an African/Asian lesbian film and photography industry is inherently different from a white lesbian industry, because we have different cultures and racial backgrounds. My desire is that in the midst of battles for funding, and while picking through the labels for our work, we are able to be strong and continue to be defiant Black lesbian film-makers and photographers.

Articles

Pratibha Parmar interviewed by Lloyd Wong, *Fuse*, Summer 1990.
Pratibha Parmar interviewed by Ian Rashid, *Bizzarre*, Spring 1992.
Pratibha Parmar in conversation with Isaac Julien, *Square Peg*, no. 19, 1988.

Chapter eight

A Literary Movement

Anita Naoko Pilgrim

Part one: A movement of Black lesbian literature

Black lesbians in Britain are enormously creative, sharing many kinds of art forms among ourselves. Although we treat each other's and our own art with the respect and admiration it deserves, we are cut off in many ways from mainstream success. As Black, as women, as gay, we are marginalized. We rarely have any idea how to approach galleries or publishers, and may continue working for years, content to share our creations with friends, and not risk the possibility of huge personal rejection from the mainstream organizations. This is entirely understandable given the racism, sexism and heterosexism we struggle with in our daily lives. We protect ourselves by guarding that most precious exposure of our souls: our creative work.

Sometimes we have succeeded in organizing representation for ourselves, usually as Black women rather than as Black lesbians. Black Womantalk publishers are an example of this, as is Maud Sulter, who set up Urban Fox Press in 1989 to publish both her own work and books by other Black women. We present a lot of work in anthologies and newsletters, but few of us manage to get an entire book. Suniti Namjoshi, Jackie Kay and Meiling Jin were the first out Black lesbians living in Britain to be properly represented in this way; Barbara Burford, Maya Chowdhry and Maud Sulter also have collections of their work available. Most often we present our work at readings and as performance. This is a vital and wonderful part of our literature, but we must also try to recapture our work for the future in books, tapes and videos.

This is the first complete published essay on British Black lesbians in literature. It covers a long, wide and rich field of study, and I hope that it will lead to more critical studies of our literature. Although it's frightening to contemplate tampering with the delicate process of creation, I believe that it's essential for the well-being of our art to have and to hear praise and criticism.

'Art and culture represent a storehouse for sorting and ordering ideas. Some of the material housed there will undoubtedly be lumber which can only be cleared by a sensitive and informed critical response to the work produced by artists,' wrote Akua Rugg in the introduction to 'Brickbats and Bouquets' a collection of her reviews for *Race Today.*[1] As Black lesbian women we are a triply oppressed minority. Therefore, our most obvious requirement is support. Even our published writers are shy of calling themselves poet/writer/artist. Many will only bring forward work for performance or publication after encouragement from friends and pressure from professionals who happen to have heard of them. But we can't trust that support if it's unqualified. We need to listen with minds as open as possible and then, as artists with faith in our own judgement about our work, to use both praise and criticism as tools to refine our work.

Literature serves a number of functions. Some writing is therapeutic and should be kept to oneself; some is therapeutic and should be shared with others who need to hear it; some is political and some vital solely for its beauty. A poem is not a poem just because it is divided into verses, but sometimes what it is saying is so important that it doesn't matter that it is badly written. There are no straightforward questions in this matter, let alone answers. It's important that we value our own and each other's work enough to make it public, and to question it when it's out in the public arena.

I based this chapter on Dorothea Smartt's piece, 'From My Eyes ... Zamis Publishing Poetry 1984–1988'. She wrote several introductory paragraphs, followed by bio-bibliographies of zami (women-loving women) writers. In the first section I set up some parameters and structures within which discussion about British Black lesbian writing can operate; and for the second section to give case herstories of individual writers. What follows is a representation of writers of African and Asian descent living in Britain. I include famous writers with whole collections of work available on the shelves, and also the literary work of women who don't call themselves writers. I wanted to get a picture of where inspiration comes from and what influences the form and structure of Black lesbian writing, but also to see how writers earn a living.

While researching Black lesbian writers I came across some women who were now in relationships with men. This made me rethink the definition of lesbian. Lesbian to me means loving women. It doesn't mean not liking men. When someone has written a sensuous poem about making love with her female lover, and has subsequently moved into a relationship with a man, that doesn't make the poem straight. I repeat, there aren't even straightforward questions in this one. As I trawled through anthologies trying to pick out and define scattered pieces as British Black lesbian writing, I thanked the ancestors that it's not something you can box up neatly.

The one clear decision I made was not to include Black lesbian writing from the USA. Audre Lorde's *Zami*, for example, is of vital importance to us, but as with all work from the USA, it's literally coming from a different place. Reading *Zami*, I responded equally to the familiarity of a Black woman's relationship with women and to the strangeness of a Black woman's life in the USA. There is a strong sense of a close relationship between Black American women and Black British women. African-Caribbean poet, Dorothea Smartt, writes:

> Connecting medium;
> BlackAmerican cousins
> meet
> BlackEnglish sistahs
> connecting beyond cultural colonization.[2]

However, Black Americans have often overshadowed their Black British sisters, and are often used by white people to effectively deny our contribution and existence. It's six years since Barbara Burford and Jackie Kay (along with Merle Collins) were interviewed by journalist, Valerie Mason-John, in Britain's Black national paper *The Voice*, about the high profile of Black American women writers in England. Burford suggests this is because Black American women pacify the white liberal conscience. During this interview she said: '... publishers are not interested in Black women living in Britain because they are looking for another *Color Purple*, a story about Black women in pain'. Six years later, very little has changed: if you ask British people about Black women's writing they will name Toni Morrison or Alice Walker. However, it is true that we can find much strength and wisdom in Black American literature, but it won't give us the familiar description of commuter life in Britain so vividly conveyed in Black British writer Barbara Burford's short story, 'The Pinstripe Summer'. We need this reflection of our own realities in order to sit with confidence on trains.

What is British Black lesbian literature? We can talk about a body of writing by Black women who define, or used to define, themselves as Black lesbians. British Black lesbians write in a variety of styles and employ many different forms: they sometimes use patois or spell words to convey how we say them rather than how they are spelt; Scottish words are sometimes prominent, as is the influence of rap and the work of white American poets. The extent to which a writers' emphasis is on Black, lesbian or environmental issues varies from one Black lesbian to another. We aren't a homogenous mass and so we should one day be placed in the different literary movements currently operating. Of course, we share much common ground with other Black people, especially heterosexual Black women writers, and with white lesbian writers. However, Black lesbian literature is not just a fusion of these two with an extra dash of feminism and race awareness. It is unique, in that it reflects our many identities surviving in a white Western world.

A quick flick through anthologies of Black women's art will usually yield at least three-quarters of a book written by Black lesbian women. At a grass-roots level, we are freed by our lesser involvement with men: we don't have to pretend to be less able in order to bolster his male pride, and we are less often restricted by having to put time, energy and scanty finances into bringing up children. However, when it comes to being published and publicized, more Black heterosexual women are succeeding. In order for a British Black lesbian to print a properly representative volume of poetry or the novel she really wants to write, she will have to be out to family, friends and the general public. As writers expressing some elemental truths, we feel uncomfortable unless we do produce properly representative work.

A great deal of Black women's literature and art (including that by Black lesbians) is cross-discipline: that is, cross-European discipline. Some other cultures also produce art that crosses many disciplines. For example, in Chinese, Japanese and Korean calligraphy, a poem hanging on a scroll on the wall is also a painting. In my interview with her, Avril Rogers-Wright talks about the way that storytelling in Sierra Leone incorporates songs. Whether because of this cultural influence or some other reason, many Black women operate comfortably in a number of media forms: Maud Sulter is well known both for her fine art and for her writing; Razia Aziz's projects (see interviews) include paintings, photographs and poems. Black people, African, African-Caribbean and Asian, are successful songwriters, combining music and poetry.

The socio-political circumstances of our times inevitably have a powerful effect on us. For example, as I was discussing above, being lesbian may make it hard for us to be mainstream, but not being in daily contact with men may free us creatively. Our work is both affected and inspired by racism in many different ways. Carmen Tunde wrote a poem called 'Bus Stop', a straightforward and clear description of the humiliation of a racist insult, and a poem, 'Contradictions', where with extraordinary sensitivity she tries to disentangle herself and us from the mess of racism and its origins:

> Can we really blame the new men
> for the lies they were told by the old men?
> Can we really blame the new whites
> for the lies they were told by the old whites?

Anymore than
blaming the women for lies told
and retold between us?
Anymore than blaming the black and brown
for the lies retold between us?

But am I to talk of a calm tolerance,
A calm tolerance![3]

Some poetry I've heard talks derogatorily of white people. We have a right to our anger about fascism and colonization, but to turn racism round into white-hating doesn't seem to be the way forward. Those of us who are of mixed racial heritage or were brought up by white carers feel uncomfortable when we hear this kind of work, and some of us start muttering in our heads, 'not Black enough for you'. These issues can be addressed in better ways. In Barbara Burford's title story from *The Threshing Floor*, for example, she begins to address some of the valid questions of Black–white dynamics in the context of a Black woman mourning her dead white lover, with whom she had a positive and fulfilling relationship. Avril Rogers-Wright's unpublished poem, 'Skin', is 'dedicated to the children of this Blessed Paradise from the East to the West to the North to the South'. She writes:

And if anyone
should speak badly of my skin,
I will say who is that strange one?
Don't they know who I am, at one
with my sparkling jewel?[4]

Rogers-Wright conveys pride, joy and anger without having to blame white people indiscriminately.

Writing as Black people living in the African and Asian Diaspora, we are constantly answering the impertinent question, 'where are you from?'; even in Maya Chowdhry's superb, sexy poem 'Cherries', where she expresses the satisfaction of sex, there are several questions and answers woven into the piece that relate to this question. In the poet/actor/performer, Michelle Asha Warsama's performance piece, *I'll Take the High Road*, we find an exploration of the beautiful homeland we dream of: 'the land where the elephants live', a place built from strange colonial notions of noble savages and fabulous ancient civilizations, which has been part of our education in England. Warsama's heroine, Angelis Queston Bury, is on a noble Arthurian quest for the silver key to free Africa from its troubles, but she is told:

> Now if you really want to help me
> Then go back home.
> STOP LIVING IN THE LAND INSIDE OF YOUR HEAD.[5]

In an evocative description of the reality of life in Africa by Bernadine Evaristo, we are not protected from the ugliness, and the familiar-strange beauties come through with a reality that is not enhanced by comparison with the ugliness which it couldn't exist without:

> Men sell cassava chips wrapped in paper,
> spiced with chili-salt and lemon,
> and the smells of the fish markets,
> the meat markets stench the air.[6]

Barbara Burford's short stories reveal an intimate knowledge and sense of belonging in the English countryside, as in her brilliant short story, 'The Pinstripe Summer', where a Black woman commuting to work develops a powerful and fulfilling relationship with a valley she sees through the train window. Any one of us who has spent part of her life in the countryside will respond to her descriptions of the valley. We will recognize, too, the feeling of belonging, the sense of reaffirmation in spite of the strange looks we get when we tell unenlightened people we're from up North or Cornwall. Later in the same story, Barbara Burford makes a reference to Africa:

> Dorothy heard the beads in her hair before the woman came in: It took her straight back to her childhood. Reading those terrible H. Rider Haggard books, because they were the only

ones in the library that spoke of people like her. The sound reminded her of the noise that she had always imagined the Zulu warriors made as they ran into battle.[7]

Here, it is clear that this is a mythical Africa, and explains why it is that Dorothy, and so many of us, stand with one foot in a dreamland. Not that this need be a bad thing, especially since we are dealing with fiction. One of Burford's finest poems, 'September Blue', describes herself as being

drowned deep in a life
like blackstrap molasses.
Only the occasional tiger flash
of an enraged golden eye
to show where I still lived.[8]

The dream becomes metaphor and gives a particular strength to the poem. A white poet could describe her life in terms of molasses – so sticky as to make it virtually impossible to move – but for Burford to talk about 'blackstrap molasses' is to refer (so delicately that we register it without noticing) to the West Indies where molasses is produced, to an identity as a Black woman and, in so doing, to hint at the race issues which may be part of what holds her fast.

In our work we frequently use patois or other ways of conveying our own English language. We also find ways of incorporating the other languages we speak. Avril Rogers-Wright is currently working along lines suggested to her by the work of Tejana Chicana lesbian writer Gloria Anzaldúa: 'the first line people write in their mother tongue and then they translate it' (see interviews in Part Two). We write at ease with the forms or rhythms from the many cultures to which we belong. Avril Rogers-Wright grew up listening to stories which contained a lot of singing, and this comes through in her poetry:

Skinnnnnnnnnnnn
without my skin
I will die[9]

Patience Agbabi grew up in Sussex and North Wales, but African drumming rhythms are an acknowledged influence for her. Similarly, in the second verse of Razia Aziz's poem 'Envy/The Colonizing Mind', there are evocative messages of India:

> Oh beloved
> how can I piece you together again[10]

The appeal, 'oh beloved', evokes Indian poetry.

One negative way in which we are affected by living and working in a Eurocentric culture is the lack of positive language to describe African and Asian people. Returning to Burford's story, 'The Pinstripe Summer', there are two Black women characters. Willoughby is briefly described, but Dorothy, through whose eyes the story unfolds, is barely described at all: '. . . although she was tall, assured, and always well groomed, she was not the desired type, colour or age, for a status symbol personal assistant'.[11] Is she light-skinned or dark-skinned? There is an assumption that she is of African origin, because she reads H. Rider Haggard in an attempt to find people like herself. But is she directly from Africa living in Britain, or from Africa via the Caribbean and now resident in Britain? Did she have her hair straightened? Or cropped? The questions and answers are numerous, and show how extremely difficult it is to write good descriptions of ourselves. In the first place, we are operating with a racist terminology. There are hundreds of words for fair skin, ranging from swarthy through dark (i.e. nicely tanned) to the English rose. What words we have for our skins may be tainted by racism. It is suspicious that they often refer to food: chocolate-coloured, coffee-coloured, cinnamon. Should we describe Black British women as gazelles, bringing up images of African savannahs? It came home to me recently just how strong the influence of colonial literature is. I was rewriting one of my stories, making the two central characters Black rather than white. Gradually, I began to question exactly what I was dropping, and why, in my description of the white women. Similarly, what language was I adding, and why, in my portrait of the two Black women?

Another possible reason why we find it hard to write physical descriptions, especially of the main character of a story, is that we don't think of ourselves in that way. We don't walk about, get on buses and buy spinach constantly aware of the shape of our eyes or the shade of our skin and hair. These are artificial ways used to divide and rule; this is a culture geared to identifying people in terms of a few arbitrary physical characteristics. White people may write stories, and never describe the central character, but everyone assumes, nevertheless, that 'I' is white. We do have the right to write stories and curse people out for not assuming the central character is Black, but I believe it would be better to get beyond the sloppiness of a lack of proper description. I don't know why, but in Burford's 'The Pinstripe Summer' I imagine Dorothy to be light-skinned and Willoughby to be dark-skinned. These details are important to me, and not just because I am a light-skinned woman who has worked in offices with dark-skinned women. I've filled in Dorothy's appearance for myself. It could be argued that this is a satisfactory way of allowing more Black women to pattern ourselves on to a given character. However, I also pattern myself on to Willoughby, whom I imagine as dark-skinned, and I've spent a lifetime patterning myself on to white women from Jane Eyre to Germaine Greer. I believe it is important that we specify, to allow ourselves that fantastic bump of grounding when we meet a person on the written page who is exactly like us. For me it happened once: a Japanese-American lesbian in a factual book complained that women from other cultures assumed she was passive. I felt completely real for a few moments. This is why it's vital that different racial groups be represented to us in all media of communication, regardless of what percentage of the population we constitute.

Another possible reason for this lack of description is the way in which we are forced by the white culture around us to think of our own Blackness as 'other'. It then becomes hard to acknowledge that it is 'self' in many persons' descriptions of Blackness.

Is it only Black lesbian poets who make use of such vivid flower metaphors in poetry about our lovers' cunts? I haven't come across any white poetic versions of Carmen Tunde's splendid poem, 'The Flower' or Jackie Kay's 'Peony': 'sex full ripe as thick sensuous lips . . .'[12] Black lesbians also have a similar literary relationship with the sea. It has a female persona, it responds to the moon, it seems to express many emotions in raging storms or warm waves, and its strong surges and currents make an ideal metaphor for women's orgasms: sea-bed life, mussels, oysters hint of vulvas and vaginas. Valerie Mason-John's 'The Alex' uses the sea in many ways to describe the feminine:

> She groaned
> Crashing her huge waves all over my body.
> Foaming and spraying her juices,
> Drenching me with her waters,
> Saturating me with her minerals,
> Embracing me with her waves.[13]

Singer and songwriter, Adeola, uses the sea as a metaphor for love in some of her lyrics:

> Love is an ocean
> Stretching further than I/eye can see;
> It's still and in motion,
> Bound by tides, yet running free[14]

Realizing that we are lesbian can affect us, in that at times we are frightened by our love for a woman or by the homophobia around us, and because of the heterosexism we have internalized. This may be intensified, as many of us risk losing our Black communities if we come out. Because we are affected by cries of 'white man's disease', people try to make us feel like traitors for being true to ourselves. Collective editor of Black Womantalk, Gabriela Pearse, writes in her poem, 'Patricia': 'Don' fear mi dear/you are loved'.[15]

Our literature is imbued with many influences, including our upbringing and birthright, which are sometimes dictated to us by our circumstances, sometimes a matter of choice. Being Black, and a lesbian means that we have a multitude of personas with which we can identify. There is a Black lesbian community which we rely on and refer to, and in which we sometimes fight among ourselves, just as you do in any family. As Avril Rogers-Wright says in her interview: 'We have created our own family system and our own kinship.'

Much of our writing is also important to the mainstream, whether or not it is intended to be so. A song that is clearly lesbian can have relevance for a heterosexual audience:

> I need two, two loving hands,
> Moving so slowly, til I just can't stand it,
> Keeps on getting stronger babe, til I got to let go[16]

In Patience Agbabi, we have a Black lesbian poet who chose to write a poem about sex aimed at everyone ('Sex is', see page 166). Jackie Kay's poems, 'Dance of the Cherry Blossom', about a gay male couple who are HIV-positive, and 'Dressing Up', about a transvestite, reach across the community to voice feelings for others in the most generous spirit. We aren't locked into our identities, and sometimes we explore multiple identities. See, for example, Maud Sulter's 'Drich Day':

> Walk through ruins
> of castles ancient, a priory
> tombstone cold as death itself
> of people past, children lost
> to disease, poverty, the harsh
> reality of life[17]

The 'people past, children lost' are the ancient Scottish people who lived in the castles, but isn't there also a hint of African people, children, still dying today? Both are personally essential to Maud Sulter.

Sometimes our lesbian identity may be expressed as delicately as our presence is unfelt in the world: 'Love came to Dorothy McDermott so gradually, with such tensile insidiousness, that although she had not been consciously aware of its spangled ambush, she was able, once knowing, to plot the ways and steps of its arrival.'[18] Barbara Burford goes on to describe in beautiful detail the growing relationship between Dorothy and the valley she sees from her commuter-train window. The growing relationship between Dorothy and Willoughby, the Black woman who comes into the story to teach Dorothy how to use computers, is hardly stated:

> 'And have you?' she asked, suddenly wanting to know. 'Found the man of your dreams, I mean?'
>
> Willoughby looked at her for a long moment, her face normally so open to Dorothy unreadable. 'No,' she said, and changed the subject.[19]

That's about as obvious as it gets. Admirable restraint on Burford's part, and yet she told us at the start.

In the same way that we are affected and inspired by racism, so are we affected and inspired by the abuse which has been inflicted on us as children and as women. Some of us have had to take extensive periods out of our working lives in order to disentangle the multiple threads of unacknowledged racism, heterosexism and the effects of child sexual abuse. The bitter fruit of these experiences are poems like 'The Violation in Secret' by Carmen Tunde (child sexual abuse), or Jackie Kay's 'Some Nights in Brooklyn and the Blood' (adoption by a white Scottish family), or Maud Sulter's 'Act of God'. These are poems that don't hesitate to scream the truth, using poetry's cut short lines to convey their emotions: bewilderment, rage, barely contained terror, grief.

Much of Black lesbian literature is performed rather than published, which gives a unique essence to Black lesbian writing. Adeola's words sound quite different when heard with the music, but this is also true of the poetry. Performance poet, Patience Agbabi wrote in an article for *Africa World Review*: 'As in traditional Africa, I don't like to make a distinction between music and poetry when it is performed.'[20] Her work acquires a quite different feel after you've heard her reading. The importance of live performance means that venues presenting Black women's readings, such as Apples and Snakes, are vital. Since writing this chapter, two events promoting Black women's creativity, Sauda and Word Up Women's Café, have disappeared. This is a tragedy with far-reaching effects, especially in the case of Word Up with its 'open mike' space where new poets could get up and try their work out in a friendly, supportive atmosphere. We need these venues and

I hope that the need will be felt sharply enough for them to be reorganized.

Live performances are vital to us, but we also need to record our work. Since we lack the finance to stage such projects, there are no publicly available videos of our performances. Although Zamimass (a Black lesbian organization promoting the cultural upliftment of Black women's creativity) have produced a tape of poetry, you can't buy it at Virgin Megastore or even in lesbian and gay bookshops. Books are the most accessible way of spreading Black lesbian literature at the moment, but there are very few publications, and even the anthologies rich in lesbian contributors aren't solely devoted to lesbian writers. Similarly, anthologies of Black women's writing like *Black Women Talk* and *Don't Ask Me Why*, published and edited by the Black Womantalk collective, are not devoted to Black lesbian writers.

Of course, homophobia, sexism, racism, etc. conspire to keep us off the printed page. As Razia Aziz remarked in our interview, being published is often also a middle-class privilege. It is bewilderingly difficult for (even a middle-class) Black lesbian to work out where to send finished pieces, unless she happens to hear of a Black women's anthology being put together. Publishers are notoriously slow at reading the hundreds of manuscripts sent into them, and many (not all) require that the manuscript be typed. A Black lesbian poet once said to me at a party, 'You're a writer, you can tell me, what is typed, double-spaced on A4 paper?' We need workshops, like those which used to be provided by local government funding, where women can learn technical basics, leave alone writing skills.

The women's presses – Virago, The Women's Press and, especially, Sheba Feminist Publishers (whose collective must be composed of at least two Black women out of the four members) – are of vital importance. But in such difficult times, even these publishers tend to invest safely in Black American writers rather than risk publishing Black British women. In addition, Araba Mercer of Sheba told me they have great difficulty getting Black women to contribute to the many anthologies they publish. Much of what Sheba receives is also about important topics but badly written, and writers will refuse to 'tidy it up, not change it but tidy it up. They'll say, “no, this is my story”.’ After an upbringing in which racism, sexism and heterosexism have all contributed to repressing aspects of our work, it may not be surprising that we are wary of people who want us to change it. However, we must learn to have a strong idea of what our work should be, which can be enhanced by professional editorial help when this is appropriate, rather than perceive this help as bad advice. We get nowhere by rejecting professional advice wholesale. The hardest part of writing is the editing. Rarely are we so lucky as to write a piece that doesn’t need changing. Building the skill to identify what works in our writing and why, and then consciously developing that writing, is difficult. Professional editorial help can be a godsend in this process, and we must regard the desire to help develop our work as the huge compliment that it is. Which do we prefer? The person who says, ‘Yes, this will do, I (and you) can make money on this piece,’ or the one who says, ‘I’m impressed enough with your piece to want to spend my valuable time on it with you.’

Another aspect of published Black lesbian work is that it consists of small pieces only. Poetry, short stories, one novella:

> Fiction was, as fiction still is, the easiest thing for a woman to write. ... A novel can be taken up or put down more easily than a play or a poem ... living as she did in the common sitting-room, surrounded by people, a woman was trained to use her mind in observation and upon the analysis of character. She was trained to be a novelist and not a poet.[21]

Both Virginia Woolf and her prime example of the sitting-room observer, writer Jane Austen, had servants to do their housework. Jane Austen had a desk to herself at least, if not a room of her own. Sometimes it is possible to take two hours or even half a day out of a life filled with jobs, cooking, children, supporting your girlfriend, in order to work solely on a poem or a short story. Writing a novel may take anywhere from six months to ten years and it isn’t something which can be taken up or put down easily. Few Black women have either the time or the money to set aside for such a long-term and financially dubious project, and we are trained from girlhood to be modest about our skills. We find it hard to believe we could write best sellers or great works.

I have every confidence that several such novels will be written. In order for us to see them published, we must give each other support but also fair, useful criticism to ensure our literature is worthy of the spirit of our community. In the following section, I speak to five Black lesbians of African and Asian descent who have contributed to the wealth of Black lesbian literature through both published and unpublished work and performance.

Part two: creative voices

Patience Agbabi

Chorus

Some like it with a he and
some like it with a she
some like to use the four-letter words and
love is a many splendoured thing but
some like to stick to three and
some like to OTT
some like to kiss
sex is sex is

Straight sex is recreation
same sex is revelation
S M sex is a negotiation
safe sex is masturbation
some like it in
and some like it out
and some like it in out in out
and think that that's what it's all about

Sex is a thing you think of when
you're feeling warm and free
often it goes hand in hand with
sexuality
sex is what you think it is

167: A Literary Movement

there's no authority
helps you to lose and find yourself that's
how it meant to be.

Some like it with a he
some like it with a she
some like to use the four-letter words and
love is a many splendoured thing but
some like to stick to three and
some like it OTT
some like to kiss
sex is sex is

Sex is the talk of the nation
sex is under legislation
sex is what society's based on
sex is misinformation
sex is an excuse to be sexist
sex is an excuse to be a rapist
anti-gay and lesbians, racist
sex is sex is

Women are said to ask for it
if their skirts are above the knee
Africa and Gay men are blamed
for causing HIV
few at the top control our thoughts
throughout history
those whom they fear from ignorance
they call minority

Some like it with a he and
some like it with a she but
some like to think we should all conform
to the nuclear family
some like to charge a fee but
some pocket the money
and make a business
sex is sex is

Some like to get a hard-on
some wear designer condoms
some call it contraception
some STD protection
some don't have anything to put it on
they cope with menstruation
it's all of this
sex is sex is

Some like it with a he and
some like it with a she
some like to use the four-letter words and
love is a many splendoured thing but
some like to stick to three and
some like it OTT
some like to kiss
sex is sex is

Some want L.O.V.E.
Some stay A.L.O.N.E
Some think it A.C.E. and
sex is . . . sex is

Basis of society
sex is . . . sex is
Something we must set free
sex is . . . sex is[22]

Patience Agbabi is a Nigerian British performance poet, who was born in 1965. She grew up in Sussex and North Wales, fostered by a white English working-class family, and studied English Literature at Pembroke College, Oxford. She lives in London and works part time in medical publishing to supplement her income. Her work as a poet involves performing in venues like Apples and Snakes, pubs, clubs and schools. In a recent article in *Africa World Review* she writes:

> Taking performance poetry into schools is important because it injects life into one of the most despised art forms

> in this culture. Poetry is still seen by many as an elitist pastime, a collector of dust on the top shelf of libraries. Poetry is not expected to address or be relevant to the masses. At a school in north-west London, one student admitted that she expected me to be a White man in a suit. The workshop was one of my most successful.[23]

One of Patience's tutors at Oxford told her that if she wanted to be a writer, she couldn't be anything but fourth-rate, and that very few people write well about universal issues. Patience ignored this attitude, because she believed that many people are capable of succeeding. It made her all the more determined to write, because she knew he was wrong. Another tutor's insistence on the significance of each individual word, however, influenced her writing in a positive way.

In her study of the English literary tradition she often found that she was not gripped by the poems she read. Agbabi could appreciate that they were good writers, but they didn't reach her soul, and she wanted to reach people's souls: 'I write against the Great Tradition – it's important that I have read those people because I'm writing against them. I'd recommend anyone who writes to read a lot just to get a sense of what poetry is, before doing it for oneself.'

Patience also felt it was important that she went into the library and took out as many recordings of poetry as she could:

> There's a danger of forgetting that poetry was an oral tradition and still is. That's why I have to perform as opposed to just publish. Everywhere had an oral tradition. Because the African one is still happening it's seen more.
>
> I'm also inspired by rap music. It connects on a very deep level with me. I'm influenced by dub and African drumming rhythms. My poetry is more musical because I hear it in my head before it's on the page. I feel I'm in the middle of the literary and the oral traditions. People see them as two separate camps and I see myself as bridging the gap.

When asked if this reflects her Black identity in white society,

Patience laughed and replied, 'Yes, I suppose I've always seen myself as bridging the gap.'

In her article in *Africa World Review*, Patience talked about rap artists who publish their lyrics: 'They are saying, our words are important, if you did not catch them the first time then we will make sure you do the second. We deserve to be listened to just as we deserve to be read.' She added:

> We have learnt the English language the hard way – too many of us have been silenced en route, and we have now reached a stage in history when we own it. We can articulate our own disparate and diasporate view of the world in our own words as the great oral and literary traditions make an alliance in popular culture.[24]

Agbabi writes about her many identities. She straddles both the Black and the white culture, having been brought up in a white culture, with white foster parents. As a Black woman who is also a dyke, with a multicultural working-class background and a middle-class education, she refuses to be pigeon-holed. She also writes in many poetic styles and uses a wide range of personae. Her performance work tends to combine political ideas with entertainment.

In the *Africa World Review* article she also spoke about the divided reaction from her Black audience to the political nature of her work. People may complain either that she hasn't covered a specific issue or that they're tired of political Black poetry, but Patience stressed: 'We do give each other a tremendous amount of support and I think we are reaching a stage where we realise our diversity and celebrate it rather than see it as a weakness.' She explained:

> My poetry comes from anger at the injustice in the world. Women in this culture are not expected to show anger and my poetry has surprised Black and white audiences alike who were perhaps expecting more humour. Although I enjoy performing I dislike the Black and White Minstrel legacy we have had to endure. At one stage in my career I deliberately withdrew humour from my set so that I would

get taken seriously. I am not afraid to use profane language if it is appropriate to the theme and I do not ever want to whitewash my art.

When Agbabi referred to specifically Black artistes she said:

> Certain poetry I hear from Black writers – that is writers full stop whatever their sexuality or sex – it's got more energy about it. I don't know what energy, perhaps anger because we've just suffered for so fucking long.
>
> When people say art is a luxury, I say it's a need. The reason it's become a luxury is because it's been eliticized. Of course it's seen as a luxury if it's performed by very few.

Agbabi has a strong sense of the relationship between herself and her audience. Seeing her live is to be at one end of a concentrated connection through which the powerful mood and message of her work is transmitted.

Razia Aziz

I

He sits exalted
among the broken piece of me
highly and lonely
in his ghostly eminence.

Graven against the spirit of
sacred geometry
austere against elegance
removed against the passion of
intimacy with the divine.

If I am indeed
in the heart of the goddess
then his flint has pierced me
erect in the hard-cast image
of a greedy god seeking to shatter the flower
of sensuality.

Though the ugliness of human evil abounds
nothing matches the envy
of the colonizing mind.

II

Oh beloved
how can I piece you together again,
remake you whole, you
who have entered
and altered,
whose perfection
haunted the invaders of distraction
whose grace they sought
to pervert,
rather than erase,
defile,
rather than destroy,
to possess,
and in possessing poison?
Unpublished
Oh beloved
how shall I avenge you
when your youth is gone
and of innocence nothing, for nothing
matches the envy of the
colonizing mind.[25]

Razia Aziz was born in 1965 in Hammersmith Hospital and went back to Nigeria, aged only a few months, to be with her parents (both of whom are Indian) until she was six, when she returned to England: 'I was desperately unhappy about what it was like when I came here. Coming to England felt like the single most traumatic experience of my life but it took a long time to admit that to myself.'

Both her parents were doctors, and Razia talked about the need to respond to class issues as a Black middle-class person, denying neither the oppression of racism nor the advantages of class:

> I was defining myself as a lesbian by the time I was sixteen. It wasn't a simple process but it wasn't one I see as having been traumatic. I think it was a good and positive choice.
>
> In terms of political influences I was introduced to feminism by an Asian woman a few years older than me when I was about ten, and that was my first real awareness of any political movement. Growing up in the family I grew up in I was aware of third world politics, but in a much less explicit way, particularly the conflict in Palestine. I actually remember the 1973 war, watching it on the news, and the feelings that were around about the plight of Palestinian people. But that wasn't presented to me as an ideology, it was almost at an emotive level.

Aziz went on to read Social and Political Science at Emmanuel College, Cambridge, and then do an M.Phil in Development Studies at Sussex University. While at Cambridge she studied Marxism as part of her course, and also began looking at lesbian and gay politics and the concept of Blackness. It was at this time in her life that she started identifying as Black. Although she had always been aware of racism, she was perhaps not conscious of the way it affected her.

Aziz worked for six months as a minicab driver and then came to London to work with the women's legal project, Rights of Women (ROW). Although she was employed as a Black women's worker she found herself doing a lot of work with white women. Her time spent at ROW marked a period of transformation. Her father died, she met her current partner and things were chaotic at work:

> I went from a situation where I was talking about racism but still colluding in it, and came under a lot of attack from Black women. That's where I was presented with a choice, that's when I recognized that I had to actually choose Black women, I couldn't just be Black, I had to choose myself. It wasn't enough to say, 'I'm Black, let's all sit together, we all suffer.' As Black people our oppression does not unite us, it

divides us. What unites us is our creativity in responding to oppression.

Currently still living and working in London, she plans to move back to India, but is under no illusions about this step: 'It's in the nature of who I am that wherever I go in the world I'll always be an outsider. It'll be the same in India, not just because I'll be an England returnee but because I'm a Muslim.'

As a teenager she had a short story published under a pseudonym, and has in hand a project (completed on a counselling course) comprising eight photographs and poems, as well as other short stories, poems and travel writing. She describes herself as a potential writer:

> I haven't yet written what I would really like to write. I don't conceive of it as a particular piece of work. For me the real creative skill, whether you're talking about writing, dance, music, signing is the ability to be a channel (and it's a discipline, a skill and it's inspirational) to that energy in the universe which is creative and life-affirming. Sometimes when I've been brave enough not to control what I'm trying to say, I open my mouth and something beautiful comes out. For me writing is the same but harder. Some of my most effective writing has been in letters which convey what is moving me without the clutter of words.

Aziz describes how one of the poems in her current project, 'Knitting', began for her in Waterloo Station when she only had a scrap of paper with her:

> Before crashing, the wave,
> Before drowning, the storm,
> Before bending, the wind,
>
> These lines came into my mind as a rhythm, then the words just came into my mind. It was something that wanted to be written. For me that's what inspiration is about. There's a space in your existence which you nurture and which invites

things into it that want to be created, and if I knew how to create that space so it always existed and I could always get access to it, I would be the happiest woman on this earth. Then I think – what are the things that stop me?'. That's when you can see the connection between the oppression you experience and why it's hard to bring things into the world. All those things like: Am I good enough? Is it my language? All that is to do with racism, sexism, class, heterosexism, but it's also existential. Whoever you are you have to answer this question for yourself.

Aziz concluded with the question, 'How do you create that space in your life?'

Jackie Kay

Been thinking of this black woman
the doors that were closed to her
the places outside she had to sit
waiting
whilst some of her band
ate inside the colour of skin that allowed.

And yet
she created all those women in
that voice that could surprise out a laugh in you
or pull down pain in you.

When she's in a low-down groove
I think of the women that came
before her –
the black women who had masters
and who scrubbed the low-down floor
and the women who come
after her –
the black women who have bosses
and who scrub the low-down floor.

She takes me round my world
long since she gone
long since she gone.

And I know
that black man hangs still
that strangefruit
on the paw paw tree.

The beat goes on and
the dream misses a beat between
each leaving and each loss
and then finds the note again –

'love me or leave me or let me be lonely'
those women who could be so independently Blue.

Reach up and catch this note Billie
high up in that gloomy sky
hear this note dip down
to all those places we are scared to go
to all those fears we're frightened to meet
you went to those places
you sang through them and deep down into them
and you dreamt
and those dreams are on record.

On record.

There are so many voices we aint never
heard nor know of;
But I can see you Billie
your full lips kiss my dreams.[26]

Jackie Kay was born in Scotland in 1961, where she was brought up by her white adoptive Glaswegian family. She is of mixed racial heritage with a Nigerian father. She graduated from Stirling in 1983 with a BA (Hons.) in English Literature. Of her first collection of poetry, *The Adoption Papers*,[27] *Poetry Review* said, 'a wonderfully spirited, tender and crafted contribution to Scottish writing, to black writing, and to the poetry of our time. It is a work of the utmost generosity and truth'. *The Adoption Papers* received a Scottish Arts Council Book Award, the Saltire First Book of the Year Award and the Forward Prize. It focuses on a Black Glaswegian girl adopted by a White family, and gives a voice to the daughter, adoptive mother and imaginary mother: 'I've used my experiences as a springboard to create the book.'[28]

Jackie Kay's book of poetry for children, *Two's Company*,[29] won the Signal Poetry Award. Her first play, *Chiaroscuro*, was presented by the Theatre of Black Women in 1986; her second, *Twice Over*, by Gay Sweatshop in 1988, with subsequent performances in Vancouver and San Francisco (both are published in collections by Methuen). Jackie Kay has written pieces for TV and two more plays: *Every Bit of It*, about Bessie Smith, and *Twilight Shift*, about two male lovers in the mining community. Her second collection of poetry for adults, *Other Lovers*, was published by Bloodaxe in 1994:

> I have always enjoyed being entertained and believe that films, theatre, poetry readings and paintings can feed you. If somebody identifies with my work I take it as a huge compliment. Writing is all about communicating and it is important to me that people who read or watch my work feel involved in it.

In an interview in the *Guardian*, Kay expressed her concern about the lack of recognition of Black women writers in Britain. She highlighted the fact that although the USA appears to foster Black women, with the success of Alice Walker and Toni Morrison, we should not be complacent:

> There's a fashion in the US at the moment for African-American women, but it will die down. Many Black writers who came to the fore during the Harlem Renaissance in the twenties have been forgotten. Zora Neale Hurston died poor, and was buried in an unmarked grave.[30]

Kay hopes that through her work, and that of other Black women writers, the same does not happen to us in Britain:

> Kay is angered when the critics categorize black women's writing as autobiographical, and challenges the critics who still insist a woman's novel should deal with feelings and emotions. She said: 'My writing contributes to changing people's consciousness about racism, sexism, and prejudice. Black women writers in Britain are exploring identity, sexuality, status, and our position here.'

She went on to add:

> I am Black and Scottish and a lot of writing explores various areas of complex identities. I am always interested in the person who is on the margin, who is being discriminated against on whatever grounds, colour, religion, sexuality, sex. . . . The list is depressingly long. I am interested in creating work that challenges stereotypes in an original way. (Hopefully.)[31]

Maya Chowdhry

she looks up
the needle swaying
under the weight of the words
red thread scratching the
outer seams of a silk kameez.

she can't recognise your
almond eyes dripping into the cloth
your body has changed
become distorted
your tawny skin seems
different because it has lain
under a woman's hand.

she thinks luckily she's
already measured your
breasts, your hips, your
inside leg because now

she doesn't want to put
her tape-measured hand there.

it's no longer
a woman inside thigh
the measurement has
expanded
become an unknown domain
a terrifying territory.

and now your clothes
are one size larger
the cloth hanging wide around
your breasts
your inside thigh
and your salwaar
tight around your ankle
you can hardly get them on.[32]

Maya Chowdhry is a film-maker, photographer, live artist and award-winning writer. Her mother is of English and Scottish heritage, and her father is of Indian descent. She grew up in Glasgow, and is now living in Sheffield. Her work has been published in *Putting the Pickle Where the Jam Should Be*,[33] and on tape with *Climbing the Mountains*. Her poetry and radio play, *Monsoon*, were selected for the 1991 Young Playwrights Festival on Radio 4, and for *Talking Poetry* on Radio 5 in 1992. She also won first prize in the 1992 Cardiff International Poetry Competition with 'Bridges of Dust'. She has performed her multimedia works in Los Angeles, Edinburgh and London, and was recently commissioned by the Institute of Contemporary Arts (ICA) to produce a live art piece, *The Sacred House*, which combines poetry, narrative, images, movement and theatre. Her work is also published in numerous anthologies. She describes herself as a writer, performance poet, live artist, film-maker, multimedia artist, photographer, teacher, consultant, director, producer and screenwriter. She is most definitely a woman of many talents: 'I write for film, radio, TV, and theatre including my own performances. I write plays, screenplays, poetry, and short stories. My work varies in content and theme, but always draws on life experience.'

Chowdhry is also influenced and inspired by everyday observations, by travelling, different landscapes, sea, city and country. While writing this chapter, she was preparing for a trip to the USA, to see her lover and to be inspired by a different environment for a while: 'I am influenced by people I meet going to the bank, on the bus, in the gym, in cafes, nightclubs, on my doorstep. I am influenced by other Black women writers, and other lesbians around the world.'

Avril Rogers-Wright

(For The Black Lesbian Support Network)

To those that have come.
Remember
our laughter
rich and bubbly in us,
our open doors
chinwagging from the window.

I want you to come.
To the warmth
positive selves Blackwomeness
to know a solace,
before
meeting the wolves in sheep's clothing.

To know that you came.
A lasting memory
of beautiful flowers
that you are or were
one of us,
before teething to bloom
in your new home.[34]

Avril Rogers-Wright was born in 1963 in Freetown, Sierra Leone (one of the countries to which free people went after slavery was abolished). She explained that the tradition she grew up in was a very oral tradition, where few people had TV. Hence, people spent time talking, telling stories and performing pieces of theatre. Books were scarce. When she returned twelve years later, to her disappointment the situation was much the same:

> Most of the storytelling was based on morals. A lot of the stories had songs to them and that had a big influence. I was used to people being free with their emotions. If someone sang, no one was going to turn to them and say you've got a terrible voice.
>
> White literature, for example Nadine Gordimer, was more easily available than African literature, but I remember when I read them I couldn't completely relate to them. We didn't grow up calling ourselves Black, we called ourselves African, or by our country's name. Our school curriculum was very English-based. We were learning things like fucking Shakespeare in the middle of Africa.

She left Sierra Leone at the age of sixteen to spend a year at school in Nigeria, and then came to England where she trained as a nurse. She has done a lot of jobs since to survive, and has always had to support herself in work other than her writing. She now lives and works in London. She is best known for her poetry, but has also written short stories and novellas. She began creative writing at the age of nine with narrative cartoons.

Rogers-Wright's work is very much about deconstructing the myths society has built up around people or the individual. For example, her poem, 'Red Queen: Red Rain: Red Blossom', works to dispel the shame women feel about menstruation. She had the following to say about her motivations and inspirations:

> Being in England made me lean towards protest poetry. On the one hand it brought out my creativity, but on the other hand it stifled my creativity. We're forever talking about race. What I'm writing about could be the same as what someone wrote about a hundred years ago. What's the point of my writing if society won't listen to its artists.
>
> What influenced me more than anything else were aspects of the tradition that went on back home. We were a very spiritual people. It was a Muslim and Christian country and

people shared their celebrations. I cherish that peace between people of different religions. We had Masquerade. Masquerade happened at Christmas, Boxing Day and Easter. On Christmas night, around 2 a.m., the men would start blowing their horns in the bush. For me that's one of the most erotic sounds.

The Western way is: there is the devil and the devil is such a horrible, terrible thing; whereas in Africa, in Christianity there is Hell and damnation but in between there is the Masquerade and a devil you can dance and have a good time with.

My greatest influence is nature. I love nature, so all my poems are saturated by nature. As much as I admire what we've achieved as human beings, for me nature is the epitome of civilization because there's something for everyone in nature – the amount of living forms that are all interconnected. My being alive as a woman, as an African and as a lesbian/zami is continually reaffirmed by nature, because there is that constant differentness; whereas (particularly Western) society says, 'Oh well, as a lesbian you can't exist', but there are many different kinds of trees.

Other writers inspire her, particularly Black women writers:

They have literally saved the lives of many Black women and stopped us being flung into a mental institution. A few men inspire me, such as James Baldwin, Wole Soyinka, but I get more inspiration from female writers.

The way that I see life, a child is born with knowledge – wisdom – and the way society works either enhances or destroys that wisdom. Other writers reaffirm it in people. … Writing doesn't come easy because English is not my mother tongue.

Avril once burnt her English dictionary in a fit of rage, only to have to go out and buy another. She also talked about the difficulties of trying to express the sounds of Creole in writing. She's currently working in a form of expression developed by Gloria Anzaldúa:

She talked about immigrant people having forked tongues.

> The first line, people write in their mother tongue, and then they translate it. We have created our own family system and our own kinship. We continue to break down barriers – like the Berlin wall – between us. I have been influenced by many other cultures and I value that. We can sit down and talk to each other, share food and even trade with each other. There's a bit of my work which is very much about celebrating our connections.

She concluded: 'I write from situations that move me, both with anger and passion. My fascination is for the birth of a new civilization. If we have a more organic and caring economic system, what would life be like?'

Note: Since this chapter was written, Sheba Feminist Publishers (the main publisher of Black lesbian writing) has folded for financial reasons.

Notes

1. Akua Rugg, *Brickbats and Bouquets.* Race Today Publications, London, 1984.
2. Dorothea Smartt, 'Connecting Medium', in Bernadette Halpin and Dorothea Smartt (eds.), *Words From the Women's Cafe.* Centerprise Publications, London, 1993.
3. Carmen Tunde, 'Contradictions', in Da Choong, Olivette Cole-Wilson, Bernadine Evaristo and Gabriela Pearse (eds), *Black Women Talk Poetry.* Black Womantalk, London, 1987.
4. Avril Rogers-Wright, 'Skin'. Unpublished.
5. Michelle Asha Warsama, 'The Land Where the Elephants Live', from *I'll Take the High Road.* Part reprinted in Halpin and Smartt, *Words from the Women's Cafe.*
6. Bernadine Evaristo, 'Mombasa Old Town', in Da Choong *et al.*, *Black Women Talk.*
7. Barbara Burford, 'The Pinstripe Summer', in *The Threshing Floor.* Sheba Feminist Publishers, London, 1986.
8. Barbara Burford, 'September Blue', in Barbara Burford, Lindsay MacRae and Sylvia Paskin (eds), *Dancing the Tightrope.* The Women's Press, London, 1987.
9. Rogers-Wright, 'Skin'.
10. Razia Aziz, 'Envy/The Colonizing Mind' (unpublished), from an untitled project.

11. Burford, 'Pinstripe Summer'.
12. Jackie Kay, 'Peony', in Burford *et al.*, *Tightrope*.
13. Valerie Mason-John, 'The Alex', part 1, unpublished.
14. Adeola, 'The Dark Side of Georgia', from *Crystal Visions*, Shango, 1993.
15. Gabriela Pearse, 'Patricia', in Da Choong *et al.*, *Black Women Talk*.
16. Adeola, 'Slow Burning Fuse', from *Crystal Visions*.
17. Maud Sulter, 'Drich Day', in *As a Black Woman*. Akira Press, London, 1985.
18. Burford, 'Pinstripe Summer'.
19. *Ibid.*
20. Patience Agbabi, 'Learning the language', in *Africa World Review*, May–October 1993.
21. Virginia Woolf, 'Women and Fiction', in *Women and Writing*, intro. by Michele Barrett. The Women's Press, London, 1979.
22. Patience Agbabi, 'Sex Is', in Halpin and Smartt, *Words from the Women's Cafe*.
23. Agbabi, 'Learning the language'.
24. *Ibid.*
25. Aziz, 'Envy/The Colonizing Mind'.
26. Jackie Kay, 'Blue Notes For Billie', in Da Choong *et al.*, *Black Women Talk*.
27. Jackie Kay, *The Adoption Papers*. Bloodaxe Books, Newcastle upon Tyne, 1991.
28. Valerie Mason-John, 'Pride of place', *Guardian* (Women's Page), 1991.
29. Jackie Kay, *Two's Company*. Blackie Children's Books, London, 1992.
30. Mason-John, 'Pride of place'.
31. Valerie Mason-John, 'Black, British and proud', *The Voice*, 10 November 1987.
32. Maya Chowdhry, 'The Seamstress'. Unpublished.
33. Maya Chowdhry, Shiadah Janjua and Seni Seneviratne, *Putting the Pickle Where the Jam Should Be*. Write Back/Jag Rahi Hai, London, 1989.
34. Avril Rogers-Wright, 'The Coming-Out Welcome', in Da Choong *et al.*, *Black Women Talk*.

Books

Adeola, *Crystal Visions* (tape), 1993, Shango.
Paul Beasley, *The Popular Front of Contemporary Poetry*, Apples and Snakes, London, 1992.

Barbara Burford, *The Threshing Floor*. Sheba Feminist Publishers, London, 1986.

Barbara Burford, Lindsay MacRae and Sylvia Paskin (eds), *Dancing the Tightrope*. The Women's Press, London, 1987.

Da Choong, Olivette Cole-Wilson, Bernadine Evaristo and Gabriela Pearse (eds), *Black Women Talk Poetry*. Black Womantalk, London, 1987.

Da Choong *et al.* (eds), *Don't Ask Me Why*. Black Womantalk, London, 1991.

Shabnam Grewal, Jackie Kay, Liliane Landor, Gail Lewis and Pratibha Parmar (eds), *Charting the Journey*. Sheba Feminist Publishers, London, 1988.

Bernadette Halpin and Dorothea Smartt (eds), *Words from the Woman's Cafe*. Centerprise Publications, London, 1983.

Audre Lorde, *Zami, A New Spelling of My Name*. Persephone Press, 1982.

Akua Rugg, *Brickbats and Bouquets*. Race Today Publications, London, 1984.

Sheba collective (eds.), *Everyday Matters No. 2*. Sheba Feminist Publishers, London, 1984.

Dorothea Smartt, 'From My Eyes ... Zamis Publishing Poetry 1984–1988', in *What Lesbians Do in Books*.

Maud Sulter, *As a Black Woman*. Akira Press, London, 1985.

Virginia Woolf, *Women and Writing*. intro. by Michele Barrett. The Women's Press, London, 1979.

Articles

Patience Agbabi, 'Learning the language', *Africa World Review*, May–October 1993.

Valerie Mason-John, 'Pride of place', *Guardian* (Women's Page), 1991.

Valerie Mason-John, 'Black, British and proud', *The Voice*, 10 November 1987.

Chapter nine

Several Faces of Discrimination

Anne Hayfield

Introduction

In writing about Black lesbians, I have referred to the experience I have gained while working in the Black lesbian community for several years. I am unable to quote any research, because no large-scale studies have been carried out on how discrimination affects Black lesbians. Instead, I have looked at what has happened to me, my friends and my allies within the Black lesbian community.

In any examination of the discrimination that Black lesbians experience in Britain, we must examine the racism that exists against all Black people, the sexism against all women and the homophobia against all lesbians and gay men. These discriminations are inseparable; as Black lesbians we belong to all three categories and therefore experience these oppressions simultaneously. While my writing on this topic may paint a depressing picture, it is worth remembering that Black lesbians do manage not only to survive but also to flourish in what is an increasingly intolerant society.

Some facts

Since the mass arrival of African-Caribbean and Asian communities in Britain during the 1950s and 1960s, discrimination and prejudiced attitudes against us have not changed. Racist abuse, both verbal and physical, has not disappeared. In fact, the racism and discrimination perpetrated against us have just become more sophisticated during the past forty years. Too many people in this country believe that racism is a thing of the past. Similarly, homophobic abuse towards lesbian and gay men has not changed during this century. In fact, since we have become more visible, attacks on the homosexual communities have increased. Despite this, the general public also seem to think that lesbians and gay men are more accepted than we were ten years ago.

Part of the reason why people are influenced by these false impressions has to do with the way the media has reported equal opportunities developments. During the 1980s the tabloid press were fond of running stories which gave the impression that people from minority groups were being given preferential treatment. This has not been the case. Equal opportunities were developed to look at whether services gave everybody an equal chance. An example of irresponsible reporting of equalities issues occurred in 1993, when the residents of the Isle of Dogs in London elected a councillor from the far-right British National Party. All the press coverage focused on the fact that the white residents of the Isle of Dogs believed that their Black neighbours were being given the best-quality council housing. This was clearly not the case, and the local authority concerned had the statistics to prove it. The media, however, typically reported what the white residents thought, and not the actual facts or figures.

Black lesbians have a curious relationship to all this. For the most part the media generally ignore us: where are the Black lesbian characters on TV and in film? The media also ridicule any form of support that is offered to us. We are wrongly accused of taking jobs, homes and other services away from the white heterosexual majority. If we are employed, it is assumed that we have the job solely because we are Black lesbians, and that we have no other skills or experience to offer. Black lesbians are oppressed by both personal attitudes and systematically by institutions. We experience multiple discrimination in the form of sexism, racism and heterosexism. Yet we are often scapegoated and ridiculed for being a minority within a minority and so, with the warped thinking of the majority, it is assumed we receive special treatment.

Some of the responsibility for this must go to the media. The rest of the blame lies with the Conservative government, which has been in political power since 1979. Senior Tories have, with tedious regularity, attacked minority groups in this country. This includes making sick jokes about the very existence of Black lesbians. When a Black lesbian councillor, Linda Bellos, became leader of a Lambeth council in 1985, she received a venomous attack from the far-right wing of the Tory party, and was also made a scapegoat by the Labour Party whenever the Tories wanted to attack Labour MPs. For the Conservative Party and the media, councillor Bellos became the mascot of the 'Loony Left' during her two years in office at Lambeth Council. The Tories continue to attack minority and oppressed groups of people, and conveniently blame them for many of the problems that we have in society today.

The law

Until recent years it could be said that lesbians had been ignored by the law. There is the old story about how Queen Victoria had not believed that two women could have sex together, so, therefore, the criminal offence was applied only to gay men. The 1967 Act which decriminalized sexual activity between men also presented them with a series of problems. There are many ways that gay men still fall foul of the law, by virtue of a range of criminal offences which have no heterosexual equivalent.

Lesbians, in general, do not have these problems. We are seen as 'mad and not bad'. It is extremely rare for lesbians to be prosecuted for sexual offences. However, it is possible for lesbians to be charged with causing a breach of the peace if they were to show affection in public. This is the sort of offence that has been used against lesbians on marches when they kiss or hold hands. As Black people we are already a vulnerable target on the streets. The police have labelled us as a 'high risk' category of people who will cause trouble in public spaces. Public affray, mugging, pickpocketing and drug trafficking are just a few of the crimes on an endless list of offences which they consider to be endemic in the Black communities. This type of insensitive policing, and the fear of being picked up under suspicion and charged, has deterred many Black lesbians from going on lesbian and gay marches. The relatively small number of us at such events means we are more visible and are, therefore, in more danger of being picked up by the police.

During the past few years we have witnessed a series of parliamentary pronouncements affecting lesbians and gay men. These are commonly referred to as Clause 25, Section 28, Paragraph 16 and the early day motion on AID.

Clause 25 is an attempt to criminalize sexual relations between gay men. As the law stands there are more restrictions on how and when gay men can have sex than exist for lesbians or heterosexuals. Clause 25 will have a minimal effect on lesbians; however, three other clauses pose a very definite attack on lesbians, with a special blow for those of us who are mothers. The most infamous of these, Section 28 of the Local Government Act 1988, was an attempt to stop local authorities from 'intentionally promoting homosexuality'. It is worth remembering that no local authority has consciously tried to encourage their residents to change their sexuality from heterosexual to homosexual. Lesbians can take some comfort in the fact that the legislation is so poorly worded that it is doubtful it has achieved any of its main aims. For example, it was originally thought that it would stop local authorities from funding lesbian and gay voluntary groups. Although some councils have refused grants to groups, others have survived with their funding intact. Section 28 is, however, often used as an excuse for a local authority to refuse to provide services to lesbians. It is, in effect, a bigot's charter.

Section 28 has been well documented. Part of the section states that a public-funded school should not 'encourage the teaching . . . that homosexual relationships are acceptable as if they were a pretended family relationship'. This has clear consequences for lesbians who are mothers. Lesbian mothers, both Black and white, need reassurance that their child is not going to be disadvantaged in a school system which is designed for the needs of children from heterosexual families. Although it has never been tried in this country, teachers should have the freedom to validate the experience of the child of a lesbian mother. Teachers should be able to use books which depict children from a variety of backgrounds, including those children who have Black lesbians as mothers.

Paragraph 16 refers to a consultative document on the Children Act 1989. The paragraph deals with fostering and adoption. While it states that the local authorities' primary duty is to the welfare of the child, it does ridicule the notion that lesbians can make good parents. It has always been extremely difficult for lesbians either to foster or adopt children. But this government pronouncement made it clear that lesbians do not have rights equal to heterosexual people. This is a sad situation for Black lesbians, in particular, as many will have good parenting skills as either biological or non-biological mothers. Many Black lesbians would like to foster or adopt. There is also a disproportionately high number of Black children in care who would dearly love a home. Paragraph 16 has not made it impossible for Black lesbians to foster or adopt, but it has certainly made it much more difficult.

An early day motion is a parliamentary device whereby an issue can be debated in order to see whether legislation is needed. In 1989, there was an early day motion which aimed to prevent single women and lesbians from being given Artificial Insemination by Donor (AID) at infertility clinics. This service enables women to be artificially inseminated so that they can have children without having a man in their lives. Predictably, Tory MPs were outraged when they discovered this. Although the number of women who had this treatment in the past was very small, the government wanted to control infertility clinics and so introduced a licensing scheme. A clinic that was seen to be offering this service to lesbians would face losing its licence. The clinics would also help by testing semen, so that if a lesbian found a suitable donor she could have the semen screened for the HIV virus by the clinic.

The services of the infertility clinics have always been more accessible to white middle-class lesbians. This is because the clinics would vet all applicants, and so many Black lesbians might not have been found suitable because of racist and classist assumptions. Also, the service was quite expensive, so few Black lesbians would have been able to afford it. For these reasons Black lesbians do not have access to the clinics, and so those who want to get pregnant are at risk of contracting the HIV virus. Although this was pointed out in parliamentary debates, the government did not seem to care.

In retrospect, within a matter of a few years lesbians have moved from a position of invisibility in the eyes of the law to having a number of oppressive laws aimed at encouraging discrimination against us.

Immigration

Immigration legislation is the most potent form of legitimized racism in this country. Britain is an imperialist power. As such, it grew wealthy from a series of complex transactions which robbed parts of the Caribbean, Asia and Africa. This form of trade is still going on today. The rich Westernized countries pay a minimal price for the natural resources, crafts, foodstuffs and minerals belonging to our countries of origin. As a result, these nations remain, in monetary terms, poor.

This economic disparity has meant that many Black people have come to the West in the hope of earning a decent living. In Britain, Black people were encouraged to come here in the 1950s when there was a labour shortage. Our mothers and fathers were drafted in to work in the transport system and in the National Health Service, which had been established as a result of the 1942 Beveridge Report on Social Insurance and Allied Services. Black people worked in the lowest paid jobs in both industries, and this is still true today. Theoretically, it used to be the case that a Black person had the same right to live and work in Britain as a white person born here. This is not the situation today. Those rights have been eroded, sometimes retrospectively, so that some Black people who have been living here have found themselves in difficult circumstances. It is clear from the imposition of immigration laws that Black people are not welcome here. It is worth noting that in 1992 the EC was being 'sold' to the British people by the Conservative government, with an assurance that it would encourage freedom of movement. Borders would disappear and everybody would be able to live and work in the other European countries. In reality we are now witnessing a Europe that is barricading itself against the rest of the world, and Black people in the EC will find it more difficult to maintain links with Asia, Africa and the Caribbean. Many European countries have a worse reputation for racism than for Britain. For example, Germany has always had the category of guest workers, and has never allowed migrant workers full citizenship. Britain is the only EC member that has a Race Relations Act.

Immigration is also an issue for lesbians and gay men. The concept of immigration is based on the heterosexual unit and blood relatives. It ignores the fact that same-sex partners cannot get married and so, if you happen to fall in love with somebody who is not a British citizen, your relationship is doomed from the start. This is not the case for all countries: our Common Market partner Holland allows same-sex couples to live together legally; and Australia, which in many ways has a similar constitution to Britain, also allows same-sex partners to stay together. Britain can, under its immigration rules, allow lesbians and gay men to obtain refugee status to enable them to stay in this country. This is because, by definition, a refugee is somebody who has a genuine fear of persecution as a member of a particular social group. In many countries of the world, people who love someone of the same gender are under the threat of long prison sentences or worse. This could become a big issue for the lesbian and gay community in Hong Kong, when the British government makes the hand-over in 1997. When the colony returns to the People's Republic of China, many lesbians and gay men who live in Hong Kong will find themselves facing persecution. Many live in fear that the British government will not help the lesbian and gay community to live in dignity, and will instead leave them to face several years' hard labour just because of their sexuality.

Employment

Paid work is important because it gives an individual status, confidence and money. It has been my personal experience that all too often I have seen Black lesbians failing in terms of paid employment. As a group, few of us have been able to achieve and sustain success. The reasons for this lie in the discrimination that Black lesbians face in the labour market on the grounds of race, gender and sexuality. When looking at racism in the labour market, all Black communities in this country have had to live with higher rates of unemployment than the white communities. This is the reality we have had to cope with ever since we arrived in Britain over five hundred years ago. Racial discrimination in the labour market has not been solved by the Race Relations Act 1976. See, for example, how the law operates in one particular area – recruitment. A Black lesbian may go for a job, have an interview and then not be selected. Instead, the job goes to a white man, who has fewer qualifications and less experience than the Black lesbian. Without inside information, how can she prove she has been discriminated against? The burden of proof is on the Black person to show that racism is operating. The law could be changed so that it is, rather, the employers who have to prove that their actions are not racially motivated. Many of the cases of racial discrimination at recruitment level have only been won because the employers have been blatantly racist: for example, when they openly state that they will not employ Black workers. Employers may also get caught if they are ignorant about the law. The law is not sophisticated enough to deal with the type of racism which is endemic in British society. The effect of the Race Relations Act has been to treat the worst cases, which has helped a few Black people to win moral victories. Overall, however, it has not generally improved the economic position of Black communities in this country.

Another fault of the Race Relations Act is that it defines racism as the oppression by one racial group over another. Consequently, the law can be used against Black people by white people. Community organizations who want to employ Black people for the best possible motives have had the Race Relations Act used against them. The whole notion of employing Black people to improve the welfare of other Black people is now under examination. Many white liberals are not willing to accept that there are some jobs, such as providing welfare services to Black people, that are better carried out by other Black people. We know, however, that front-line Black workers are needed because many Black people have a healthy distrust of the majority of white community workers. A case that illustrates this point well concerns the Tottenham

Under Fives project and what happened when they tried to appoint a Black worker. The project wanted to appoint a worker of African descent because they had many African-Caribbean children in their care. A white person complained of being racially discriminated against, and took them to an industrial tribunal. The Tottenham Under Fives lost their case because they had other Black workers. The idea that you can keep a racially balanced workforce is now under question. It is almost as if the courts are saying, 'One Black worker is OK, but two is excessive.' The case went to appeal, and from the judgment it would appear that only having a non-English speaker can be cited as a genuine reason for employing a Black person. This is a dangerous situation, because there are many circumstances in which a community group might want to employ a Black worker where language might not be a major consideration.

In August 1992 the tabloid press ran a series of stories about a housing project that wanted to appoint a Black lesbian. The project ran a hostel where a considerable number of residents were themselves Black lesbians. The nature of the work involved a great deal of personal contact with the residents. It would seem obvious to all that the best person for the job would be a housing manager who was herself a Black lesbian and therefore had specialist knowledge of the problems that Black lesbians face. The post was to be funded by the Department of the Environment (DOE), but after it had seen the job advertisement the funding was refused. It is also quite likely that the department leaked the story to the tabloid press which, true to its nature, used racism and homophobia to ridicule the project. 'Why is this job not going to a white man with a family to support?' they screamed.

The government minister in charge of the DOE at that time was Michael Howard. This is worth mentioning, as he was one of the principal people involved in getting Section 28 on to the statute books. The DOE wanted assurance that the post would be open to everyone before they would agree to fund it. That was their understanding of equal opportunities. Whether the group ever managed to resolve this situation successfully is doubtful. To my knowledge the funding for this post was never reinstated. The significance of this event is how government power can be used to persecute Black lesbians, and while doing so, subject small community groups to vitriolic attacks from the tabloid press to make a political point. For the record, because there is no specific legislation on lesbians in relation to discrimination, it is perfectly legal to advertise for a lesbian worker.

The Sex Discrimination Act 1975 has failed to change the reality for millions of working women in this country. Twenty years ago, most women could be found in the lowest grades of the health, education, secretarial and manual sectors. Today we are still there. It is worth noting that the reason often cited for the failure of women to move up the career ladder is that we are not able to take on extra responsibility because we have children to look after. Many lesbians are childless women, but they are still not getting promotion.

An illustration of how the Sex Discrimination Act 1975 fails women can be seen by what has happened to women who have trained for the construction industry. Manual work appeals to many women who do not want to work in an office or the caring professions. The appeal of building work like carpentry or plumbing for many Black lesbians is that it is better paid than the more 'traditional' women's jobs like cleaning. It is also something that you can do on a self-employed basis, and so avoid the worry about discrimination from employers and co-workers. Building work uses skill, not necessarily strength, and can be very satisfying. To a certain extent many women have been encouraged to try the building trades, with the establishment of courses designed to train them in non-traditional skills. Thus, many Black lesbians have the qualifications, but building firms still regard a woman carpenter as a joke. Many of the building firms that exist have only a few employees, and it has not been possible for the Equal Opportunities Commission to have any sort of influence with this type of employer. The Sex Discrimination Act and the Equal Opportunities Commission have, however, enabled some middle-class Black women to enter the professions. This has been their major achievement.

Lesbians do not have any specific protection in the workplace from unfair dismissal. In the majority of workplaces, being discriminated against because you are a lesbian is still not talked about or, if it is, it is a source of ridicule. For this reason many lesbians do not come out at work, and of those who have, many will leave their employment because of heterosexism, and a few may even be sacked. Black lesbians are especially reluctant to come out at work, because we are already coping with the dual burden of racism and sexism. We do not want to add more to our plate. It is also important to make links with the other Black workers, who will probably be heterosexual, and Black lesbians will not want to risk losing this important form of support, regardless of how informal it may be.

For the Black lesbian who does not come out at work there is the problem of lying about her life outside work. This can be demoralizing as it also means that if you do have a major catastrophe, such as a relationship breakdown or housing problems, there may be no one at work who can give you support. The Black lesbian who has to maintain this sort of distance from her colleagues may also disadvantage herself in other ways. She may not be invited to the informal work gatherings that can be important in developing her career.

Sex and sexuality are often regularly talked about in the workplace. We can thank the tabloid press and women's magazines for keeping these topics in the public consciousness. This makes it difficult to avoid questions about whether or not you have a partner. For some Black lesbians this may mean that if they say they do not have a boyfriend that they will find themselves being 'set-up' with somebody. Many lesbians, both Black and white, hate the annual ritual of the Christmas party.

People often wrongly assume that only blatantly out lesbians have problems at work. This is not the case. Many Black lesbians face problems because they have been forced out by a colleague's insensitive and homophobic actions. It is wrong to assume that not being out at work somehow means that you do not experience heterosexism. A Black lesbian who has to spend forty hours a week listening to homophobic comments will experience a range of emotions, including stress. Indeed, Black lesbians need to have excellent stress-management training to cope with this constant tension, and should always acknowledge and applaud each other for being so strong.

Housing

Many studies have shown that Black people, when applying for public housing, have been given the most unpopular type of accommodation. When applying for council housing, we have been dumped on the problem estates and housed in slum conditions. The poorly maintained council accommodation which is available to Black people is often unsuitable for Black lesbians, for many reasons. Only single women with children have an automatic right to council housing, although they can often languish in a bed and breakfast for months and sometimes years. This means that the likelihood of a single Black lesbian getting housing from the council or local authority schemes are slim. For those Black lesbians who are mothers or who are co-parenting, living on council estates has a number of problems. The architecture of these estates means that neighbours are in close proximity, which makes it difficult to keep your private life to yourself. There is often a permanent threat of violence: excrement through your letter box; burglary; graffiti; vandalism; as well as verbal abuse and physical assault, are all part of the fear and reality of homophobia and racism on a housing estate.

The private rented sector is effectively closed to many Black people because of high rents, and we also have to deal with the prejudice from private landlords, most of whom are white. Even when Black people can afford the rents, the widespread racism often means that the properties are rented out to white people. This same racism is repeated in the dealings of private accommodation bureaux and estate agents. One solution that white people have found to the problem of high rents in the private sector is to share flats and houses with each other. Racism and homophobia again prevent many Black lesbians from taking this option as there will be difficulties for us in sharing with white heterosexual people. Also, because some of us live in isolated areas where there are few visible Black lesbians about, it becomes difficult for Black lesbians to enter into this type of arrangement with each other.

Buying a home has been a way of finding decent housing for some Black people. Again, our economic disadvantage means that this is only accessible to a small proportion of the Black communities.

Single homeless people have no automatic right to public housing. Some of the people who fall into this category will be living in self-help housing co-ops, which have gone some way to providing housing for lesbians. Many of these housing co-ops have grown out of the white middle-class squatter movements of the 1970s. The problem associated with this type of housing is that, firstly, you have to 'do your time' living in accommodation in a poor state of repair before being offered anything that is half-way decent. Secondly, the skills that are needed to run housing co-ops are associated very much with the ethos of white middle-class attitudes. There is, for example, a lot of liaison with local authorities, and maybe the Housing Corporation as well. For these reasons, Black lesbians who have joined co-ops often feel that they are not really part of them. Only a few Black lesbians have been housed by co-ops in houses converted into one-bedroom flats.

The current political climate has led many local authorities, including ones run by Labour, to abandon housing co-ops. In the past, where properties were considered too run down to be let out to homeless families, local authorities allowed co-ops to renovate them. These properties have been used to house single homeless people, both heterosexual and lesbian and gay. However, in recent years, councils have found that these schemes are unpopular with local residents. Once councils agree to local residents' demands that the houses should be let to families, they are guilty of the worst form of heterosexism. As a result, the housing co-ops which gave relief to a few lesbians and an even smaller number of Black lesbians are now themselves in decline.

Housing associations have been useful in providing accommodation for single people. These organizations were set up by a Tory government to provide cheap public housing. It is also important to point out that many have adopted and implemented equal opportunities policies which cover women, Black people, lesbians, gay men and disabled people. The overall impression is that these organizations, which are relatively new to the scene, have implemented their policies much more effectively than the local authorities. However, housing associations have been forced by legislation to keep their rents in line with market forces. Or, in other words, they are under pressure to charge higher rents, a development which may well lead to more people being made homeless.

Also, little thought has been given as to the suitability of housing association accommodation for single Black lesbians. Living in a one-bedroom flat or a bed-sitter can be a very isolating experience, and housing associations have not really addressed this problem. Furthermore, because some areas of London are more overtly homophobic than others, many are geared more specifically towards the needs of heterosexual families. A young Black lesbian may find herself living in a nice new flat, but one which is expensive and miles away from any visible community or her friends. How does all this affect the average Black lesbian? Too many have found themselves in their thirties and forties without a suitable home. They may have lived with partners who are mothers and have had to leave once the relationship has broken down. Few providers of public housing allow joint tenancies to lesbians, and on the break-up of a relationship one partner may find herself homeless. Many Black lesbians will have slept on friends' floors for months at a time. They may have lived in draughty houses that are poorly maintained and can only provide temporary relief. In the large cities it is a common sight to see people sleeping on the streets, most of these being white and male. That does not mean that Black lesbians are not homeless – it just means that we are among the hidden figures of the homeless.

Overall, the Conservative government has implemented policies which have created a drastic shortage of affordable housing in this country. While their ideology has encouraged the sale of council houses, they have refused to allow local authorities to replenish their stock by building more houses. The Conservative government has some strange and frightening ideas about the shortage of housing in this country. A few government ministers have let it slip that they do not believe there is a shortage, putting the blame rather on the breakdown of the heterosexual nuclear family and the fact that people leave the parental home before they get married. With ideas like these influencing housing policy, it is no surprise that Black lesbians see housing as their worst headache. Of course, most young lesbians and gay men do not have the option of staying at home until they are married; when coming to terms with our sexuality, marriage is inevitably not on the agenda. Whatever relationship develops in later years, many young lesbians will have to leave the parental home, or possibly be thrown out, once they have come out to their parents. Housing is therefore a special issue for young lesbians and gay men, both Black and white.

In an ideal world it would be possible for lesbians to be housed in communities of single units so that a Black lesbian would be near other Black lesbians. Here, we could give each other relief from the discrimination we all experience. More importantly, we would be able to learn from each other how to survive as a Black lesbian in a world that is made for, and by, white heterosexual men. Some houses might be adapted so that groups of Black lesbians could live communally. Sadly, all this is far from the reality. The needs of Black lesbians in relation to housing have not been sufficiently researched for any provider of housing to be able to offer the solution that is needed.

Education

A good research topic for someone to carry out in the future would be to look at the age at which an individual lesbian comes out and to see what effect it has on her educational achievements. My guess would be that the earlier a lesbian comes out the more damaging the effect will be. Coming out while still at school will almost certainly mean that a lesbian will be bullied. The sad fact is that schools are the places which are least equipped to deal with heterosexism. Section 28 has meant that lesbian and gay teachers have one more reason to fear losing their jobs. It has also meant that any discussion of sexuality in the classroom has to be closely scrutinized.

Section 28 and recent government plans are aimed at stifling such progressive developments in our schools as equal opportunities policies. These policies would have had two beneficial effects: they could have prevented the witch-hunt of a number of lesbian teachers, and have allowed some discussion of lesbian and gay issues in the classroom as part of an introduction to the diversity of society and a promotion of tolerance. If a school has an equal opportunities policy, then it is more likely to be able to provide progressive counselling services to a lesbian who does come out, instead of telling her that it is 'just a phase' and that she will grow out of it. In some cases she may even be treated as if she has a psychiatric problem. The government has also taken information on HIV and AIDS out of the compulsory part of the curriculum. The effect of this is that parents can control whether or not a child receives information which could save his or her life.

Lesbian mothers need to know that their children will not be bullied because of their mother's sexual orientation. Few lesbian mothers would feel confident about the school offering support if this happens. Also, children may need help coming to terms with their mother's sexuality and the school should be able to provide this kind of help. What is much more likely to happen is that a lesbian mother would be blamed for any problems that the child may have.

The government has tried forcing schools to publish league tables showing how well their pupils have achieved in terms of academic success. This performance indicator is meant to demonstrate how 'good' a school is. As a result, there has been a huge increase in the number of school expulsions, as children perceived as having problems are thrown out. Surveys have shown that a disproportionate number of these children are Black. Among the hidden minorities, it is probable that some of these children might have developed behavioural problems as a result of heterosexism, aimed at either their parent's sexuality or their own.

Local Management of Schools (LMS) is another recent government development. One of the aims of LMS is to get more parents involved in the running of their children's school. This idea sounds fine, but in practice it is white middle-class families which often have the time, the resources and the educational background to join the board of governors. It is likely that the needs of minority groups, such as Black people and lesbians, will be ignored. This is especially true in view of the present government's contempt for progressive teaching ideas and anti-racist education. The government is also responsible for encouraging schools to 'opt-out' of local authority control. One effect of this is that the schools no longer need to adhere to the council's policies on equal opportunities.

Diverse communities could be reflected in the educational materials that are available in schools. However, we are further away from this than we have been for years. The move towards anti-racist educational materials faces constant vilification from right-wing forces. Many teachers are now arguing that certain children's books have given Black children a negative self-image and so should not be used. Progressive educationalists have also pointed out the damaging effects caused by the traditional Eurocentric view of history, and its portrayal of Black peoples as victims.

The movement to get lesbians and gay men shown in a positive light has never really got off the ground. This was illustrated by the argument that grew up around the book, *Jenny Lives with Eric and Martin*. In 1986 Haringey Council had set up a Lesbian and Gay Unit to look at whether lesbians and gay men were getting a fair deal from the local authority. The unit started its investigations with the education service, and encouraged schools to foster positive images of lesbians and gay men. This 'Positive Images' campaign was deliberately confused with the book *Jenny Lives with Eric and Martin*. By coincidence, this book was published by the Gay Men's Press, which happens to be based in Haringey. At no time did the Haringey Lesbian and Gay Unit plan to introduce that particular book into the borough's schools. The link was made by several right-wing groups who wanted to use scare tactics to discredit the work the unit was doing on lesbian and gay issues. These right-wing groups were also the same people who attacked the Council for trying to encourage anti-racism.

Coming out at college can be a rewarding experience for many lesbians. Most universities have groups for lesbian and gay men called Gay Socs which, although dominated by white gay men, do help many lesbians to feel good about themselves. It will often be the first time in their lives that they have come into contact with more than one other lesbian. However, few Black lesbians will feel comfortable in this environment. White lesbians and gay men can be just as racist as any other group of white people. If a Black lesbian wants to be fully accepted by white lesbians and gay men, then for a good deal of time she will need to keep quiet about her race. Coming out as a Black lesbian can mean putting up with isolation: your peers may stop talking to you, sharing their notes and inviting you out to social occasions. An out Black lesbian can feel like a social outcast. This homophobia, coupled with racism, can lead to Black lesbians either leaving courses or underachieving academically.

In colleges and further education establishments, groups of Black students stick together in both informal and formal groups. A Black lesbian will only be allowed to be a part of this if she is prepared to remain quiet about her sexuality – in effect, to make herself invisible. Problems can and do arise for Black lesbians while at college, when they lack support from both Black heterosexual people and white lesbians and gay men. Black lesbians also have to deal with the combination of racism and heterosexism from college lecturers. Internal procedures which allow a student to complain about discrimination are rarely sophisticated enough to take into account the needs of a Black lesbian.

Racism in the lesbian community

Black lesbians are oppressed by the institutions that govern our lives, but we are also subjected to racism on a personal level. This racism is often hardest to deal with when it comes from other lesbians. White lesbians, regardless of whether or not they define themselves as feminists or socialists, often cling to the privileges that have been given to them because they have a white skin. This racism has been experienced by all Black lesbians. It is present everywhere, including the services which are supposed to be open to all: conferences; political gatherings; nightclubs; and in the bedroom. White lesbians have the same racist stereotypes of Black women as the rest of the white population. Women of African descent experience all the negative stereotypes and attitudes reminiscent of slavery: we are seen as 'sexual beasts', savage and more exciting because we have 'animal urges'. This all goes back to the white notion that Black people are uncivilized, less intelligent and therefore more prone to behaving like animals. Asian lesbians are seen as passive and exotic. Images left over from Colonial days depict Asian women as weak, more feminine and willing to suffer anything – the 'Madame Butterfly' stereotype.

Clubs run for and by lesbians are also riddled with racism. For example, there have been many instances where Black lesbians have been refused admission. If our white 'sisters' are gracious enough to let us in, we are often ignored, have trouble being served at the bar or have to share space with white lesbians who, through wearing racist and fascist regalia, make it plain which side of the racial debate they are on. Much of the fashionable dress which is currently worn by lesbians and gay men bears more than a striking resemblance to the uniform adopted by skinheads, who are, after all, card-carrying fascists. Such fashion – swastikas, Nazi uniforms, chains and dog collars – is particularly prevalent within the lesbian and gay SM community.

Many of the organizations that are meant to represent lesbians and gay men ignore Black issues. While this has been addressed in some quarters in recent years, it is still possible to find lesbian and gay community groups with no representatives of the Black lesbian and gay community. The most glaring example of this is the Stonewall Group. This was set up to campaign for lesbian and gay equality around the time that Section 28 was going through Parliament. They have never made any apology for the fact that they did not intend to represent the needs of Black lesbians or Black gay men. I have been told by one of their ex-workers that they believed it was Stonewall's intention to ignore the wider community.

I recently experienced racism from a white lesbian who was organizing a national conference for October 1993 under the banner, 'for all lesbians'. A woman from the Lesbian Link conference contacted me at work – Lesbian and Gay Employment Rights (LAGER) – with a request that we should facilitate a workshop on issues in the workplace. During the early part of the conversation she told me that there had not been a lesbian conference since the late 1970s. I pointed out that there had been two Black lesbian conferences, one in 1984, the other in 1989. There was silence. It was obvious that she did not think that these counted. When I told her I was Black she revised the original idea of a workshop for all lesbians and suggested that I could run one for Black women only. I then told her that I felt she was denying my expertise in the area of lesbians and employment. She replied that I had got the wrong end of the stick, that I had misunderstood her and that maybe she should write it down – the implication being that I did not have sufficient command of the English language (I was born and brought up in Britain). She also asked me if I was a lesbian – obviously the concept of being both Black and lesbian was difficult for her to grasp. When, coolly and calmly, I pointed out her racism, she refused to apologize, but made some excuse about the organizers all being volunteers. I also found out that none of the earlier suggestions I had made to another member of the conference planning group about including Black lesbians had been taken on board.

This example is not meant to single out that particular conference planning group for any public admonishment. Sadly, what it does illustrate is that every time white lesbians organize a conference, we can be sure that the same scenario is being played out. Will they ever learn?

Homophobia in the Black communities

It also has to be said that Black lesbians are on the receiving end of another form of discrimination from their nearest and dearest. Black communities can be homophobic. This feature of our lives as Black lesbians is particularly damaging when we remember that these communities are made up of extended family and friends. It has to be remembered, however, that there is a racist stereotype that Black people are more homophobic than white people. This is based on the belief that Black people are less sophisticated, less civilized and more ignorant than white people, and therefore more prone to homophobia. This racist myth also lets white people off the hook because it is white society which has the power to institute its homophobia.

Religion is very important to many Black people. The teachings of most of the major religions have taken a fairly neutral stance on same-sex love. However, they have been interpreted by patriarchal society as homophobic. It also needs to be pointed out that religion has been used to deny equality to other groups of oppressed people. Disabled people have been thought of as 'evil', and of having no sexuality at all. It has been assumed that their disability was a punishment from God. Many of the world's white supremacists try to justify their beliefs by using religion and the concept of 'a natural order'. Of course, we must also not forget how many religions treat women.

Another popular misconception is that Black lesbians do not exist outside of Western culture. There are several reasons for this. Because lesbians are a minority we are often omitted from history. Also, the dominant view of history is Eurocentric: we are not told of the achievements of Black people, either men or women, but only how our countries should be grateful to white people. Several of my Black lesbian friends have tried to uncover the truth for themselves, but have been discouraged. It is up to us as Black lesbians to uncover our past. We have our work cut out for us.

Conclusion

Discrimination against Black lesbians is both complex and wide-ranging, and I acknowledge that I have only scratched the surface of the problem. There are, however, many positive aspects to being a Black lesbian. We can have sex without worrying about getting pregnant. There is a much lower incidence of sexually transmitted diseases, including AIDS. Our sexual relationships are more intimate, fulfilling and orgasmic. Our personal relationships, in general, can be free from heterosexist stereotyping, and we can live a more independent lifestyle. For me, one of the best things about being a lesbian is that I do not have to put up with men. Black lesbians can and do lead happy lives, drawing strength from the fact that we have rejected all the received heterosexist brainwashing. We can be content in the knowledge that our hearts have won.

The issues of racism in the lesbian and gay community and homophobia in the Black communities are further discussed in a pamphlet called 'Shot by Both Sides', which is due to be published by Lesbian and Gay Employment Rights in 1994. Please also read *Making Black Waves*, by Valerie Mason-John and Ann Khambatta (Scarlet Press, 1993).

Chapter ten

Behind Locked Doors

Quibilah Montsho

Some harsh facts

Black lesbians living in a white society are under constant pressure. We are faced daily with descriptions of ourselves as stupid, aggressive and insane or bad from the people who have power and influence – politicians, police, psychiatrists, etc. – simply because we are Black. We are very hard pressed to find anyone anywhere within the establishment who is willing or able to give us any positive representation. Black people grow up in an environment which subjects them to racist beliefs, attitudes and values. The treatment we receive in British society from the judicial, educational and employment services also reflects these same prejudicial standpoints. Similarly, the National Health Service, as part of the state system, has only ever been able to provide healthcare which reflects its inherent institutionalized racism. Therefore, I believe that as many as 60 per cent of Black lesbians in this country have had, or will have, some experience of the mental health system during their lifetime.

In the 1990s as much stigma exists around the issue of mental health and illness as there was one hundred years ago. Yet during this same century massive changes have taken place in the development of mental health services, changes which white professionals would describe as improvements. However, as far as the Black lesbian communities are concerned, our experiences within psychiatry are negative, because we are subjected to a system which is both racist and homophobic. As far as society's mainstream perspectives and opinions are concerned, we are culturally, economically, socially and politically invisible, and the case is obviously the same within psychiatry. Thus, it is difficult to quantify the widespread effects the system has had on us, but our own life experiences speak for themselves. This information may frighten us, but mental illness – as defined by the professionals and misrepresented by society's agents, the press and the media – is a fact in the lives of many of us. We need to recognize that it has developed into a weapon used by the state to justify our institutionalization and the labelling and treating of many of the behaviours which are readily observable throughout our communities. Having lived alongside such a varied manifestation of behavioural differences, and taken them in our stride for thousands of years, we have plenty of experiences which tell us that the way to treat someone different from ourselves is to accept them, and to provide care and support where necessary.

However, it is our survival of slavery, colonization and cultural displacement which has left many of us with a legacy of what our oppressors may call 'antisocial' behaviour. The triple oppressions of racism, sexism and homophobia may even heighten this notion of antisocial behaviour. This oppression does not stop here. If we are placed in psychiatric institutions, there are a number of reasons why our behavioural patterns may become even more exaggerated. Firstly, because we are Black we are therefore more visible. Secondly, we are culturally different to white patients, and therefore communicate and express ourselves in other ways. Finally, it may be the first time in our lives that many of us have been taken away from our Black communities and placed in a white environment. This experience alone is enough to distress all Black people placed in mental institutions.

Mental health and illness are purely subjectively defined, and in this country, what is defined as mentally ill is determined and controlled by white straight men. In relation to Black people, mental illness is a synthetic phenomenon, born out of the subjective mind of the white heterosexual male. During the latter part of this century, the immigratory patterns of Black people in Britain have provided the much sought after chance for ambitious opportunists to invent new forms of mental illness, diagnoses with prognoses (forecasts), treatments and therapies to match, all of which reinforce the racist concept that Black people are more prone to mental illness. As Black lesbians, we more often than not experience the undesirable side of the psychiatric system. These experiences range from a series of visits to the local GP for help and/or advice following difficulty in sleeping, to a home visit from the duty psychiatrist (called in because of, for example, 'strange behaviour', to forced and repeated hospitalization following a diagnosis which has a good prognosis if we submit to the system. The treatment we receive at the hands of the psychiatric profession does not address our specific and different needs and requirements.

From our viewpoint, the discomfort and pain of emotional, psychological and cultural dis-ease manifests itself in many ways. It is the howling woman, who starts up at eleven o'clock at night and continues for the next eight hours; the woman who brushes the invisible dust off her seat for ten minutes before sitting down; she who talks non-stop to herself while no one listens; the woman who cannot venture beyond her own front door; and many others like her, in whom, if we are honest, we will recognize ourselves. How many of us can say that we have never 'gone mad', taken all we can handle, wanted to kill ourselves, smash everything up, or just have a sub-machine-gun for the day? I believe there are few of us who have been lucky enough to escape such thoughts and feelings. We may not want to admit it openly, but we have all been there, and the only difference between those of us with a mental illness label and those of us without it is the experience arising from the label itself. Hence, many of us have nervous breakdowns but are fortunate enough not to come into contact with the mental health system.

What is mental health?

A worker at the Brixton Community Sanctuary in London, Alan Leader, gives the following bleak picture of the country's mental health system:

> This country does not have a mental health system, it has a mental illness system. It functions by responding to what it defines as crimes in the lives of ordinary people, who it then goes on to label as mentally ill, and more often than not, incarcerate, either literally, socially or psychologically, by a continued process of medicalization through drug dependence.

In a system which operates with the 'well-being of society' at the top of its list of priorities, it must be difficult, if at all possible, to provide a service which can fully address the needs of the people it purports to help and support. If it relies heavily upon the administration of major tranquillizers to control people, it can very easily avoid any serious examination of the social, emotional, cultural, psychological, mental and physical needs of its clients. Instead, they can quickly become prisoners, sometimes literally, in hospital or in their own homes, completely at the mercy of those who have promised a service which they clearly cannot deliver. Mental health is about just that. It is not about the absence of any diagnosable illness. It is about ensuring we receive enough of whatever we need to maintain a good standard of emotional, psychological, mental, spiritual and social health. It means having a good level of self-esteem, valuing ourselves and our opinions, and developing a sense of purpose in our lives, with goals, ideas and ways of working towards the things that mean a lot to us. It is about being free to achieve the things we are capable of, and realizing our full potential – politically, educationally, in employment, with our families, in our leisure time and in all our relationships. Furthermore, mental health is about being able to find a friend or professional to trust in the bad times when we feel ill, desperate or suicidal. Mental health is having the confidence that we will receive the caring and support we know we need.

While someone can be defined as mentally well by their community, this is of little concern to the psychiatrists and psychologists. Once a person crosses the line in the direction of mental illness, they are seen as the responsibility of the state, a potential threat to innocent people, and therefore the subject of the behaviour-controlling professionals. Theirs is the responsibility to control, by whatever means they see fit, and the law fully supports them in this. Behaviour which society deems antisocial and which they believe constitutes 'a danger to themselves or others' is essentially the cut-off point. Once such behaviour has been brought under control, often with the use of mood-altering drugs, and the subject has proved that s/he can play their life by society's rules, they may then be returned to the 'normality' of the outside world.

Harassment: victims of myths

A single mother struggling to make ends meet, to feed and clothe her child, pay for the roof over their heads, as well as finding enough cash at the end of the week to pay the bills, will be offered little or no attention by mental health workers. If she reaches a point where she feels she cannot carry on, and then forgets to feed the child, stops paying bills and does not want to speak to anyone, only then do the mental health services show an interest. Similarly, the 'powers that be' are far too quick to step in when the stress of full-time work proves too much and we need a break; or the neighbours play that same old tune at full blast at one o'clock in the morning again; or the security guard follows us once too often down the aisle at the supermarket. Showing concern when we reach our limits is really of little value. When we need it most is before we reach that 'breaking point'. Many of us resent these people who have set themselves up as professionals and experts, who invade our lives when we are at our most vulnerable, and then discard us when it suits them.

Clearly, then, it seems that little is being done to keep people well, and to provide us with the support we need to maintain our mental as well as our emotional and psychological health.

Rather than interpret petty crime, truancy and aggression as the angry symptom of racism, the state prefers to label us as Black delinquents with chips on our shoulders, uncontrollable, sick and mentally ill. Accepted opinion and working practice dictate that we treat those labelled mentally ill as disreputable, untouchable and, in some way, sub-human creatures. The mentally ill are referred to, rather than talked or listened to. They are not comforted, supported, sympathized with, or otherwise provided with the life-giving requirements afforded to people who have not been categorized as mentally ill. Many Black lesbians have been sectioned under the Mental Health Act 1983, because society has not understood our cultural habits and expression, languages and race. Like all lesbians, once we become 'patients' under the mental health system, our sexuality is perceived as abnormal or a symptom of our 'madness'.

Whether the professionals like to admit it or not, it is a fact that psychiatry is a rigid system which operates through a practice of control. It has adhered stubbornly to the myth that only the professionals know how to deal with someone who is threatening to kill himself, or everyone in his block of flats. Similarly, only they can deal with someone who is convinced that there are people on the TV who are trying to kill her, or another person who believes there is a man under the stairs who is affecting his thoughts and actions. And for most people, who have no personal experience of this system, every patient is perceived to be extremely dangerous. Some even believe they must be tiptoed around, through fear that they may just creep up at night and slit a few throats in passing. It is this myth which has fed the idea that people with a psychiatric history have some evil or violent secret past, that they are to be feared, locked up and the key thrown away. Of course, the media has played its part in bolstering such misinformation. There is no shortage of badly and inaccurately written newspaper articles, composed out of pure prejudice, which achieve nothing more than perpetuating the image of the 'mad axeman' or the 'crazed killer'. In the 1980s, during the media coverage of the Broadwater Farm riots in London, and the subsequent trials, such phrases were indeed used to describe Black people.

Psychiatrists themselves like to believe that their labelled clients are responsible for a major part of the violent crimes committed in this society, but this is simply not the case. The reality is that only a minority of people labelled as mentally ill commit such acts. I believe most violent crimes are committed by those who never have and never will come into contact with mental health professionals. Indeed, it is usually the professionals themselves who are the perpetrators of the most criminal acts. They force the patients (innocent people) into hospital, on to drugs, and into a way of life which they could never have foreseen. I believe that this behaviour must constitute one of the most socially acceptable, state-financed atrocities currently in existence. The only difference is that these acts are not called crimes. They are considered to be measures carried out in the interests of society, and are fully condoned by laws drawn up by people who have no interest in preserving the well-being of the vulnerable and the weak. A walk through the psychiatric wards of a hospital would perhaps reveal such a reality: quiet and sedate 'in-mates', who sit around looking bored or try to control the drug-induced twitching and shaking, while others play cards or darts, drink tea and wait submissively for the next round of medication.

Our triple oppressions

When a patient labelled as mentally ill is also a Black lesbian the situation worsens, because the system is set up only by and for white heterosexual people. Anyone falling outside this norm is unlikely even to find a listening ear. It is not possible to complain of racism, sexism or of homophobia in a psychiatric setting, because in psychiatry such attitudes do not exist. It has evolved, and was created, within a context incapable of recognizing these differences between people except in psychiatry's diagnostic terms. For example, homosexuality is still considered by many as a mental illness which can be cured. Significantly, it is these imbalances of power – racism and heterosexism – which can make Black lesbians ill in the first place. In the words of a consultant psychiatrist from Birmingham, Dr Sashi Sahidharan: 'Psychiatry takes every type of behaviour and gives it a label.' If this is the case, then even insignificant movements like scratching the head, noting down a TV programme and smoking two cigarettes one after the other can be interpreted as symptoms of the illness which the psychiatrist has already diagnosed. Therefore, complaining of racial harassment, homophobia or sexism may also be interpreted as displaying an aspect of paranoid psychosis suppressible by either increasing medication or prescribing additional drugs. In fact, they have even invented a mental health illness. The professionals claim it is innate for the Black community to smoke marijuana, which has led to the development of so-called West Indian Psychosis and Ex-Psychosis.

There is much to be said about the discrepancy of treatment forced upon Black as opposed to white people, and it should be noted that it is unlikely that a Black lesbian will willingly come out to a member of the psychiatric profession, for fear of further labelling, drug treatments and general victimization. This will render us even more vulnerable to harassment from the hospital staff. As far as psychiatry is concerned, lesbianism is simply a perversion, a deviation from what is normal. Being vocally or otherwise overtly positive about being a Black lesbian is only likely to be interpreted as a manifestation of that perversion.

Surviving the system

The big issue – certainly as a hospital in-patient – is simply one of survival, by whatever means possible. Far from providing a safe place for rejuvenation, it has been described as a system which is capable of 'eating you alive'. Imagine the prospect of being isolated, sometimes literally, in a building from which you have no exit, in which you are followed everywhere, including the toilet and bathroom, where you have no privacy, and instead share a dormitory-style 'bedroom' with twenty other people. Imagine facing a military style line-up twice daily for a drug cocktail which you know will knock you out, muddle and confuse your thoughts, slow down your ability to walk or move at all, and induce drunken speech. Such is the prospect and life for many people who have lived within that system of terror, pain and humiliation. As Black lesbians we do not cope well within this system. It is entrenched with white values and cultural habits, and for many Black lesbians, British food and the British cultural routine are enough to make them crawl inside themselves, which can, in turn, trigger off what is defined as 'odd or antisocial behaviour'.

Not only are we faced with a system bolstered by laws which are motivated by protecting the freedom of others at the cost of removing our freedom, we are struggling with professionals who are themselves corrupt. They say that the majority of in-patients are in hospital on a voluntary basis; this claim is not as clear as it may seem. We are tricked into agreeing to go into hospital, wrongly believing that this will in some way save us. The doctor simply says, 'if you don't come in voluntarily, I'll put you on a section, and I'll make you stay'. It has been done, so we should never assume that they possess any integrity. In reality, the Mental Health Act can detain a person for anything from four weeks to life. A psychiatrist often has the final say about the length of stay, and with the subjectivity which operates around mental health, how can we possibly trust a straight white man to treat a Black lesbian with any degree of respect, let alone justice.

As Black lesbians we are all too aware that simply to exist in this country, or any other place which is not our country of origin, requires a great deal of strength, commitment and perception. In the psychiatric system the case is no different. Indeed, it is that much more acute, because the state has the right to take away our liberty, our children, our homes, our innocence and, for the most unfortunate, our lives. Without any law which can protect us inside we can easily die, and no one will be there to witness the account. Make no mistake, our lives are on the line when we come into contact with the mental health system. When we experience dealings with heavy tranquillizers and mood-altering drugs (the effects of which can never be properly predicted), it raises the question, how do we manage to survive at all? How can we function in a system where to be other than heterosexual and white, with the values and expectations of that group, means that you are devalued, negatively categorized, and treated for the rest of our lives as a label rather than a person. I believe that in such an environment it is clearly very dangerous to make any declarations about our sexuality, if they can be avoided.

However, Black lesbians have no choice about declaring our Black identities. Our identities are always visible, by how we look, dress, speak, act and eat. If we make accusations of racism we are labelled as the aggressive troublemaker on the hospital wing. When Black lesbians are forced into corners by the racist behaviour of other patients, we are all too often ignored by hospital staff. Many of us have had to resort to our own brand of justice. In the violent situations which can result, four hefty 'nurses' piling on top of us, threatening to call the police, it is usually we who are charged with assault, while the racist patient walks free. Rarely is there any acknowledgement of what caused the Black lesbian to become verbally abusive or physically violent. Instead, she is locked up in solitary confinement and labelled as dangerous. With this constant threat of racist abuse from both patients and staff alike, it seems there is no place for us within the established psychiatric services.

If you are white you may be offered psychotherapy, but if you are Black you will probably be given major tranquillizers. If you are white and (assumed to be) straight you may be offered occupational therapy; but if you are Black, and the records expose you as a lesbian, you will probably face solitary confinement if you don't conform, or for any dispute, argument or refusal to eat hospital food and take medication. Patients who display an independent, thinking mind are often confined in solitary away from the rest of the patients. In fact, if the staff take a dislike to you for any or no reason, the consequences can be the same. Racism coupled with homophobia can play a large part in explaining why members of staff dislike Black lesbians, or find us difficult to cope with.

Black lesbians have faced, and do face, some of the most horrific experiences at the hands of the professionals in the name of mental healthcare. It is not unusual to find ourselves in the office of a psychiatrist, after a visit to our doctor, social worker or the local police station to report a crime committed against us. In the same way that the criminal justice system acts to incarcerate or frame us, so it is with the mental health system. It is all too easy and advantageous for the power-holders in this society to voluntarily commit our minds and bodies to the hands of the psychiatric services. For example, if we take broken or otherwise faulty goods back to the shop, the shopkeeper all too quickly assumes that we are trying to steal from him: as far as they are concerned, all Black people are thieves. In no time at all we are in the police cells, screaming and protesting against the injustice of being wrongly and coercively held in custody. The same basic assumptions are made if we approach professionals for assistance or advice about childcare, benefit difficulties or any of the other problems that we face every day.

It needs to be acknowledged that such irrational actions on the part of the power-holders is not an unusual occurrence, as our experiences regularly testify. How we find ourselves in such situations depends largely upon the way in which we are viewed by the people in power: white people in authoritative professions. Without a doubt, the list of racist misconceptions is extensive: aggressive, stupid and particularly prone to mental illness, we are also usually unemployed and 'scrounging off the state'; often we are single mothers, incapable of acting responsibly or taking care of ourselves and others; certainly we are hostile to people in positions of authority, and are usually either drug- or gun-addicted, often both. This is a heavy millstone to lay around our necks, but lay it they do, and unless we happen miraculously to fit their fictitious and stereotypical criteria of what a Black woman is like, they will provoke, interrogate and subjugate us until we do. With their self-fulfilling prophecy firmly in place, they can then proceed to treat us in the way they assume all Black people should be treated: with contempt, lack of sympathy or understanding, and maximum (and sometimes life-threatening) drug doses. It is clearly a no-win situation, in which we can often feel forced to succumb to their preconceived ideas.

Recognizing our needs

Many of us grow up speaking languages other than English. This is seen to be a problem when we come into contact with a system which is geared to deal only with English-speaking people. Rather than acting as a spur to improve services, this is actually used as an excuse to assume that the person who does not understand or speak English well is not only mentally ill but stupid too. The professionals use it as an excuse to add the label, 'uncommunicative', which in turn becomes another symptom of the illness they have already diagnosed. In this context, it is impossible to find help or support at any level which is truly useful. Indeed, in this setting, the mental health experience becomes an even more isolating nightmare. A listening and understanding ear, together with the motivation to carry on, is the most important service we can offer someone who is defined as mentally ill. If there is no one willing to look after us at home during our time of emotional crisis, state-financed mental healthcare is all that most of us will ever have access to. The NHS claims that it would cost too much to employ interpreters, and that it is unrealistic to provide the food we are accustomed to eating. They also argue that if we are given special treatment, everyone else will want it. Certain questions need to be asked: When will NHS attitudes change for the better? What real chance is there of positive changes happening? How long do we have to wait for these changes? The refusal even to consider the importance of providing a quiet and private space to pursue our religious practices; failure to acknowledge the necessity for us to be free from ridicule when we wear our own African and Asian clothes; and a lack of respect for our wishes about spending time with our families and whether they should be informed of our whereabouts, represent just a few of the issues which need addressing.

As Black people, our cultural expression could and does help us to deal with the constant battles facing us because of racism and anti-lesbianism. Such a vital means of creativity and activity should not be denied us simply because we find ourselves in hospital. There is overwhelming evidence of links between creativity and mental health, but rather than explore this area the psychiatric system attempts to quash all traces of our inherent abilities. Such a denial must contribute to the difficulties we are already experiencing within the mental health system. The way the Mental Health Acts work, the psychiatrist and other doctors can, and literally do, force us to take drugs, despite the often incapacitating side-effects. This is given greater value than any other element of the 'care plan'. No real weight is afforded to activities such as poetry, painting, music or discussion – all crucial aspects of our expressive cultures. However, once physically and mentally incapacitated, we are unable to enjoy activities which may help us experience and deal with our feelings positively. This goes some way towards demonstrating the misuse of an authority wrongly given.

Even under conditions where the use of drugs is employed instead of a more appropriate treatment, the very least that the professionals could do would be to inform us fully of all the usual and possible side-effects. They could also give us a choice as to whether we take them or not. Furthermore, such a choice should be placed beside those alternative therapies involving creativity and self-expression. However, psychiatry being the system of repression that it is will never accept that, so it is up to us to look for other alternatives.

Some alternatives

The alternatives we choose will depend upon our particular situation. Some of us are fortunate enough to have family and/or friends who are willing to look after us in times of crisis, who are able to offer intensive and constant support when needed. However, as Black lesbians some of us will have chosen to live openly with our sexuality, which may be unacceptable to our families and friends. In such a situation, we will not have the luxury of choice when it comes to mental healthcare. Those of us lucky enough to benefit from the intensive support of family or friends can often avoid unnecessary hospital admissions. Our unpaid 24-hour carers' support and commitment network in the Black lesbian community should not go unmentioned. Indeed, in the future Black lesbians may well have little or no choice when it comes to looking after our relatives/friends who carry the mental illness label. As a matter of course, our unpaid carers are usually better equipped to visit daily, to ensure that the person is eating, resting and not becoming completely isolated. However, they may not always want, or be able, to offer the level or type of support that is needed. In any case, the NHS should still be available to provide a sensitive and caring service which is non-judgemental, non-invasive, non-coercive, anti-racist and non-homophobic.

However, a patient's recovery can be dependent on the varying levels of support she receives from friends, family and lovers. Maintaining contact with patients is of invaluable help. The facts show that those who receive regular visits are more likely to 'escape' from the hospital in the long run. If a woman is heavily sedated or severely distressed and upset, she may say anything. Therefore, it is important that people close to a patient offer support by attending the case conferences which are held by members of the psychiatric professions. However, be prepared for the struggle it may entail to obtain the right to be present at such meetings. Making allies and friends while in hospital, and maintaining those relationships after discharge, is another way in which

Black lesbians can cope with the experience. Of course, staff are hostile to the forging of such friendships, which they see as leading to troublesome or uncooperative patients.

The importance, therefore, of incorporating alternative measures during our confinement in the oppressive psychiatric system cannot be overemphasized. The reality is that once we are forced on to heavy drugs, we can become both physically and emotionally addicted to them for the rest of our lives. For some of us the addiction can be preferable to the idea of coming off the drugs. Very often it seems that we are trapped in a no-win situation. As Black lesbians we are indicted for being ignorant and stupid if we do not know what our rights are in hospital, but troublesome and a threat if we try to exercise them properly.

It is unarguable and a gross indictment that for Black lesbians the psychiatric system has little, if anything, to offer. When we look for alternatives, it can be difficult to distinguish between what is and is not helpful. For most of us the pressure to carry on with the pretence that we are managing just fine is too great to even consider taking time out. One method of temporary consolation we may resort to is drugs. Be it legal or illegal, drugs, both hard and soft, prescribed or not, provide a lease of life for many of us. Eating disorders, alcohol abuse and self-sabotage behaviour are just a few of the methods employed by Black lesbians to deaden their inner pain. The hard fact is that although the initial boosting effect of these coping mechanisms may be welcome, usually the longer-term difficulties they create only increase the burden that we are forced to carry. Having said that, at least the drugs we actively choose to take – the illegal drugs – provide us with some relief for short periods. In the case of the drugs we are prescribed by the psychiatric profession to control what has been labelled as 'undesirable' behaviour, the negative effects are so extensive that they often outweigh any 'good' the drug may be doing. Despite this, the professionals still tell us that we do not know how to choose what is best for ourselves. We can hold jobs down, look after families, participate in all types of social and leisure activities while taking heroin, cocaine and marijuana, but on Largactil or Clomipramine it can take all day simply to get out of bed. We are better to be trusted to make these choices for ourselves. However, taking illegal drugs like marijuana, cocaine, heroin, speed, crack and ecstasy, or using food and alcohol to survive this cruel world, may prevent us from being sectioned under the Mental Health Act, but they do not facilitate our recovery from the abuses we have had forced upon us. Hence, it is not enough for us to just survive, we need to begin to recover and live.

Outside the walls and boundaries of the mental health system there is available an almost limitless array of alternative therapies. Homeopathy (one of the oldest and most effective forms of treatment), hypnotherapy, relaxation, reflexology, massage, meditation and the simple but effective person-centred counselling have all helped Black lesbians avoid the mental health system. However, they are expensive forms of treatment, and therefore are not readily available to most of us. The following quotes are from lesbians of African and Asian descent who have had first-hand experience of the mental health system, and of some who have tried alternative therapies:

> I had breakdowns for ten years, but since I started homeopathy, I haven't had any.

> I have been admitted to hospital five times, but since I found a reliable counsellor who was prepared to listen to me, and to forget about judging me, I've learnt to stop even thinking of psychiatry as an option.

> For so long, I felt as if I just couldn't relax. My body was like a cold, hard object, but with the help of my counsellor, and the use of hypnotherapy, I've finally managed to learn how to let go, and have been able to think seriously about coming off medication permanently.

> With the help and support of my counsellor, who visited me at home when I couldn't get out, and a friend who visited me every day and co-ordinated a 24-hour care plan, I avoided going into hospital, and found a way out of the 'merry-go-round' of psychiatry.

The results and experiences speak for themselves; the real alternatives are found outside psychiatry, as many of us already know. The most inhibitive factor, of course, is that we are usually forced to turn towards private practitioners to find these other choices. However, all is not lost, because a number of women have been able to find, after years of searching, ways of turning the existing services around for their own benefit. By exploring Well Woman centres, Rape Crisis centres and setting up self-help groups, more and more Black lesbians are finding ways to get the help and non-judgemental support which it now seems is beyond even the sights of the 'conventional' treatments available. However, what is also important to stress is that despite the fact that these alternative treatments include informal means of care and support – from family, friends and agencies such as Rape Crisis centres – which can provide non-judgemental counselling free of charge (in the few instances where they have managed to employ Black lesbian counsellors), this in no way absolves the state and the NHS of their responsibility to care for us. At best, this informal model of care could act as a blueprint for the future planning of care by and for Black lesbians. It is never safe to assume that Mum will look after us, or that our partner will 'sort something out', because this is unfair to them and to ourselves. The crucial point here is that we can and do take responsibility for ourselves in a society which fails to care even for its own. What we now need is sufficient spending power from the state to enable us to develop the services, which we already know how to employ and tailor, to meet all our needs.

As Black lesbians, even our existence has yet to be fully acknowledged by the white male world of psychiatry, let alone the fact that we are extremely dissatisfied with the treatment we experience. In the meantime we are continually faced with compulsory hospital admissions, invasive drug 'therapy' and a lifelong sentence of labelling. We are still fighting the same battles that our mothers and grandmothers fought, but have never been clearer about what it is we want: treatment with the respect, compassion and the care that we deserve. We have grown up in a space where we are all too familiar with doing things for ourselves. When this becomes a very difficult task, we need and deserve a gentle hand to support us. The 'Big Brother' approach has never and will never wash with us. So we are left, as usual, with the lot of putting pressure on the state, directly and indirectly, formally and informally, to listen to what we have to say about our own experiences. Until the power-holders face up to their responsibility, we will be here to pressure and argue with them, to do whatever it takes to ensure that we get the services we want and need. What is clear is that most Black lesbians have a lot to heal from, and the mental health system is most definitely not the only answer.

Chapter eleven

Healing through My Own Eyes

Ulanah

Setting the context

I am a Black woman of African descent who was born in Jamaica. I have lived in England for twenty-seven years, some of which was spent going to school in Manchester where I lived with my family. I am a mother of a two-year-old son. I moved from Manchester in the late 1970s to study for my first degree in Psychology, and have lived in London ever since. I now work as a healing artist, after being trained as an educational psychologist, rebirther and Psychology lecturer. Soon after moving to London, I became involved in the women's movement of the late 1970s and early 1980s, and joined the Brixton Black Women's Group (BBWG). It was here that I developed my consciousness as a Black woman. I learnt the importance of working together as Black women when I became involved with the Organization of Women of African and Asian Descent (OWAAD), which was initiated by some of the women involved with BBWG.

During my involvement in the Black women's movement during the 1970s and, to some extent, with the political movement and mobilization of all Black people around the repressive and racist strategies of the state, I soon became aware that many women living in the West were beginning to go through a spiritual awakening. We were becoming pioneers of change. As Black women we were also beginning to perceive ourselves as powerful sources, and rediscovering our spiritual ability to be creative in our own lives and in the world. We were aware that we could make choices.

It was within the women's movement that I discovered the diversity of choices available to women in defining our sexuality. I was confronted with lesbianism and recognized that a preference for a woman's way is part of who I am. I have never been happy about labels, and still feel the same way today. I am an open, developing human being who values all the choices we make in living our lives. I have no need of labels for my sexuality, and seek to join with others on my journey rather than to judge and separate.

I remember having homophobic feelings before joining the women's movement and I also remember, later, feeling that every woman should be a lesbian or relate to women. Both these positions are equally righteous and judgemental. I don't relate to either of these opinions any more. Many of us are choosing to include men in our lives, and to embrace male qualities that are positive. Some of us don't have much of a choice, as we have been presented with the challenge of raising male sons. For those who choose to renew their relationships with men and have sexual partnerships with them, I say that this choice is as valuable as any other. However, I believe lesbian relationships are more of a sanctuary – offering peace and tranquillity, togetherness and support – than any other form of sexual relationship. Trusting, being vulnerable and open, accepting and compassionate is not an easy task when our early learning has taught us that relationships are not safe places. Relationships of all kinds can be hard, abusive and extremely painful. Our healing and wholeness lie in the recognition of what we share as human beings.

This account of spiritual awareness is the product of approximately ten years of conscious commitment to my own spiritual development. It has come at a time in my life when I have gained a clearer view of what healing really means for me. My spiritual journey in my adult life has taken me through the practices of Buddhism, meditation, yoga, spiritual retreats, Rosicrucianism (an esoteric movement of spiritual renewal), African/Asian spirituality and related workshops. It is also the product of seven years of group and individual therapy with women, most of whom were lesbian-identified. Most of all, this chapter is about the hills and valleys in my life, and the dependency and yearning for approval, the loneliness, the sense of abandonment and the fear of living.

My healing journey began at the foot of the most honourable and aged neeseberry tree in the Caribbean island of Jamaica. Great, silent, ancient spirit rising eloquently into a blue blemishless sky, forming an umbrella from the sun and a playground for lizards, humming birds, piniwalli and insects of all kinds. The tree's sturdy limbs reached out, sure-footed and wise. From here I could drink, until I was giddy, the eddy mixture of panic, life energy – the energy of the animal and plant life around me, and the energy of my things unforeseen. Each week, it seemed women in white with coloured head-dresses hinting of Africa would pass by, single-mindedly heading for the balmyard, the healing ground. Here, spirit and soul would be transformed through songs, words of power, dance, trance and prayer. Futures would be read through divination, and baths of herbs, kananga water, Florida water, salts from the sea and mineral baths would, with rituals, reawaken the inner fire. I would run to the gate so that I could see these awesome women close to. Their purpose was one with the divine. Their heads were held high, with eyes that could turn you to stone. In the small village of Leith Hall, St Thomas, people looked upon these women with deference and great respect. All understood that there was more to life than could be seen. Spirit was alive in St Thomas, and no one questioned it.

When the full moon shone it was midnight, blue with a haze of white. It seemed to spray everything with a clear-as-crystal glowing light. When it played with the strings of my heart's harp, I knew that there was something special in the waking and waning of the moon. My passion for spirit began to rise. Occasionally, at night the Kumina drums would ring out, and we would dance our ancestors' dance of possession until it was light. Conversing with our ancestors, dancing with giddy movements and rolled-back eyes. People said the ancestors were meant to mount their loved ones, relaying messages from the world beyond the grave. Nobody questioned, when a cup was thrown on the dung heap among a rubbish tip at the back of the yard, everyone was forbidden to touch it. No one did, even the children knew they might be struck dumb, or stricken with an unknown illness, which could cause their death. Spirits had handled this forsaken cup, and now it was plagued.

My visit to Jamaica triggered off a whole set of memories, which would soon fundamentally change my life.

Remembering Who I Was

Remembering

Self, catapulted out of body, I went wandering and was lost. In space, in time, dismembered pieces of who I was went roving. And I was left behind to wonder where I went, and who I am. To die a death.

Hollow drum, empty vessel and lifeless carcass – my soul had taken flight. And I was out to lunch – glazed eyes. Members of myself fragmented, cast asunder, to worlds beyond the seen. Where I wandered in limbo, until it was safe for my return. A nation's dismembered body parts were cast into sea. Strewn over a million different places. Until her beloved did gather them. So she could be RE-MEMBERED. And so will I find wholeness, through RE-MEMBERING who I am. The pieces of my selves, my soul – being separated from its temple.[1]

Remembering who I am

I have always felt like a kind of emotional bottomless pit with an insatiable need for love and recognition, and when I decided to accept and acknowledge the facts of my personal history, I could see why this was. Aged two years I, along with my siblings, went to live with my grandparents in a house with two rooms. The reasons why we had to live with our grandparents were unclear, but I suspect they were related to lack of money. However, it is interesting to note that my parents also experienced early childhood separation from their parents. After this one year away from my parents, my father left for Britain to prepare the way for our education in the universities of England. My mother took us back after one year, and two years later we joined our father in England. When I look at my two-year-old son today, I often remember what my early childhood separation meant to me. My son's vulnerability, and his adoration of me, triggers off painful memories. Before I accepted these painful personal facts, my fear of rejection and abandonment was not completely rational or comprehensible to me.

I never knew my parents, and still yearn for their embrace. I spent all of my adult years looking for recognition through love, relationships and primarily through career and educational achievements. I was an emotionally dependent and needy individual who found it almost impossible to function outside of a symbiotic relationship.

I don't remember the exact moment in 1990 when I seemed to lose myself, to separate from who I knew myself to be. I don't remember the actual moment of disconnection or the specific event, although I do know it had something to do with the collapse of my business. My business seemed to slip away slowly into a deep, dark well, a well so deep that I could no longer see the light above, inside or around me. Interestingly, this all apparently began after I had made a major spiritual manifestation through creative visualization and psychic attunement. I had managed to attract all the way from California a spiritual companion who shared my approach to healing, and who also dreamt of a centre of healing for all Black women. She was like a waking dream: beautiful, dynamic, powerful and an incredible healer. During my period of dis-memberment – a time which was also potentially joyous – I felt completely alone and lost. Who had I become? My head weighed heavy with concerns, primarily financial. My heart thudded endlessly. My stomach was in knots. I didn't know where to find me inside myself, let alone any spark of the divine. There was absolutely no light. It was as if I was in the middle of one of the tightly wound knots in my stomach – I was a tightly wound knot. The way to unravel myself was a mystery to me. I could not scream out aloud for help. I had lost my power to undo myself, a power which had belonged to me for so long.

I shook with fear and trepidation, I, a proud peacock, was now only able to lie down and take what seemed like punishment for my colossal ego, my lack of judgement and business acumen. I couldn't remember ever feeling like this, although I know the memory for pain is sometimes extremely short. However, it seemed to be the worst hell I had ever lived through. Worse than being left in Jamaica without my parents. Worse than the shocking cold weather of Manchester when I first arrived in England. Worse than my realization that I could never find satisfaction in a relationship with a man, and also worse than the realization that I would not find the fulfilment and cosiness I dreamt of with a woman. I seemed to lose touch with my faith in myself, my Godself and my Spirit within. I didn't read, meditate, write or do anything which was life-enhancing. It was as if I was just waiting for death. I felt I had no right to life.

These feelings came to a head during the height of my career as a rebirther, counsellor and consultant trainer at the beginning of the 1990s recession. It was small comfort that millions of others were experiencing their own personal deaths and crises with me. So I dived when the economy took a dive, submerging myself in despair, lack of self-belief and self-pity. When my business disappeared in front of my eyes, the bottom seemed to have dropped out of my world. I bled with disappointment and shame at my inability to care for my lover, who had sacrificed a well-paid job and a Ph.D, and had left friends and family in California to join me in England. Because of my financial crisis I was unable to give her the security she needed to settle into living in London. She came straight into poverty and financial struggle. The pain caused between us was intense: sadness and anger were the weapons ranged against us. I had failed. I wasn't good enough. I wasn't worthy of success. I couldn't handle it.

These decaying thoughts pulled me further down to the bottomless pit. They made my face vacant, my eyes dull and my body language very heavy. I chose to forget that I was heavy with a child inside me throughout this painful time. My lover told me I was beautiful, but I still felt like shit. I felt guilty for selfishly deciding to be a parent at the same time as we came together as lovers. My ego had told me I could handle it. It was as if my swelling stomach was a testament to my failure, and my lack of judgement.

Throughout this time my place of refuge always beckoned me, but I did not always answer the call. When I heeded it, I could be still and simply feel my breath. The tightness of my chest. The air struggling though my nasal passages. I was afraid of life itself. The breath of life was to me like a poison that I was forced to drink daily. I pulled in just as much as I needed to stay alive. Breathing shallow and narrow. Limiting myself. Breath was indeed God. Without it we die slowly. Without this breath I was separate from God, from life, from Spirit, and myself. Sometimes I wanted to heal myself to prove that I could do it alone, although I knew in my head that this was ridiculous. But the urge to say 'Fuck 'em all, I need no one,' was irresistible, because of the legacy of my childhood and the pain of having waited all my life for the love of my parents. I had lost the belief in the possibility that someone else could care for me. This belief was so deep that most of the time I was not in touch with it.

When a workshop leader on a personal development course suggested that I had needs and needed people, I was flabbergasted, insulted and confused. How could that be? I had survived for a long time, it seemed, without people to take care of my needs, and hadn't died. To me a need was something one had to have to stay alive. I was still alive and therefore had survived without them. My angry, neglected child within believed that I only needed water and food to survive. Intellectually, I knew that one could die physically and emotionally without love and emotional nurturing, but that truth was too painful for me to deal with . The workshop leader, whose skills I had been admiring throughout the day, now seemed to have it all wrong. In my vulnerable state I could not hear the truth (it was only years later while in therapy that this truth liberated me). I sank into denial to protect myself, living a lie. I took refuge in some other distraction to take me away from the facts that I have needs worthy of attention, and that my quality of life depended on the satisfaction of such needs. When my therapist also suggested that I needed people, my suppressed anger emerged: I wanted to decapitate her there and then. Eventually, however, we worked through my years of self-denial and fears together. Gradually I began to feel pride in my ability to rise out of this difficult situation.

Black lesbians in crisis

Imagine an erupting volcano, a gigantic earthquake, with repeated explosions coughing up rocks and belching hot liquid, shooting intense colours like a canon, a frying heat, scorching its own insides with lava. Imagine being no longer willing to be invisible, to sit silently, content with all the lies you have been told in the past, the lies which have denied you the power and the ability to transform your own life. And then imagine the volcanic eruption exploding inside, creating chaos with your emotions, and the suppressed power unleashing itself like a thick heavy current, slow and treacle like, taking its time to be acknowledged. It is the awakening to revitalized energy, the dying of the old and rebirth of the new amidst the destruction of an old security. The raging furious heat of the volcano and earthquake prepares the way for reconstruction. Destruction precedes creation. The eruption is the divine, universal fire burning through old structures and eradicating them, transmitting their energies to a higher vibrational level. The burning and incinerating cleanses, throwing up creative, productive energy.

This is the Black lesbian in her healing crisis, in her state of pain and disintegration. It is her joblessness, homelessness, bereavement, sexual and physical abuse, isolation and lost love. These devastating and world-shattering experiences can make us undergo a state of decay and death. Black lesbians might even wish for physical death, or turn to coping mechanisms like drink, drugs, food and self-destructive relationships to dull the pain. The urge to heal, for many of us, can be a phenomenal and overwhelming fear of the truth. Although it may hurt to let go and begin healing, the promise of peace beneath the pain is inviting. Black lesbians who made the choice to heal are healing their world. We are choosing to heal from sexual abuse, male violence, racist abuse, homophobic attacks, addictions, childhood neglect and all other forms of powerlessness and victimology. It is no surprise that there has been a growth in the number of Black lesbians who choose to heal and develop their spirituality through Buddhism, and various other religions like Islam, Yoruba, Sankara and Christianity. Many of us are seeking out spiritual altars and committing ourselves to spiritual practice. We are remembering our creativity, re-evaluating our physical and mental diets, and committing ourselves to self-support and healing. Most importantly, many of us are exploring the notion of the Goddess who is internal to us, and exploring our divine nature.

Spirituality

Spirituality means of the spirit. It is an awareness of the unity of all creation and an understanding of our place in the cosmos, acknowledging our connection to all living things, to nature and the universe – an integral part of a dynamic whole. This understanding offers a sense of completeness – of being connected to a wealth of power beyond our physical and intellectual body.

My life and work is an acknowledgement of Spirit. Spirit is the life-force of every living element, the essence beneath the skeletal frame and the bodily tissue. Spirit is the divine, creative Goddess – energy. It cannot be destroyed, neither does it die. Spirit exists on the various levels of nature: fire, water, earth and air. It is also present in animals and through the life energy of our ancestors who no longer live in the flesh. All these forces are of a divine nature, and can be used in spiritual development and healing by acknowledging their presence within and around us.

I believe:

- We are all divine beings with a higher self vibrating to positive forces of good.

- We have within us all we need, and all we need to know.

- All our pain is based on a sense of being un-integrated and separate from ourselves and who we really are.

- Healing is becoming whole and reconnecting to our inner power, our divinity.

- Healing is about joining our heads and hearts, and about joining with and forgiving others.
- There is no real and profound healing without a connection to Spirit, and the embracing of it.

Spirituality is using our inner beings, our internal universe to assist us in negotiating our way through life. To live a spiritual life means being open to guidance by Spirit, to align our physical body with our Spirit. Living a life guided by Spirit requires the stilling of the conscious mind, and a surrender and suppression of the ego. It means focusing on the divine energy within and around the motivating force of life. Spirituality is about evoking the Goddess within each individual, through the tool of meditation and spiritual attunement. Therefore, the Goddess is expressed in every living human being. Becoming wholly integrated is a life-long process, but with commitment it is a certainty. Spirituality is not a religion, it doesn't involve the worship of an external creator separate from the human being. It is not moralistic or judgemental, blaming or punitive. It does not constitute a set of rules and regulations about how we should live our lives.

Commitment to a spiritual path promotes an increasing humility – an acceptance that we suffer and are in need of healing. In the spiritual path we are all teachers and students at the same time. We recognize our power to transform, and we acknowledge our need to learn and be healed. We become willing to open ourselves up and to be known by others. We begin to understand that we are more than just our physical body, more than our mind and our personality, feelings, emotions and pain. We are all divine beings with a higher self vibrating to positive forces of good.

I also believe that illness, disease, imbalance and discomfort show that we have forgotten who we are. This is the shamanic notion of healing. Forgetting who we are creates thoughts and actions that lead to an unhealthy lifestyle, where we search for fulfilment outside ourselves through addictions to substances, drugs and material possessions. This path eventually leads to illness and dis-ease. It is a universal signal that we are imbalanced and unintegrated. What follows is the volcanic explosion. We decide enough is enough, although sometimes our external circumstances decide this for us. Our world turns upside-down, crumbles and disintegrates. Our frame of reference shifts. Unaware of who we are or where we are, we lose our identity.

An altar: a place for healing and spiritual attunement

My altar is often alight with candles whose colours vary according to my spiritual needs. The colours ring out their vibrating sounds at a pitch and rate which creates the peace, courage and confidence I need. In my state of immobility, paralysis, helplessness and powerlessness, when every move I made seemed to culminate in a dead-end street, and obstacles seemed to come from nowhere, the fighting fire energy of Shango (a Yoruba life-force) was epitomized in a red candle. Its flame poured into me a slow, increasing sense of power, and helped to clear the obstacles from my path. When I didn't have one cent to my name, bills couldn't be paid and the wolves crept stealthily to my front door, I beckoned the energy of Oshun, the Yoruba goddess of fertility and abundance, through the yellow rays emanating from a yellow candle and its flame. An iridescent candle burnt throughout the gloom of my grey years. At least one candle was kept alight, but often there were many. They represented the flame of my life energy. The light without reflecting the light within, ringing out a reverberating Yes! to life. The light speaking of my right to be alive, to be visible. Often I would see a lonely flame within a deep, dark abyss, like a rescue flare in the midst of a vast expansive sea.

Like each candle, I possess a body. The wax – my flesh and temple walls – destined to crumble and dissolve, returning to the earth. The flame is the light of my soul, my spiritual essence. My inner Godself. My higher self above the candles' fire, detached from earthly cares and fears, safe from the forces of death, destruction and separation. My higher self resonates with higher principles: love, compassion, peace, acceptance, abundance, health, harmony. And so in the candles I burn, amid the flame, I find an inspiration reflecting my glowing, alive and radiant self. This healing light continues to guide me out of my darkness, drawing me closer to myself, to my centre. The candles' energy burns slowly through the way, symbolic of the death of my ego.

This infinite, indestructible light is a promise of hope, of change and transformation. Healing takes place at my altar, it is the place where I can still myself. Eyes closed or open, but attuned to the light. It is my sanctuary, my place of refuge and my temple, where rituals of reverence, thanksgiving, blessings and prayers are offered. Upon my altar there are always flowers, a single one or a bunch, representing the abundance of the universe. Like my self, they grow if nurtured by light. The flowers and their powerful healing are always pleasing to me. They calm me, uplift my Spirit, inspire and renew me. They till the soil of my mind, making way for new seeds to be planted. The flowers honour me, my Godself, my creator, and give thanks for life. They represent the impermanence of life: we all grow, evolve, decompose and become one with the earth.

The ritual of thanksgiving is also a tool of healing for me. Sweet fragrances of incense made from flowers, herbs, or bark burn on my altar. Frankincense, myrrh and sandalwood raise my mind out of darkness, thrilling, pleasing and awakening my soul and spiritual essence. The scents relax, calm and soothe me, turning my attention inward. The vapours hoist me along their spiralling trail to the clouds, where I can tarry for a while and hear what I need to do. The upward spiralling movement is meditative in itself. I place a bowl of clear water at my altar, which offering draws the negative energies out of me, transmuting vibrations and raising them to a higher level. The energy of the water lifts and carries me out of my gloom. Whenever depression overwhelms me I sleep with a bowl of water beside by bed. Clear and unadulterated water is the life-giver and source of all life. Water with herbs and salts bathe me in a purifying ritual of blessings and healing.

Sounds for healing

The human voice is one of the finest tools we have for healing the body and spirit. It helps to reawaken the spontaneous and creative child within. In toning the word 'om' (pronounced 'aum' – the sound embodying spiritual power in Indian religion), a subtle, inner sound can sometimes be heard during meditation or in other states of higher consciousness. It has been known to move women into an alpha state – a state of bliss, where fleeting movements of integration are experienced. Through the use of chants and sounds, we can move into a place where we are undisturbed by the stress of modern life, a place where we can replenish our energies.

Chanting: Nam myoho renge kyo

'Myoho' is the power of revitalization, the emergence of the higher state of life – the Buddha state within us. 'Renge' is the cause and effect of the emergence of our Buddha nature, in terms of benefit, happiness and fulfilment. 'Kyo' is the thread or link of life, connecting everything through sound and vibration and, specifically, the sound of the Buddha state which is 'Nam-myoho-renge-kyo'. 'Nam' is the act of summoning this law from within us and putting it into action in our lives and environment by chanting the Nicherin Shoshu Buddhist chant, 'Nam-myoho-renge-kyo'. This chant can rid us of our sense of grief, and send messages out for prosperity. There are many Black lesbians turning to Nicherin Buddhism, Zen and Friends of the Western Buddhist Order to help with their healing process. When I was penniless, each Wednesday for three weeks my lover and I chanted, burnt candles and incense until the remortgage came through. When it came the bank took it all, destroying our plans to shop for clothes and accessories for my newborn baby.

Words of power

The power of words vibrates and shapes the world like a virus transforming the culture it inhabits. My words make me who I am. They magnetically connect me to the circumstances and events mirroring all the words I use. My words come out of my beliefs, reinforcing those beliefs and my actions. My body assumes the shape and energy of my words, through its stance and posture. Words can maim, and create armours to protect us. My grandmother's words often surface in my mind: 'Wha sweet you wi sowa yu.' (What gives you pleasure gives you pain.) 'If yu want good yu nose have fi run.' (If you want to be successful then you must go through the pain.)

We are all victims of words – Black lesbians are victims of racist, sexist and homophobic words every day of our lives. No wonder we need to heal from such a negative assault on our self-esteem and empowerment. Damaging words remain imprinted on the mind for years, through the repetition and conditioning. If we have a belief that we are not worthy, we can often sabotage our own success. Today, I now use words of power to affirm me, light me up, enfuse me with energy, make the cells of my body tingle and my aura brighten. I have reclaimed words and learnt to use them for my good. I chant, sing, write and read words. I breathe them and speak them out aloud to my reflection in the mirror. I shout words to the trees, whisper them beneath my bed sheets and visualize them in emblazoned neon lights. The following are examples of healing words which can be used every day:

- I am perfect just as I am.
- After joy then there is much more joy. I am worthy of success.
- I have the right to be here.
- I am worthy of life.
- I am an individuation of God. I am God.

Breathing to heal

My rebirthing experiences have taught me about the power of the breath. Breathing is the life-sustaining process that brings the Spirit into balance. As we breathe, we strengthen our connection to the source of life, and the creator. Therefore, breathing must become a conscious practice in our spiritual development and healing. The more conscious we become of our breath, the more conscious we will be of our feelings and inner life. We will become conscious of the creator and receive enlightenment and guidance from the depths of our being.

Many women have stopped breathing right down into the abdomen. Sexual and physical abuse, the desire to have flat stomachs and the fear of being completely alive can affect the way we breathe. Breathing is the art of mindfulness and awareness. It is being aware of the cup you are washing in the sink, experiencing it, and not wondering what you will buy from the supermarket. It is being aware of the person who is making love to you, experiencing it, and not wondering what you will be eating for dinner or how you will cope with your exams tomorrow. Being mindful can be learnt through meditation by counting each breath up to ten as you breathe in and out, repeating this process for five or ten minutes, and then, without counting, following the flow of the breath in and out for another ten minutes, focusing on the point of the body where the breath enters. Each stage can be as long as you like. Three deep, long breaths right into the bottom of your abdomen, extending it to the full, can be a perfect tonic in any moment of stress, major trauma or catastrophe.

Healing in relationships

We do indeed need others to support us in our healing. To provide a mirror for us in our process. To be a model for loving, accepting and caring for ourselves. We need a space where love can heal us and lift us out of our despair and sense of hopelessness. At times we need a healing space with someone who can act as guide, facilitator or workshop leaders, someone whose role is to flow with love for us, regardless. It is vital for us to practice qualities which enhance our development and the growth of those we choose to be in a relationship with. We need healing attitudes and guidelines as a framework for all our relationships. In my healing relationships, my intimate relationships and my self-work, I have been guided by a number of principles, values and attitudes, some of which have produced phenomenal changes within the one-to-one therapeutic relationship, and within the context of a workshop or training experience.

Healing principles

It is important to remember that as Black women we have all been victims of racial abuse, together with the many other forms of abuse which white women experience. When Black lesbians have relationships with each other we bring a legacy of hurt which has perhaps been sitting there for years. The fact that we are relating to somebody who shares some of the most painful experiences of racism, and rejection from our Black parents because of the racism they have been subjected to, can trigger off some of our most painful memories. Therefore, our relationships with each other can become places where we perpetuate self-abuse and abuse of our partner. If we steer ourselves to confront our pain, we can begin to heal and create nourishing relationships. No matter who a Black lesbian chooses to have a relationship with, it will be potentially abusive if the process of healing is dormant. Committing ourselves to our healing can only give everyone concerned a better quality of life.

The following principles are to be used in relationship to one's self and one's personal growth, as well as in our relationships with others:

Compassion A warm glow of complete acceptance and love for self and others, where one places oneself in the other's shoes in order to empathize with their emotional experience. The listener within us is able to experience the feelings and fears of the sharer. This connecting or uniting experience heals the sense of separateness from the sharer providing strength and support through the process of healing. The key quality required here is compassion, because of the subtle detachment that the listener needs to maintain in order to remain aware of the power and the ability of the sharer to overcome and transcend the painful and limiting conditions she is living with. With detachment, the sharing of empathy is an empowering experience, as opposed to the dis-enabling quality of sympathy.

Developing compassion or *metta* (loving kindness) to oneself and others can be done through meditation practice. First, as you sit to meditate, you focus on yourself and wish yourself compassionate and loving thoughts. This can be done by remembering something enjoyable in your life. By visualizing yourself and saying, 'May I be happy. May I be well. May I be free from all suffering,' or by saying, 'I am' instead of 'May I', one can develop compassion and *metta*. In the second stage of this meditation you visualize a friend (not a sexual partner) and transfer the words and loving feelings on to them. In the third stage you visualize somebody neutral (postperson/shopkeeper/ticket collector, etc.), and try to do the same. In the fourth stage you visualize somebody you are in conflict or angry with, and try to wish them love and kindness, accompanied by the affirming words. If anger arises, neither try to encourage nor suppress it, rather stay with it and just let it pass. Eventually you will develop metta for this person. In the final stage send it out into the world, to all human beings and living things. You may find it difficult, you may even cry, but with regular practice you will begin to see a change in your life, because what you give out will become more positive, attracting more positive things into your life.

Unconditional acceptance and valuing We need not do anything or be anything to be worthy. Neither our acts nor our thoughts or intentions disqualify us from self-worth. We are valuable and unique divine beings with a purpose to fulfil. This quality allows us just to be, without straining to be what we think we should be, or to gain approval. It allows us to practise forgiveness for our destructive acts, thoughts and intentions. When we receive this quality in a healing relationship we can breathe a sigh of relief that we really don't have to perform or do anything to be of value.

We often get caught up in business and activity, in order to justify our existence. In other words, we can only allow ourselves to live if we can prove that we are doing important and worthwhile things – making a contribution. When our healing crisis immobilizes us, as was the case for me, we have an opportunity to learn to value ourselves even though we are still, insular and inactive. We learn that, regardless of what state we are in, joy, strength or despair in people is OK.

A non-judging attitude We are taught to be selective in our valuing of others. Some people are good, others are bad. We categorize, judge and place a value on people according to their sex, class, race and numerous other attributes. Our judgements are absolute and final. Once the judgement is passed and the category is made, that is it. No change. No escape. We judge ourselves in much the same way. We compare and compete. Sometimes we win, other times we lose. The stress put on ourselves to be the best, to be correct, to be right on and have the correct political line is enormous. We separate ourselves from each other with our judgements. Allowing people and ourselves the space to change facilitates change. It is a healing experience to stay in the moment, to accept people as they are right now, knowing that they can change when they so choose; to be aware, and to acknowledge that we too have idiosyncratic behaviours which need changing. Healing is humbling and connecting, it relieves the stress of always having to prove our righteousness. It joins us to others. Not judging is about believing in others' ability to be transformed. To believe in the intrinsic good of everyone.

Response-ability Like many of you reading this chapter, I have often felt like an innocent victim, helpless and powerless in the political and social system. I remember being almost perpetually angry, my clenched fist held ready to hit out at my oppressors. If only ... I would angrily think, and then I would be more fulfilled, more successful and happier. Healing is about acknowledging our power to act. It is about empowerment, the ability to respond and the ability to initiate. We have a sense of being important and instrumental in our personal world and in the universe, and we begin to feel that we can make a difference. As we begin to accept our power to create and be constructive, complaining and blaming others becomes a useless exercise. It drains away valuable energy and leaves us feeling disempowered, helpless, angry and jealous. When women in a healing crisis prepare to accept their ability to create and respond, there is terror and more anger at the fact that they can no longer absolve themselves of responsibility and action. When the acceptance of power comes, we become like oceans swelling with energy, rising with force and power.

Risking Change and growth is risky business. It involves taking new steps, trying out new strategies and experimenting. If we focus on the possibility of rejection, we limit our growth and imprison ourselves within our own fears. Restoring ourselves to a complete whole is about taking risks. Healing relationships provide a safe space and practice ground for our new choices, a place where we can try out our new behaviours.

Opening up to experience Few of us know how to exist in the present and experience the exact moment of now. We are either thinking of the past or the future. Sometimes we regress into a role we played in past relationships, playing out an old scenario. Opening up to experience the present and now means that we become more awake to life and can move through our problems without falling back into the same old patterns. Through the practice of meditation, using mindfulness by following the breath (as cited earlier), we can learn to experience the present.

Accepting detours and plateaux I often struggled with the course of healing and group work. I had a strong belief in mistakes being failures, which proved to be unproductive for my own personal growth. As long as I continued to view my healing crisis as an experience which came out of a failure, a mistake, the longer I remained stuck and dis-enabled. The longer my disgust and embarrassment with myself persisted, the stronger and more pronounced my ego became. My healing really began when I saw my crisis as a detour, a point of learning and rejuvenation. An opportunity to rest from my business. An opportunity to grow. Then I recognized that I was not in fact as special or different as I thought. Indeed, my sense of humanity was enhanced by a joining with others who had taken detours in their learning. I began to accept the troughs and peaks that are an essential part of our personal and spiritual growth. The detours burn through the ego leaving us emptied of pride and loftiness.

These principles have healed and nurtured me through the most difficult periods of my life. They are gifts that I offer to people through my work. One of the greatest gifts a person can ever receive is to be validated as a human being, and to be guided in developing skills that can empower them. Validity is not a conditional thing, we are valid regardless of our misguided actions and beliefs. In time, healing relationships can support and nurture us by the use of *metta*, compassion, forgiveness, self-acceptance, valuing, a creative responsible attitude to ourselves, risking, thinking good thoughts about ourselves, refusing to stay in the past, accepting our detours as learning opportunities and not judging. In fact, when we turn within to that still, quiet space, we find that the nurturing qualities we need are right there inside of us. It is the divine energy, the higher self, the spirit within us that possesses all the love, peace, power and healing we could ever need. Practising spiritual attunement enhances our ability to resonate with higher qualities of unity and wholeness in our daily routine. This is what spiritual argument is basically about.

The spiritual healer, whose task it is to facilitate the spiritual development of her client through her use of divine energy, acts as a channel which opens to receive and use this energy to facilitate healing. She also assists her client in the process of opening, in order to channel divine energy for use in her own healing. Healing is a work of love, where compassion supports and transforms.

Note

1. Ulanah, 'The Temple of the LIVING GODDESS'. Unpublished.

Books

Tich Nhat Hanh, *The Miracle of Breathing*. Rider, London, 1991.
Iyanla Vanzant, *Tapping the Power Within: A Path to Self-empowerment for Black Women*. Writers and Readers, 1992.
Sangharakshita, *A Guide to the Buddhist Path*. Windhorse Publications, Glasgow, 1990.

Thank you to Namonyah for her care, compassion and commitment to the truth, and for her knowledge and commitment to African/Asian spirituality. And to Valerie Mason-John for her compassion and patience with me during the writing of my first published piece, and for her knowledge of Buddhism.

Chapter twelve

Holding the Banner High: Several Days in the Life of a Black Lesbian

Tina Kendall

My friends are always threatening to write the sitcom of my life. I do have an unconventional way of thinking, acting and sorting things out, which for some reason my friends find quite hilarious, and some are most probably driven quite mad. The following account is to set the record straight, and to explain how I got to be a lesbian and where I am today. Our lives as Black lesbians need to be documented, celebrated, told and retold, so we can laugh and cry about our experiences together.

The build-up

It wasn't as if living in foreign parts was something new for me. Doing a Modern Languages degree in the 1970s had meant that I was always swanning off to places whose names I could barely pronounce. Research is what I used to call it. I was in the right place at the right time, when I landed myself a job teaching at Dijon University. At least I could get my mouth around the word Dijon, and the job turned out to be really good. The university had a white male specialist in Black literature, which was referred to as Commonwealth and African-American writing. I was fortunate enough to have conversations, even if only at a superficial level, about Black writing, which was and still is one of my passions. The words of Black writers touched me as no other writing had ever done before. Exploring the different writers, and stumbling across women like Toni Morrison (who was not well known in the 1970s), was like finding my way home. I had a secret dream stashed right away that I never mentioned to anyone: that maybe one day I could also contribute to 'home' by becoming a writer myself. However, I needed to work out how to wipe out all the negative messages that society sends to Black women. How did a young Black woman gather together enough belief in her own creativity to be determined enough to become a writer? During this time Black writing was by far my main passion. But I had other minor ones too, one of which was people.

My connections with friends of differing degrees and intensity spread from California, New York, Morocco, Southern Africa, to, inevitably, a couple of people in France and in Britain. I was living in a large and light sixteenth-century half-timbered flat in the middle of a French town, where friends rang the doorbell at all hours of the day and night. I was working hard, studying hard and keeping notebooks full of my dreams. If I had known how to muse over my scribbles, if I had dared to take myself seriously, I would have deciphered the messages about becoming a writer and opening myself up to women more speedily. I was at a time of my life when I directed most of my sexual energy to men, and had my emotional needs met by women. However, straying at times into flashes of sexual relationships with women who defined themselves as bisexual both electrified and petrified me. I used to think that love and relationships were a bit of a game. But some nights, lying beside a woman, things took on a different texture, and I could feel myself sliding into 'D and Ms' (translated as 'deep and meaningfuls'), so each time I would scurry away.

It all sounds rather flighty now. But I was also recovering from the death of my father, and from being raped a couple of weeks later by the man who broke the news to me. Somehow the death and rape had fused inside me. It had become a sticky and indistinguishable mess. I tried the odd counselling session, but it didn't seem to help. All my gallivanting, and allowing lots of people superficial access to me, no doubt sprang directly from the festering hurt which I was unable to talk about.

Gathering momentum in the 1980s

In 1982 my teaching contract ended at Dijon, and I somehow landed myself with another teaching post at the University of Philadelphia, where my closest friend, Cathy, lived. I went over for a preliminary visit, but found the omnipresent American belief that success can be measured by how much you have in the bank too much, and I withdrew. Back in France, I was unemployed, which meant that I had an additional nine months to pay my annual tax bill. The extension felt like a windfall, because I had the money already tied up in the bank. A few months later, I had acquired a working-holiday visa, a one-way ticket to Sydney and £300 in traveller's cheques. On 17 November 1982 I was knocking back complimentary drinks at Charles De Gaulle airport in Paris, waiting for the plane which was twelve hours late, and thinking of the friends I had there. Eventually, I left Paris in the freezing fog. On the plane I sat next to an Australian woman singer. We got into conversation, as you do, and I quizzed her for ideas on earning money. It was so hard to imagine life in Australia. I asked her how long she thought £300 would last me. She replied: 'Don't worry, you'll survive. Sydney's that sort of city. You never know what might come your way.'

It certainly felt rather magical when I landed. This was probably due to a mixture of jet lag, culture shock and the transformation from the depth of autumn to brilliant spring sunshine, coupled with the beautiful scent from the purple flowers of the jacaranda trees that lined the streets of Sydney. The first few hours felt so good. I was picked up at the airport and whisked back to the home of one of my former house-mates. I sensed I had made the right choice. All my trips to Germany and France had taught me how to get the most out of a place quickly. I found somewhere to live in a brilliant women's house in Chippendale, close to the city centre and Sydney's university campus. The people I already knew introduced me to their friends, so that quite quickly I had a busy social life. Australia proved to be the land of my liberation. There were lots of reasons why I went there, but it wasn't until International Women's Day (IWD) day, 8 March 1983, that I came face to face with my deeper motivation for the trip. Women's activities of all kinds were thriving in Sydney, so it was easy to acquire the contact number for the local Black women's group. Although I had attended various Black women's events in Paris and London, it was the first time I had formally belonged to a Black women's group. Tentatively, I picked up the phone and dialled:

'I'd like some information on your group,' I confessed to the woman who answered.

'Hi – are you Black?' she enquired.

'Yes ...'

'Are you a lesbian?'

Nothing like point-blank communication. 'Well, not exac...', I answered. I was hardly likely to map out my ditherings to some woman I hadn't even set eyes on.

'Oh well,' she sighed, 'at least you're not a tampax.' At this point I decided to be just as direct. 'What on earth are you talking about?' She giggled, and exclaimed: 'A tampax is what we call them – you know, the white, uptight and out-of-sight women.'

'Oh, got you,' I managed a feeble laugh and despite the conversation I still allowed myself to be coaxed along to the next meeting. It transpired to be a most significant decision.

The group was called the Rainbow Collective – a.k.a the Black Third World and Migrant Women's Group – and was a focal point for women from all over the world. Ironically, there were virtually no Koori (indigenous inhabitants of Australia originating from the New South Wales area) or indigenous women from other parts of Australia in the group. We used to meet once a fortnight, plan social events and invite each other for meals. I joined at the time when International Women's Day was looming and, because I had time on my hands, was asked to represent the group at the IWD planning-group meetings.

I dutifully trotted along on a Tuesday night and found, as you do, that I was the only Black woman in the group. That meant it was even more important that our ideas and wishes were listened to, and taken on board. This was easier said than done. You have to work through the initial lack of understanding, then the resentment, and settle for the vaguely patronizing attitudes, the unspoken, 'Oh well, if you Blacks want your own space, I suppose we just have to humour you.' A whole weekend of workshops and entertainment was being planned, so I put forward the idea of Black women-only workshops, which the planning group eventually agreed to. And, of course, there would be the march, when women of all denominations would have a chance to take to the streets together and demonstrate their solidarity.

Meetings aside, the weeks and months were flying by. After working at a playgroup, I graduated to the position of cleaner and cook. I also trained as a simultaneous interpreter, which is not an incompatible activity in Australia. My newly acquired knowledge no doubt stood me in good stead when a yob on a city centre bus spat in my face, and barked: 'You fuckin' Abo.' Expecting me to step back or yell at him, I stared without blinking, and told him: 'Wrong, I'm not Aboriginal at all, but I am conducting postgraduate research into Aboriginal traditions. Does this count?' The guy didn't know what had hit him, and scuttled off the bus at the next stop. But that was the only nasty incidence of racism I experienced. Overall, I fell in love with the Sydney lifestyle,. The fact that no one I knew had to work full time, and wages were high enough to permit a comfortable existence on a part-time salary had a major effect on people's lives. People actually had time to enjoy their creativity. All my friends were writers, film-makers, painters, sculptors and poets. Literally everyone was at it. I loved the café culture, the hanging out and reading magazines, and chatting over chocolate cake.

I found myself more and more in the company of women who had deeper emotional relationships with women, who didn't cower beneath the term bisexual, but affirmed that they were lesbians. I'd only been passionately in love with one woman before I came to Sydney but, frightened of the consequences, I had avoided sleeping with her. Whereas with all my previous girlfriends, I'd always kept most of myself locked away. I had given on one level, and withheld on another. Maybe it was the pleasure of two summers in a row that made me soften. It certainly had a lot to do with taking myself off to the other side of the world, getting right away from my family, their expectations of me, and painful episodes in my past. Comparatively few people knew me in Sydney, and I needed to cut the ties to be able to explore all the territory within me that I had chosen to classify as forbidden, before I went diving into swirling pools.

Swirlpool: 8 March 1983

The alarm rings. It is seven o'clock. I check the sun. It looks promising. Time someone swept out our backyard. That's not one of the jobs on our rota. Someone should stick it on. I am about to step out of bed when I catch sight of the lesser-spotted giant cockroach, wobbling its antennae on the floor beside the bed. I grab a book – heavy volume by Mary Daly – then put it down. Seeing as it's International Women's Day, I'll be merciful. Sue, a painter, is brewing lemongrass tea in the kitchen. She's the only woman in our house who claims to be clear about her sexuality. We nibble bagels in our sunny front room, a spider's web of pot plants. She's just off down to her studio to get on with a piece that's been commissioned but promises to catch some of the IWD events in the afternoon. She wouldn't miss my turn for the world. I do my fifty lengths in the quiet university pool. My swimming's improved so much since I've been here. Swimming daily, it seems to me, firms up your body and tones your mind. I like the way my mind floats in the water.

After a long shower, I wander up the road to Newtown where the events are taking place. I have to do some time on reception, and women arrive in droves. It's good to see the Rainbow Collective out in force; I have a long chat with Ann, a Chinese-Australian poet, painter and activist who lives in my house, and introduce her to some of the group. My stint on reception ends, and I hurry along to a workshop on assertiveness for Black women. I am in sore need of it. Growing up in a large family with younger brothers and sisters, I was conditioned always to put other people's needs before my own, to the extent that you stop trying to work out how you feel, and what you really want in any situation. And being raped fed into that.

Listening to someone talk can sometimes be like breathing oxygen. I leave the session all fired up with fresh ideas on how to tackle life. Suddenly, it is clear to me: before you can start being assertive with other people, you have to be assertive with yourself. Then lunch and my serious thoughts are interrupted: lots of joking and laughter in the canteen space which the Black women had appropriated. But I can't linger, I have to rush into town to check that all the plans for the march are going smoothly.

By a quarter to two, thousands of women are gathered in George Street, which feels uplifting in itself. The march begins, and women are striding and singing and carrying banners. There is an ambience of solidarity: the women are warm, optimistic and united as they mill around catching up with friends. A Black woman from London, who's a schoolteacher, asks me: 'Tina, can you help me with this?' Her co-bearer has just wandered off to talk with friends. She points to the banner: 'Sydney Black Lesbians', it says, or rather shouts. For a second, I feel like saying no. I don't want to give myself away. But then, on a sunny Sydney street, I align myself and take hold of the banner. I've been looking for a long time, but now I know, I have come to accept what my identity is. I don't talk very much, but inside I'm all aglow. I hold the banner high, the banner that marks the new beginning, is the turning-point. After a while, it feels like the banner is carrying me. When we reach the square, I have almost forgotten I am meant to be on stage, that I have been elected to give one of the speeches. It's normally a big deal for me to speak in public, but this afternoon has been eclipsed by another more major event and the words spill off my tongue. I talk about the forms of oppression that join Black women, and of how we celebrate our strength. After the speeches, I am interviewed by a Japanese TV crew, but cut short the questions because I want time on my own to sit and have a coffee and take everything in.

By the evening I've come round enough to head up to the Rainbow IWD party. A group of women from out of town are there, and I am introduced to a very striking Koori woman who works in Canberra, a three-hour drive from Sydney. Our co-ordinator introduces us: 'This is Tina,' she announces directly. 'And more's the pity she isn't a lesbian.' 'Whatever gives you that idea?' I respond. I grin and steer the woman off into the kitchen for a drink.

The momentum mellows: 20 November 1993

Ten years down the road, I wake up in a suburban house in Bristol, where I am currently the Poet in Residence. It is a rather grand term, but nonetheless I am very proud to be involved with the project which aims to put elderly Asian and Caribbean people back in touch with poetry. When you know how to listen to people, memories are a cluster of poems. I worked with Tom last night. He had been a reasonably wealthy farmer in Jamaica, but lost faith when the price of ginger dropped drastically. So he sailed off to Britain in 1961, and spent the rest of his working life cleaning trains. And Agnes, a disabled woman, who was talking about all the birds and flowers of her childhood, and the long walk to the market where she'd sell the family goods. I work by conducting oral and written poetry sessions, which means that you literally bring people back to life, and catch the essence of their experience. Which is all very wonderful at the time. Yet I sit on the train back to Manchester feeling terrible. Yes, I am a writer now. I succeed in supporting myself and my family through writing which, in a recession, is no mean feat. And this is one of the loveliest jobs I've had. It is very rewarding to tap into other people's lives, and to astound them with what they themselves can do. But it also feels exploitative. Building up a tight relationship with an elderly person, or in my case, twenty elderly people, then disappearing altogether once the residency ends.

Outside Macclesfield, I start to think. I should probably go over the stuff I'm reading tonight, never mind agonizing about a situation I can do nothing to change. I have a girlfriend who lives in a small Yorkshire town with a sizeable white lesbian community. A few weeks ago, one of the women invited me to read at an Audre Lorde commemorative event due to be held this evening in Bradford. It felt like a real honour, until it transpired that I was the second woman to be contacted. The first woman, who has no leanings at all towards poetry, was thought to be an appropriate choice on the grounds that she was the only permanent Black lesbian in the area.

We get back to my girlfriend's house with little time for catching up properly or getting close. I am relieved not to bump into her white South African house-mate who tends either to scowl, snub or simply ignore me. Fortunately, we Black lesbians are known to rise above these things. I drive into Bradford, the city where I was born. I always enjoy working in Bradford as a writer, probably, because I have a sense of cementing my distant childhood dream. The Audre Lorde Commemoration is an event organized by white women, which is strange somehow. As the very efficient, but all white, women on the reception greet me, I wonder why I and other Black lesbians in Yorkshire haven't got round to organizing the celebration ourselves. All the Black lesbians I know lead such hectic lives, with little time for relaxation, and little time to really take stock and prioritize projects, including such major events as a commemoration of Audre Lorde.

Wryam, the Black woman signer, waits for me and is as excited and nervous as I am. It has been really difficult selecting the different segments, because Audre Lorde's work is so outstanding and clear. How do you decide what to put together for a 45-minute performance? Eventually, Wryam decides to sign several of the poems, as there is not enough time to prepare the longer prose pieces. The Black women's poetry workshop I run before the performance is a very special time when women get together and share their creativity. We all take away a sense of our strength, a sense of how Black lesbian lives interweave, and of our infinite potential.

A break for half an hour, then straight into the performance, which can hardly go wrong when you're delivering words as powerful as Audre's. There are some sexy, moving passages, and prose extracts covering a variety of topics: meat-eating at a party in the 1950s; Black lesbians sporting poodle haircuts; older women; the plight of a little Ethiopian girl with wrists broken from malnutrition; text that tries to make sense of her cancer.

I am sharing her words with all the women in the audience, and for whatever reason, Black lesbians are very thin on the ground. Then I read a speech which she gave to a women's conference in Melbourne. Audre explains that she is in two minds about accepting the invitation, but recognizes that her visit can serve a purpose. She suggests that by accepting the invitation it will perhaps make white Australian women conscious of their treatment of Aboriginal women, a fact which is reflected in the absence of Aboriginal women at the conference.

Identifying as a Black lesbian involves a recognition of the vast amount of work we have to do. But Black women have never been afraid of getting on with work or of facing daunting tasks. Identifying as a Black lesbian means there is no sitting back: there's a world to be transformed and sweetened. And while I read Audre's Australian piece, I have a glimpse of myself walking along Sydney's streets holding the banner high. It has been carrying me ever since.

Resources

Political and social organizations

Black Lesbian and Gay Centre (BLGC)
BM Box 4390
London WCIN 3XX
Tel: 0171 732 3885

Wages Due Lesbians
Kings Cross Centre
71 Tonbridge Street
London WC1H 9DZ

Zamimass
c/o CLC/BLG 54–56 Phoenix Road
London N1

Lesbian Archive
London Women's Centre
4 Wild Court
Holborn WC2

Orientations and Shakti (London)
c/o London Friend
86 Caledonian Road
London N1

Shakti (Birmingham)
Tel: 0121 622 7351

Shakti (Bradford)
Tel: 01274 723802/722206

Black Lesbian Support Group
c/o Harehills Housing Aid
188 Roundhay Road
Leeds 8

Black Lesbian Support Group
c/o Box 26
1 Newton Street
Piccadilly
Manchester M1 1HW

Black Lesbian and Gay Bisexual Group
Tel: Bristol 0117 942 5927

Mental health organizations

Project for Advice, Counselling and Education (PACE)
(A lesbian and gay service, with Black lesbian counsellors)
Tel: 0171 700 1323

Afro-Caribbean Mental Health Service
Tel: 0171 737 3603

MIND
General advice telephone helpline: Mon–Fri 10 a.m.–12.30 p.m. and 2 p.m.–4.30 p.m.
Tel: 0181 522 1728

MIND
Legal advice telephone helpline: Mon/Wed/Fri 2 p.m.–4.30 p.m.
Tel: 0181 519 2122

Bath Black Health Support Group
Tel: 01225 461 4444

Index